SPENSER STUDIES

XI

SPENSER STUDIES

A Renaissance Poetry Annual

XI

EDITED BY

Patrick Cullen AND *Thomas P. Roche, Jr.*

AMS PRESS, INC.
NEW YORK, N.Y.

SPENSER STUDIES
A RENAISSANCE POETRY ANNUAL

edited by Patrick Cullen and Thomas P. Roche, Jr.

is published annually by AMS Press, Inc. as a forum for Spenser scholarship and criticism and related Renaissance subjects. Manuscripts must be submitted *in duplicate* and be double-spaced, including notes, which should be grouped at the end and should be prepared according to the format used in this journal. All essay-length manuscripts should enclose an abstract of 100–175 words. They will be returned only if sufficient postage is enclosed (overseas contributors should enclose international reply coupons). One copy of each manuscript should be sent to Thomas P. Roche, Jr., Department of English, Princeton University, Princeton, N.J. 08544 and one copy to Patrick Cullen, 300 West 108th Street, Apt. 8 D, New York, N.Y. 10025.

ISSN 0195-9468
Volume XI, ISBN 0-404-19211-4

Contents

Spenser's Virgilian Pastoral: The Case for September
NANCY LINDHEIM
1

The *September* eclogue, generally considered one of Spenser's ecclesiastical or Mantuanesque poems, can be usefully examined in relation to the Virgilian tradition of pastoral deriving from *Eclogues* I and IX. These poems about the land confiscations that were contemporary with Virgil's composition of his *Bucolics* offer an important insight into the content and values of pastoral ignored both by those who equate the form with Arcadia and by those who read the *Calender* in exclusively Protestant terms. The possiblity of understanding Virgil in other than Arcadian terms enables a reinterpretation of Hobbinol that gives him and the pastoral ideas he represents structural importance in the *Shepheardes Calender* as a whole.

Spenser's November Eclogue
LESLIE T. WHIPP
17

In the November Eclogue of Edmund Spenser's *Shepheardes Calender,* Spenser-Immerito includes a lament for Dido. I explore in this essay the associations of the name "Dido" by considering three different Dido poems in Spenser's November eclogue—the Dido poem which Colin offers us, the Dido poem which E. K. offers us, and the Dido poem which Spenser offers us. I find a rich tradition that allows Spenser to achieve an astonishing multivalence in Colin's lament for Dido: while veiling the instructive implications for the queen, and dangling flattering implications before her, the name also allows this brilliant new poet to advertise himself and fashion his own claim to be the new English poet by convicting his foil, Colin, of being mired in earth and time.

Spenser alludes to Lucretius throughout book four of *The Faerie Queene,* not simply to appropriate the Roman materialist for Christianity, but to argue for a Christian sexuality energized by a wildness which Lucretius reserves for his randomly colliding atoms. In his translation, during the Temple of Venus episode of Lucretius' opening hymn to the goddess of love, Spenser accentuates both the energy of the Lucretian universe and the control to which it is subject. The result is a freer embrace of sexuality than Lucretius could have countenanced, and an insistence that sexuality be channeled into action: boisterous courtship on behalf of one's beloved or one's queen.

That the faery queen mirrors Elizabeth has never fallen into question, but the poet's "generall intention" that she be taken first of all as a symbol of glory has commonly been marginalized or even ignored. Despite the virtual exclusion of his heroine from the work named in her honor, however, Spenser does afford us at least five glimpses of Gloriana and her allegorical significance, and these suffice to establish her peculiar "glory" as crucial to his conception of a "vertuous and gentle discipline." We see her variously as one whose "excellent beauty" leaves Arthur "rauished," whose earthly capital stands in contrast to the heavenly Jerusalem, whose "royall presence" is known only in memory and expectation, whose "imperiall powre" constitutes "the beautie of her minde," and even as an avowed symbol of glory whose attire comprises "all that *else* this worlds enclosure bace / Hath great or glorious in mortall eye'"; and in each of these respects the faery queen proves to be the image of what one contemporary of Spenser calls "the first and originall mistris" of the world. This primeval empress is, improbably enough, simply a pristinely radiant version of the natural light or agent intellect, already allegorized in similarly extravagant terms in the Bible's Wisdom allegories, and pre-eminent in a broader conception of "glory" which encompassed all the lights and splendors of the created world as promulgators of the moral law.

Spenser's Rehabilitation
of the Templars
GREGORY WILKIN
89

The Faerie Queene may have been read by early readers as an allegory of the history of the Templars, the Red Cross knights of the crusading period, disbanded officially as an order in England in 1312 but surviving as the lawyers' guilds of Spenser's day. In Book I Redcross falls victim to betrayal by the Catholic Church and the giant, Pride (as Spenser says of the Templars in his *Prothalamon,* "they decayed through pride"), having originally been successful against Error and the Saracens. The redemption of Redcross by Arthur recreates the fortunes of the English Templars after the inquisition of 1310.

Although the Templars were thus dissolved as an order, the treasury remained at the London Temple while the lawyers took over. Mammon gives Guyon a tour of a landscape that duplicates that of the Temple in London, the landmarks occurring in the precise order they would in a walk from the Round Temple church through Inner Temple hall, the grove, and garden, to the Thames. Books III and IV present the courtly love interval between the crusading ethos of I and II and the judicial/commercial knighthood of Spenser's time in V and VI. The trials at the courts of Mercilla and Cupid, and the solving of quests that are now brought on by "torts" here may be meant to flatter and exhort the lawyer-knights to whom Spenser dedicates the poem, Hatton, Northumberland, Buckhurst, Raleigh, and Henry Herbert, the late husband of the Countess of Pembroke, all of the Temple.

Romancing the Word:
Pre-Texts and Contexts
for the Errour Episode
LAWRENCE F. RHU
101

The initial episode in *The Faerie Queene* participates in the literary history of epic and romance as genres, especially as these kinds of narration were theorized and allegorized by Torquato Tasso. It also reflects the controversy among Elizabethan Protestants in the late sixteenth century, especially as it concerns biblical interpretation and the spread of heretical opinion. These two phenomena are related inasmuch as both pertain to "error" in one guise or another, and they thus form a revealing backdrop against which to consider the first challenge faced by the Redcrosse knight. The proliferation of episodes that threaten unity of both theme and structure in romance narration runs parallel to the widespread dissemination of unauthorized religious opinion made particularly overwhelming by the new print technology. The opening of Spenser's epic-romance registers these literary and social issues both directly and by implication.

Deconstruction
and Spenser's Allegory
WENDY RAUDENBUSH OLMSTED
111

Deconstructionists such as Paul de Man, Jonathan Goldberg, and Elizabeth Bellamy seem to challenge basic premises of traditional allegorical readings of texts like Spenser's *Faerie Queene* when they argue that there may be no connection between a text and a non-verbal phenomenon, system of meaning, or transcendental signified outside of the text. Yet, an allegorical reading of text in relation to analogue need not reduce the text to a phenomenon or meaning outside of the text. The allegorical reader relates the text to cosmos and to Queen Elizabeth as signs. The semiotics of Charles Sanders Peirce clarifies how the sign functions of icon and index mean through the kinds of physical patterns and tensions that one finds in Renaissance cosmology, psychology, and moral thought. The relation of the text to a secondary set of signs changes the way one reads the text. Movement does not dissolve names or meanings; it changes them. Spenser's language has a pragmatic, rhetorical power for reshaping signs and meanings in a cultural system that exists outside the text as well as within it. Spenser's thoughtful refigurations of cultural signs engage the power of a partial, not a radical, indeterminacy in language. Allegorical readings explore the historically particular ambiguities, conflicts, and negotiations of meaning in order to understand the edge and force of Spenser's particular rewritings of his culture.

Book Five of *The Faerie Queene:*
An Elizabethan Apocalypse
RICHARD MALLETTE
129

The second half of The Legend of Justice is not only shaped by biblical apocalypse but also is in dialogue with apocalyptic commentary of the post-Armada period, which views the Reformation as a national struggle and hails the prince as the hope of Antichrist's destruction. This essay determines how Book V partakes of biblical apocalypse throughout the final six cantos, how it forms part of late Elizabethan apocalyptic commentary, and how that commentary bridges biblical texts and the allegory of contemporary history. The great battles of the final cantos are modelled on a variety of apocalyptic battles as mediated by the commentary that depicts Philip II and other contemporary enemies as the tyrants representative of Antichrist. The Book, then, is part of the discourse of foreign policy as well as the newly developing discourse of nationalism. Hence Elizabeth plays the leading apocalyptic role as the locus of hope for the nation, just as Spain is the locus of fear. Demonized and refracted in the tyrannical villains of the final episodes, Philip corresponds to his avatars in other post-Armada apocalyptic discourse, and his numerous trouncings in this Book reflect the violence deemed necessary to defend religion and punish the sacrilegious. Hermeneutics is deployed consistently to validate bloodshed. The Belge and Burbon episodes form an apocalyptic diptych, representing the two primary approaches taken by the exegetes to the question of how to smite Antichrist, by preaching the Word or wielding the sword. The final canto, however, seems intended to present an unsettling inconclusiveness to the issues raised in the international episodes. Yet the final dour notes, too, belong to the apocalyptic view of temporal justice, which comprehends human failure as deeply as tragedy does.

The Aesthetics of Decline:
Locating the *Post*-Epic
in Literary History
ELIZABETH J. BELLAMY
161

Spenser's Book V (and its precipitous plunge into history) has long been viewed as exerting a regressive, anti-prophetic pull on the epic teleology of *The Faerie Queene*. But, to my knowledge, never has its pervasive sense of fatigue and cynicism and its presentation of a world in decay (a world that "growes daily wourse and wourse" [Proem.5]) been viewed as an explicitly (and conventionally) *epic* gambit (almost, as I will argue, as the formulaic deployment of an epic topos) in the representation of civil war. In the first part of my essay, I will offer some extended comparisons between Ariosto's *Cinque Canti* and Spenser's Book V in an effort to trace the lineaments of what I would call the "*post*-epic" as the genre of empire in decline. A key question I will consider is: what does it *mean* when an epic comes too close to (real) history? In the second part of my essay, I intend to use Spenser's Book V as the occasion for a broader theoretical discussion of the new historicism and its weaknesses in providing a conceptual framework for interpreting this, ironically, most "historical" of Spenser's books. My overarching purpose will be to offer some further consideration on how historical meaning is revealed through literature — and what is at stake for literary studies when literature and history confront one another as directly (and uncomfortably) as they do in Book V.

Spenser, Sidney
and the Myth of Astrophel
THEODORE L. STEINBERG
187

Spenser's *Astrophel* has often been regarded as something of a failure, a late and lukewarm tribute to the darling of the Elizabethans, Sir Philip Sidney. If the poem is regarded as only a tribute to Sidney, like so many of the elegies that were written after his death, this assessment might be justified. When considered from another vantage point, however, the poem emerges as a passionate statement about Sidney and the meaning of his death. A close reading of the poem indicates that far from offering a simple tribute to the fallen hero, it offers a sharp criticism of the impulses that prompted Sidney to abandon his important work as a poet for the more adventurous and less productive life — and death — of a soldier. By the time the poem was written, it had become apparent that Leicester's expedition to the Low Countries had been a failure and that Sidney's death had been just another disastrous part of that failure. Both Sidney and England would have been far better off had Sidney been true to his vocation as a poet. This point is made repeatedly in the poem, both in its narrative aspects and in the imagery of sterility that pervades the poem. Furthermore, it is reinforced by the "Doleful Lay of Clorinda" that confirms the waste of Sidney's unnecessary death while simultaneously displaying true grief over that death.

Constructing the
View of the Present State of Ireland
JEAN R. BRINK

General agreement that concepts such as "authoritative" and "standard" are constructed has not resulted in recognition of the need to reexamine the attribution of works to Spenser and standard editions of those works. To encourage this kind of critical attention to Spenser's texts, I evaluate assumptions about government censorship that have become entrenched in discussions of the *View of the Present State of Ireland,* demonstrate that the text of the *View* is unfinished, and offer a critical survey of the evidence we have for attributing the *View* to Spenser. My purpose is to show that, until the extensive manuscript evidence is fully sifted, scholars should be very cautious about legitimizing approaches to Spenser that use this highly unstable text as the cornerstone for either the explication of his work or interpretation of his life.

Gleanings
Triumphing over Death and Sin
ANNE LAKE PRESCOTT

Index

Contents of Previous Volumes

NANCY LINDHEIM

Spenser's Virgilian Pastoral:
The Case for *September*

*I*T HAS BECOME something of a truism that Virgil's First Eclogue is the most influential work in the tradition that governs
Renaissance pastoral. Paul Alpers, for example, notes that Sidney's *Apologie for Poetry* defends the genre solely on the basis of
Eclogue I, and Annabel Patterson virtually defines pastoral since
Virgil in terms of the use of this one poem.[1] I wish to narrow the
focus somewhat to explore the ways that *Eclogue* I and its pendant, *Eclogue* IX, also about the land confiscations,[2] inform our
understanding of one particular poem, the *September* eclogue of
the *Shepherdes Calender.* Implicit in this resonance and in the
eclogue's placement as a "harvest" poem towards the end of the
Calender is an argument that the paper does not pursue: that *September* is important in the design of an eclogue-book indebted to
Virgil for both content and form. My more modest purpose here
is to demonstrate that *September*'s relation to these "defining"
Virgilian poems suggests a dimension to Spenser's examination
of pastoral that deserves weight when one considers the *Calender*
as a whole.

The mere suggestion that *September* is a "Virgilian" poem will
raise some eyebrows. Discussions of the *Shepheardes Calender* that
divide the work into types—whether these are E. K.'s recreative,

plaintive, and moral or Patrick Cullen's Arcadian and Mantuanesque[3] —
place for *September* firmly in Mantuan's moral camp. Nor can one deny
Spenser's allegiance here to the concerns with the corruption of church
and society that informs the Carmelite monk's vision and give shrillness
to his tone in the *Adulescentia*. Mantuan's tone is perhaps determining
when one tries to characterize his poems. He engages in all kinds of
moral crusades and invective — against women, against cities, against
"insane" love, against ungenerous patrons — even when the point is not
ecclesiastical. Yet Spenser's special achievement in *September* is not merely
his tempering of Mantuan's tone, but his significant recovery of Virgilian pastoral.

Even a cursory examination of Virgilian pastoral will reveal factors
we would not ordinarily call Arcadian: it has no necessary relation to
ideal landscapes or to love, and its attention to poetry is more often
problem-oriented than purely celebratory. It can be concerned with the
land, politics, and history of the poet's own country.[4] Spenser could
well have understood his own treatment of religious depredation (raids
by wolves and foxes, the dereliction of shepherds) as the logical transformation of Virgil's concern with political depredation (the land confiscations); religious controversy was "politics" in post-Reformation
England.[5] Even without having recourse to the Arcadian values of the
happy shepherd, then, Spenser can be Virgilian, and he can manage it
while still being Mantuanesque.[6] Nor is this altogether a surprise; for
Baptista Spagnuoli also, writing pastoral would have meant writing
with some relation to Virgil. Thus the name "Mantuanus." *September*'s
allegiance to a double tradition — its suggestive relation to both Virgil
and Mantuan[7] — makes it a particularly interesting poem.

The gesture that most clearly defines *September* as a Virgilian poem is
of course Hobbinol's invitation to Diggon Davie to find shelter in his
humble cottage. The invitation echoes Tityrus' offer to the exiled
Meliboeus in *Eclogue* I, but the context of the gestures, being dependent on the relation between the two shepherds, is quite different in both
poems. In Virgil's opening eclogue, the goatherd Meliboeus is also a
farmer with a strong and intimate attachment to the land of his fathers.
He is being sent into exile because "barbarous soldiers," presumably
veterans disbanded after the battle at Philippi (41 B.C.), have been
given his land as a reward for their military service. His neighbor
Tityrus, an older man who herds cows and sheep, has been granted permission to remain on the land. The poem offers no reason for the
disparity in the two men's fortune: it seems unrelated to anything

Tityrus is or has done.[8] Some young "god" who held audience in Rome is responsible for Tityrus' remaining, he tells Meliboeus, though the purpose of his trip to Rome was apparently only to purchase his freedom. It is to this siuation—a man totally wrapped up in the fact of his recent good fortune, paired in dialogue with a neighbor who laments his exile from the beloved fields and the sounds that have made up his life— that Tityrus' invitation to Meliboeus to stay the night offers closure:

Hic tamen hanc mecum poteras requiescere noctem
fronde super viridi. sunt nobis mitia poma,
castaneae molles et pressi copia lactis,
et iam summa procul villarum culmina fumant
maioresque cadunt altis de montibus umbrae.[9] (I.79–83)

[However, for tonight you could rest here with me
Upon green leafage: I can offer you ripe fruit
And mealy chestnuts and abundance of milk cheese.
Far off the roof-tops of the farms already smoke
And down from the high mountains taller shadows fall.]

Perhaps no poet has ever been better at closure than Virgil, or more calculated about its effects. This is as true of the first work in his *Opera* (*Eclogue* I) as it is of the last (the famous final line of *Aeneid* XII). The emotional closure offered by Tityrus' invitation is purely formal (of the poem, not of the politics), though it is not thereby specious. The lines carry on the subtle interchange or balance—what Paul Alpers has described as suspension[12]—that has all along prevented the potential pain from sundering the dialogue itself. As readers we are grateful for the invitation, for the focus of hospitality and humane feeling it establishes in the midst of social injustice and disorder. But we remain aware that it is temporary, *hanc noctem,* and that Tityrus' ability to make the offer is the gift of the same blind fortune that has taken away Meliboeus' land. The duality of the sitation is echoed in the final two lines: the autumnal chestnuts and smoking chimneys indicate an end to the year but also a phase in a cyclical recurrence, just as the lengthening shade might indicate the close only of day.[13] *Eclogue* I is neither an angry nor a pessimistic poem; its emotional shadows come from a poised awareness of arbitrariness and pain.

Earlier readers did not understand the eclogue quite this way. The Servian allegorical tradition of exegesis, by identifying Virgil himself

Virgil himself with Tityrus, promotes both a more positive view of
that character and a more laudatory interpretation of the politics. We
read a great deal about the poet's gratitude to the young god Octavian.
Yet if we look closely at Mantuan and Spenser we can see that Tityrus
must have puzzled them in ways not reflected in these early comments or
commentaries on the *Bucolics*. In reworking *Eclogue* I, Manutan and
Spenser both fasten on the aspect of Virgil's poem that bothers twentieth-
century critics most: Tityrus' apparent insensitivity to Meliboeus' deso-
lation. They "solve" the problem by recasting the situation of their
shepherds, decreasing the disparity in their fortunes and increasing the
sympathy between them. And this is neither an arbitrary nor a sentimental solution, given the sense of human community that underlies
the pastoral form.

The point is made urgent in Mantuan: he *begins* his ninth eclogue
with the shepherd's invitation. Candidus has just arrived in Rome from
Faustulus' home province near the Mincio and Po Rivers:

> *Faustulus:* By what misfortune, Candidus, driven from your
> father's lands, have you come into these fields? Here are no pas-
> turelands or rivers, no clear springs, secure sheepfolds, or
> shade. . . . (1–3)
> [*Candidus:* I was misled into thinking this land would be whole-
> some, but I regret the long journey and leaving my homeland
> behind (paraphrase, 11. 5–11)]
> *Faustulus:* Since it has befallen you to enter safe and sound into
> these Latin groves, by the right of our fellowship of old [*antiqui
> . . . iure sodalitii*] you may enter my house here. My few acres of
> poor land yield me barely enough for my living. Yet such as it
> is, consider it yours [*quidquid id est commune puta*]. Perhaps
> some favorable destiny will come to you. Dame Fortune is
> much like the wind. Enter my hut of reeds until the heat of the
> day has passed . . . lay aside your sheephook, lie down for a lit-
> tle while, refresh yourself with a drink (12–20)[14]

Mantuan presents two shepherds whose situations differ only in that
one arrived (presumably in Rome) some time before the other; Faustulus has settled himself in a cottage and can warn the newcomer of the
dangers that await him. They are almost the same person at two different stages of experience. We are immediately struck by the openness of
Faustulus' hospitality: *quidquid id est commune puta* (1. 15). But this

impression is qualified in two ways. Noting that below its title, "Falco," the eclogue announces that it was written *post religionis ingressum* (after his entry into religious orders), we may well understand *iure sodalitii* (by right of fellowship) quite technically. Moreover, the largeness of the gesture seems to diminish as it unfolds: what opens as an apparent invitation to "stay until good fortune comes" soon develops into an offer of temporary respite from the heat. The generous compassion of the opening dwindles into the sheer conviviality of fifteen lines or so devoted to the pleasures and benefits of wine (22–31, 35–37).

In spite of much anger, complaint, and invective against the depravity of Rome, the eclogue is not pessimistic in its overall tone. Its closure abandons Virgil's pensive tension for something decidedly more upbeat. Candidus' original choice to come to Rome was voluntary, and he can take his flock elsewhere if the promise of Falco to remedy the evils of the countryside does not bear fruit. This potential savior whose name provides the title of the eclogue is a man explicitly compared to Tityrus' young god; he is, moreover, a better guardian of the flock than Argus, more skilled than Daphnis and Apollo at shepherding, in fact worthy of Christ and Peter (212–27). The final lines insist not only on the promise but on the shepherd's freedom: *Si favet iste, mane. quod si negat iste favorem, / Candide, coge pecus melioraque pascua quaere* (If he smiles with favor, stay. But if he denies his favor, drive forth your flock, Candidus, and seek greener pastures).[15]

Spenser's *September* is perceptibly different in conception, though one can easily recognize both *Eclogue* I and Mantuan IX in it. Hobbinol is like Virgil's Tityrus in remaining behind (not as a benefit of gods or good fortune, however), while Diggon Davie is like Meliboeus in being effectively dispossessed, though not exiled. He is returning home from a disastrous effort to find success in some other country; his motives are those of Mantuan's Candidus, his experience the substance of Faustulus' warnings. The difference in character between Diggon and Hobbinol is not so sharp as that between Tityrus and Meliboeus, but it remains important, as it was not in Mantuan. That Virgil's tact in sharing the materials of his dialogues is not picked up by Spenser makes Hobbinol even more of a mere interlocutor than Candidus, though his being "dependent" on Diggon for his speech paradoxically ensures a fuller sense of communication than Virgil depicted. A similar paradox can be found in Hobbinol's role itself: notwithstanding the fact that the bulk of the poem is given over to the "ecclesiastical" matters expressed by Diggon Davie, the largely "classical" or Virgilian content of what

Hobbinol says directs us to some of the central pastoral meanings of the eclogue. Less turns out to be more.

The "equality" one feels between Spenser's shepherds is the result of many overt expressions of sympathy. Such comments are so numerous that they seem a conscious attempt to "correct" Virgil's portrayal. Hobbinol's first response introduces his sympathy—"Diggon areede, who has thee so dight? / Never I wist thee in so poore a plight" (7–8)[16]—and Diggon himself sets up the conversation in terms of human emotions, needs and bonds: he is a "most wretched wight" (4) and adjures Hobbinol on what he holds most dear not to renew his old griefs and cause new woe (11–13). Hobbinol, presumably taking this refusal to talk as a conventional demurral, counters with the commonplace assurance that sorrow is a burden that can be eased if it is shared (15–18). The idea remains in our mind as we read; the length of the dialogue itself promotes the possibility that Hobbinol's assurance might prove true. Yet towards the end of the poem the theme is repeated only to be denied. When Diggon specifically says that the long conversation has *not* helped his grief (242–43), however, I suspect that we assess the situation differently. Diggon has changed for us by this time. His tone is no longer that of the man whom we heard denouncing clerical greed or of the man who, just a few lines earlier, knew how to avoid the depredation of wolves with absolute commands to "heede and watchfulnesse" (230). There was no uncertainty or moderation in his admonition to the shepherd not to play to sleep "*all* the long day: / But *ever* liggen in watch and ward" (233–34, emphasis mine). Now, just ten lines later, his pathetic question is

> What shall I doe? what way shall I wend,[17]
> My piteous plight and losse to amend?
> A good Hobbinol, mought I thee praye,
> Of ayde or counsell in my decaye. (244–47)

Just as in *Eclogue* I, Tityrus' only moment of full awareness of Meliboeus' situation issues in the invitation that provides our sense of release, so in *September,* Diggon's increased vulnerability (here it is Diggon's awareness) makes some kind of amelioration possible. He puts himself in a position where being helped will matter—and evokes an offer of aid. This then forms the context of Spenser's revision of Tityrus' invitation, which he sets elaborately in motion. First Hobbinol's strong avowal of sympathy—"Now by my soule Diggon, I lament / The haplesse mischief, that has thee hent . . ." (248–49)—then his apology for not being able to do more (no *fortunatus senex* he), and finally, the anticipated gesture:

> But if to my cotage thou wilt resort,
> So as I can, I wil thee comfort:
> There mayst thou ligge in a vetchy bed,
> Till fayre Fortune shewe forth her head. (254–57)

The explicit infusion of sympathy results in a less qualified invitation: not for "this night" or "until the heat of the day passes," but unequivocally "until your fortune changes." Hobbinol's use of the word "ligge," moreover, shows extraordinary tact: he means "take rest," but uses a word that is acceptable to a man who will "ever liggen in watch and ward" (234). Tityrus and Faustulus also responded as the "facts" of the situation permitted, but Spenser has set up his poem deliberately for this deep recognition of human need. Diggon in turn is moved. Hobbinol, he says, is a rare friend, calling attention to the importance of the moment by invoking this classical (and Renaissance) value. The words "friend" and "friendship" do not appear in the *Bucolics,* though they are a cardinal factor of the Epicureanism that underlies both Theocritus' and Virgil's pastoral universe.[18] As an idea, friendship is notably embodied in the tenth eclogue, written out of love, the poet tells us, to help Gallus in his sorrow. That the form of Spenser's *September* echoes what can be called the "envelope" of pastoral sympathy shaping *Eclogue* X ("envelope" because the sympathy is articulated at the beginning and end of the eclogue), suggests that this important Virgilian poem too is part of the configuration that forms its context.

Many of the interesting modulations noticeable between *Eclogue* I and *September* (or even between *Eclogue* I and Mantuan IX) can be accounted for by Virgil's own ninth eclogue. The first and ninth eclogues are manifestly pendant poems, both dealing with the plight of ordinary civilians during the land confiscations of 41 B. C. *Eclogue* IX already reworks the relationship between the two shepherd speakers. Lycidas seems less specifically afflicted by the land expropriations than Moeris, who is the older man, but it is mostly the shared central "action" in which they both walk along a road to the city that defines our perception of them. Putnam's description of them as "alive in a doomed land"[19] perhaps exaggerates the situation, but it reflects something of their importance to each other. Moeris tells Lycidas his story: he and another shepherd, Menalcas, have barely escaped with their lives; Menalcas has even been forced to leave the land.[20] Young and relatively untouched as he is, Lycidas still treats the experience of these other men as though it were or could be his own:

> Heu, cadit in quemquam tantus scelus? heu tua nobis
> paene simul tecum solacia rapta Menalca! (17–18)

> [Alas, can such a crime befall any man? Alas, Manalcas,
> your solace and yourself so nearly snatched from us!21]

Even beyond the double exclamation of sorrow, the details of these lines reinforce the idea of sympathy. *Cadit in quemquam* (fall to any man) immediately generalizes the human response: we are all equally vulnerable, whatever positive principles of justice we may think govern our lives. The juxtaposition of *tua nobis,* as Coleman says, "enhances the expression of intense personal loss" (IX.17n, p. 260). The use of pronouns such as *tuus, vestrum, noster* is especially resonant in this eclogue,22 creating almost uniquely a network of relationships comprised of varying though strong bonds of connectedness:

> *vestrum* [l. 10] indicates an association with Menalcas more intimate than Lycidas', yet one that Moeris shared with others . . . there is a contrast with *nostra* (12) 'the songs we country men enjoy' and *tuus* (16) 'your friend', both of which associate the two speakers very closely. (Coleman, p. 258)

This notion of community is crystallized around Menalcas: he is their *solacium.* That Menalcas' special function for the shepherds arises from his poetry allows the eclogue to explore the spiritual and political malaise of the countryside by questioning the kind of power poetry has. The answer seems to lie in this notion of "solace" — the strength drawn by the community through the expression of its delights and fears, of its aspirations to peace and harmony. In the face of military and civil force, poetry's claim to political power is specifically discounted:

> . . . sed carmina tantum
> nostra valent Lycida tela inter Martia quantum
> Chaonias dicunt aquila veniente columbas. (11–13)

> [but songs of ours / Avail among the War-God's
> weapons Lycidas, / As much as Chaonian doves,
> they say, when the eagle comes.]

In Spenser's *September* we can see how the conflation of the first and ninth eclogues works: the emphasis placed by *Eclogue* IX on mutual dependency and on the vulnerability of what men value because of the greed and insolence of the powerful is used by Spenser to define the context of Hobbinol's Tityrean invitation. The tone of *September* shares the darkness of *Eclogue* IX rather than the suspension of *Eclogue* I. (It too is the ninth poem of its eclogue-book.) Although *September* avoids Virgil's emphasis on poetry,[23] one can detect a parallel between the two arguments: Virgil's ninth eclogue is about pastors as singers and it asks how effective is song; Spenser's ninth eclogue is about pastors as keepers of flocks, and it asks how effective is care. The positive power of both song and care is severely limited. What the "broken tops of the ancient beech" (*veteres iam fracta cacumina fagos,* IX. 9) does to form our response in the one, the "Westerne wind [that] bloweth sore, . . . Beating the withered leafe from the tree" (*Sept.* 49–51) does in the other. Diggon's admonition that we must "ever liggen in watch and warde," though it apparently puts the power for success in the hands of the individual, is immediately undercut by Hobbinol's reply that such a "straight rule" does not take human nature into account:

> Ah Diggon, thilke same rule were too straight,
> All the cold season to watch and waite.
> We bene of fleshe, men as other bee.
> Why should we be bound to such miseree?
> What ever thing lacketh chaungeable rest,
> Mought needes decay, when it is at best. (236–41)

The strain on Spenser's adaptation of Virgilian material is perhaps at its greatest at this moment. The ecclesiastical reading of the stanza, promoted by the otherwise incomprehensible statement of line 238, "We bene of fleshe, men as other bee," urges us to see Hobbinol as revealing his moral inadequacy, because "pastor" is clearly to be translated as "clergyman" here. Yet if Hobbinoll is not only a religious shepherd, but the sort of shepherd that literature treats as an "everyman,"[24] the meaning is different. As a general position, perhaps provoked by Diggon's absolute "ever" and "all," Hobbinol's awareness of human limitation is both moving and clearsighted. I want to call this second tendency of Hobbinol's lines "classical," noting that the Ovidian tag of the final sentence can be seen as a signpost of such an affiliation.[25]

The strain we are discussing in *September* is a necessary result of Spenser's conception of the *Calender,* visible in all three eclogues that redefine shepherds as religious pastors. In *Maye* the tension makes its first incontrovertible appearance[26]: lulled as readers are by the simple associations of *March* and the successful harmony of politics and song in *Aprill,* they must be flat-out shocked by the discovery that Palinode's "shole of shepeheardes" who have gone out maying in the greenwood, "with singing, and shouting, and jolly chere" (*Maye*, 20–24), are in fact "faytours" heading "for the Devils stedde," who "playen, while their flockes be unfedde" (39–44). Spenser reworks the vocabulary of his earlier eclogues, substituting the "good pastor" meanings of the ecclesiastical tradition, changing his Pan of *Aprill* (Henry VIII), for example, into the great Pan of these "biblical" lines:

> I muse, what account both these will make,
> The one for hire, which he doth take,
> And thother for leaving his Lords taske,
> When great *Pan* account of shepeherdes shall aske.
>
> (*Maye*, 51–54)

Having sharply redefined the meaning of the pastoral scene, *Maye* continues to make its judgment for Piers and against Palinode. The "charm" of Palinode's love in the green world is presented early in the poem and is controverted as much by his own later lines as by any comparison with Piers. The point is even made too broadly: what clergyman could possibly say that shepherds must reap the pleasures of this world, "For when they bene dead, their good is ygoe" (66, whole passage 63–68)?

Julye, the middle ecclesiastical eclogue, seems to have this doubleness of vocabularies and interpretation at its heart, as Thomalin and Morrell constantly shift their levels of discourse.[27] Much of the argument assigns a metaphorical dimension to "high" and "low," but much also asserts a common-sense, non-symbolic literalism: there is no connection between spirituality and physical height (*Julye,* 92–104).[28] Yet the literal level of the poem will not stand up to any pressure. If Morrell really is a goatherd and goats eat well on mountains, he cannot be a bad goatherd for dwelling there. Goats require mountains, sheep valleys — there is no moral debate here, though the eclogue is set up as if there were. The possibility of more than a single standard for evaluation, what I am calling doubleness, appears in the emblems at the close of the poem, where the terms may remind us of the genuine debate of classical philosophy concerning whether the *summum bonum* is virtue or happiness:

Thomalins Embleme.   *In medio virtus.*
Morrells Embleme.   *In summo foelicitas.*

What begins in *Maye* as a choice of ecclesiastical over classical reference, and translates into *Julye*'s "recognition" of doubleness, concludes with *September*'s attempt to pull ecclesiastical material back into a Virgilian orbit. The pattern formed by the three eclogues moves into, then out of, an ecclesiastical perspective (A->B->A'), but the second "classical" position is not an equivalent of Palinode's original carefree assertion. It is not "A" but "A-prime," not Arcadian but Virgilian. Spenser uses the calendrical structure, the movement from spring to autumn, to redefine even Virgil's pastoral in terms of material derived from *Eclogue* I and IX. The advantage of this darker, more serious version of the Virgilian tradition lies not merely in its echoing the season, but in its ability to connect the Christian and classical strands of pastoral by means of the human values of compassion and fellowship that they share. The two traditions seem to converge in *September*. After *September* the secular focus on society in *October* and on the shepherd community in *November* seems totally appropriate. If we compare the classicism of *March* and *Aprill* with that of *October* and *November*—the comedy of *March* with the irony of *October* or the fused "nationalizing" of classicism in *Aprill* with *November*'s fluid movement to a Christian perspective on death that redefines but cannot root out the pagan sense of loss—we can gain some idea of the difference between Arcadian and Virgilian pastoral in the *Calender*. Paradoxically, then, if viewed against its usual interpretation, *September* ushers in the renewed classicism of *October* and *November*.[29]

In taking over some of the verbal plane we noted for *Julye, September* extends the "doubleness" to a moment that seems to probe the pastoral attitude towards experience. The relation of pastoral to heroic is too complex for discussion here,[30] but we may say that in general the decorum of classical pastoral gives us a shepherd whose psychic freedom, though real, depends on his distance from centers or figures of power. The innovation toward complexity of Virgil's eclogue-book lies in his having introduced these issues of power (or history or politics)[31] both absolutely (in the fourth eclogue) and into the lives of its characters; but the stance of the shepherds within the individual eclogues remains determined by their "class." They are without the power to shape their own lives. Tityrus' good fortune has nothing to do with his abilities; Menalcas' ill fortune comes despite his talent and presumed influence. These herdsmen live, not necessarily without repining,[32] within the situation that has been created for them. The modern reader surely, the Roman reader probably, would not react like Meliboeus, who shows no rage against his exile. But we neither fault him for his lack of rage nor praise him for his lack of envy. The issue does not present itself to us for judgment.

The reformist Christian ideals controling ecclesiastical pastoral, on the other hand, demand a much more active response.[33] What they see as crucial to their existence — the moral stance necessary to salvation — makes no distinction between shepherd and prince. In this sense the moral assumptions that govern the attitude of ecclesiastical pastoral, as Auerbach has said more generally of style in Christian literature, are classless. Our expectations of response are not conditioned by the shepherds' relation to power. Indeed, since the major stance of the shepherd-pastor is indignation against the greed, injustice, and moral turpitude of both the religious and secular orders of society, their "classlessness" makes the call to heroism absolute. And any response less than comparable indignation or commitment seems to us like cowardice, i.e., like an act we judge morally.

Thus I would prefer to read Hobbinol's apparently shocking response to Diggon's fierce accusations of political and secular corruption as a collision between two different traditions of conceiving the shepherd rather than, as is frequently done, as an exposure of Hobbinol's moral weakness.[34] The stanza in question occurs after Diggon has presumably, in "flatt" English (105), fulfilled Hobbinol's request to "speake not so dirke" (102)[35]:

> Nowe Diggon, I see thou speakest to plaine:
> Better it were, a little to feyne,
> And cleanly cover, that cannot be cured.
> Such il, as is forced, mought nedes be endured.
>
> (136–39)

Our immediate reaction is to see these lines as the negative truth of non-heroism. But the doubleness of Spenser's conception allows us the additional realization that Hobbinol's remarks fit into another scheme the poem has invoked, one mirroring different ideas of class decorum. He speaks as a representative classical shepherd, not merely as an inadequate good shepherd. The lines are of a piece with Hobbinol's speech discussed above protesting the call for eternal unbending watchfulness (236–41). Both moments, because their context is a double tradition, allow a significant tension to be suspended.[36] Without undermining the "protestant" judgment that is provoked by them, they suggest another position, neither absolute nor heroical, where a good man might stand.[37] This is an important "place" for pastoral, incidentally, which from its Alexandrian inception has doctrinally set itself up at a distance from the heroic.[38]

Contrary to this interpretation, which does not rank the traditions morally but seeks to adjust one tonally against the other, Puritan readings of *September* want to subordinate whatever Virgilian resonance they may see to the ecclesiastical concerns of the eclogue. For them the poem, either gently or not so gently,[39] finds Hobbinol insufficient. These readings, which often use E. K. to support their general interpretations of the *Calender,* are for the most part silent on E. K.'s own comment here, likely because they are embarrassed by the fact that it is exactly in *September* that he chooses to identify Hobbinol as Gabriel Harvey, the author's great friend. The identification is accompanied by fulsome praise of Harvey's achievements, guaranteeing, one would think, either that Spenser did not interpret Hobbinol negatively or that at least one contemporary close reader of the *Calender* spectacularly failed to do so. This in itself might make one question readings that insist on Hobbinol's deficiencies, even if one were not sensible to the incivility of setting up a friend for public scorn. I would suggest that Spenser treats his friend with more respect, making him the center in the *Calender* of values that Harvey would probably have supported and that have important positive weight in the whole work.[40]

If we accept the possibility that Hobbinol offers a positive position, we can then see *September* as a poem finally embraced by a Virgilian tradition that differs in emphasis from "Arcadianism." Here the ecclesiastical ideal that the good pastor care for his flock is made continuous with the concerns of *Eclogue* I and IX, in which external political forces throw the certainties of daily life into turmoil, constraining the shepherds to find whatever consolation there is in personal gestures of solidarity, whether these be Tityrus' offer to Meliboeus of shelter for the night or Lycidas' willingness to share Moeris' burden as they walk towards the city. In this reading, Hobbinol becomes the classical shepherd, not in the negative sense that he has a "fondness for an easy life" (Hume, p. 38), but in the positive (and hardly unchristian) sense that, forced to accept what fortune brings, he meets the situation by reflecting those bonds of compassion, generosity, or friendship that define the human community.

Universty of Toronto

Notes

1. Paul J. Alpers, *The Singer of the Eclogues: A Study of Virgilian Pastoral* (Berkeley: University of California Press, 1979), 65; Annabel Patterson, *Pastoral and Ideology: Virgil to Valéry* (Berkeley: University of California Press, 1988); see also Julia Reinhard Lupton, "Home-Making in Ireland: Virgil's Eclogue I and Book VI of *The Faerie Queene*," in *Spenser Studies* VIII, ed. Patrick Cullen and Thomas P. Roche, Jr. (New York: AMS Press, 1989): 119–45, and John D. Bernard, *Ceremonies of Innocence: Pastoralism in the Poetry of Edmund Spenser* (Cambridge: Cambridge University Press, 1989), Ch. 2.

2. Virgil criticism generally relates the two poems; English Renaissance discussions generally do not.

3. Patrick Cullen, *Spenser, Marvell and Renaissance Pastoral* (Cambridge: Harvard University Press, 1970), 1–26.

4. See Lupton, p. 141, on the "'historicity' of pastoral."

5. There is also a veiled reference to corruption of secular power in *Sept.* (ll. 122–28). See Anthea Hume, *Edmund Spenser: Protestant Poet*, (Cambridge: Harvard University Press, 1984) and David Norbrook, *Poetry and Politics in the English Renaissance* (London: Routledge and Kegan Paul, 1984).

6. The terminology here is Cullen's; I do not mean to imply that he is unaware of the relation between Mantuan and Virgil. See the excellent discussion of Mantuan and Virgil in Nancy Jo Hoffman, *Spenser's Pastorals: The Shepheardes Calender and "Colin Clout"* (Baltimore: Johns Hopkins University Press, 1977).

7. Bernard, p. 51, gets the final assessment of the *SC* right, though I am unwilling to grant his conjecture about which models are most "immediate": "Though Spenser's immediate models are less often Vergil than Mantuan and Marot . . . his feeling for the form of the total work, as well as for its political/cultural assumptions, proclaims his Vergilian kinship."

8. Tradition identifies Tityrus with Virgil, but the poem offers little support. The original basis for the identification is probably IV.6 (Apollo's address to the poet as "Tityrus"), but this may be (as Robert Coleman argues) merely generic humility. See notes to I.1 and VI.4, and discussion of "names" as characters on p. 25 in Robert Coleman, ed. *Vergil: Eclogues* (Cambridge: Cambridge University Press, 1977). The problem is complicated by the apparent identification of Menalcas with the poet of *Eclogue* II and III at V.86–87.

9. My text and translation are from *The Eclogues*, ed. and trans. Guy Lee (Harmondsworth, Middlesex: Penguin Books, 1984).

10. Erwin Panofsky, "*Et in Arcadia ego:* Poussin and the Elegiac Tradition," in *Meaning in the Visual Arts* (Garden City NJ: Doubleday Anchor Books, 1955; 1st publ. 1936), 300.

11. See, e.g., Jacques Perret, ed. *Les Bucoliques* (Paris: Presses Universitaires de France, 1970; 1st publ. 1964); Michael C. J. Putnam, *Virgil's Pastoral Art* (Princeton: Princeton University Press, 1970), 20–81; A. J. Boyle, ed. *The Eclogues of Virgil* (Melbourne: Hawthorn Press, 1976), 19; Coleman, 90; Stephen V. Tracy, "Theocritean Bucolic and Virgilian Pastoral: Commentary on Alpers," *Arethusa*, 23 (1990): 50–52.

12. Alpers, *The Singer of the Eclogues*, 97. The term is originally from Charles Segal, "*Tamen Cantabitis: Arcades*—Exile and Arcadia in Eclogues One and Nine," in *Poetry*

and Myth in Ancient Pastoral: Essays on Theocritus and Virgil (Princeton: Princeton University Press, 1981; essay orig. publ. 1964), pp. 278–79. It will be clear to readers of Alpers' book — and other articles — that my understanding of pastoral owes much to his sensitive readings of this literature.

13. One is reminded of course of the ending of Keats's *To Autumn*.

14. My text is *Adulescentia: The Ecloques of Mantuan* (Baptista [Spagnuoli] Mantuanus), ed. and trans. Lee Piepho, World Literature in Translation, 14 (New York: Garland Publishing, 1989).

15. If *favet* is heard as an echo from Virgil's Eclogue 4 (line 10), Mantuan could be linking the promise of Falco to the onset of a golden age.

16. The text for *The Shepheardes Calender* is taken from *The Yale Edition of the Shorter Poems of Edmund Spenser,* edd. William A. Oram, Einar Bjorvand, Ronald Bond, Thomas H. Cain, Alexander Dunlop and Richard Schell (New Haven: Yale University Press, 1989).

17. This line translates one that appears in both Eclogue 1 and Mantuan 9. In E 1 there is no answer possible, in M 9 Candidus' clear alternative is to return home with his flock.

18. See Thomas G. Rosenmeyer, *The Green Cabinet: Theocritus and the European Pastoral Lyric* (Berkeley: University of California Press, 1969), 42 ff, 105; Alpers, 86 for the importance of Epicureanism. Friendship is strongly implied, e.g., in the description of Corydon and Thyrsis, the *Arcades ambo* of Eclogue 7 and in the pronouns *tuus* and *noster* in Eclogue 9. Lewis and Short seems to indicate that *amicitia* is not a word used in Latin poetry, though the more metrically convenient *amicus* occurs regularly.

19. Putnam, 305.

20. Coleman suggests three different possible reconstructions of the situation at IX. 4 n (p. 257).

21. Lee trans., altered in first clause and printed as prose.

22. The concordance bears out the impression that the usage is not common. See René Lecrompe, *Virgile, Bucoliques: Index verborum; Relevés statistiques,* Alpha-Omega XXIV (Hildesheim and New York: Georg Olms Verlag, 1970).

23. I argue elsewhere that *October* picks up the theme of poetry that is missing from Spenser's *September,* thus becoming a companion poem that splits the interests of Eclogue 9.

24. See the discussion in William Empson, *Some Versions of Pastoral* (Norfolk, Conn.: New Directions, 1960; orig. publ. 1935), e.g., 12. Frederick T. Griffiths, *Theocritus at Court,* Mnemosyne Suppl. 55 (Leiden: E. J. Brill, 1979), 40, elaborates some of the implications of Empson for classical pastoral. Hobbinol is not a pastor-shepherd elsewhere in the *Shephardes Calender.*

25. Ovid, *Heroides* 4. 89. The speaker is Phaedra, but I believe the tag has a "life" independent of the morality of its allusive speaker. Sidney, e.g., uses a version of it — a bow too long bent that must be unstrung or it will break — quite neutrally: see the discussion in Neil Rudenstine, *Sidney's Poetic Development* (Cambridge: Harvard University Press, 1967), 3–15. For Spenser's frequent moral ambivalence about the need to rest (Guyon, Redcrosse, Calidore's truancy) see Bernard, 82–84.

26. Although *Februarie* shares some of the same tonal features as the ecclesiastical eclogues, it does not make us question the identity of Thenot and Cuddie as ordinary shepherds.

27. See Harry Berger, Jr. *Revisionary Play: Studies in the Spenserian Dynamics* (Berkeley: University of California Press, 1988), 306.

28.   David R. Shore, *Spenser and the Poetics of Pastoral: A Study in the World of Colin Clout,* (Montreal: McGill-Queen's University Press, 1985), 36–48, makes a good case for "doubleness" by arguing the sense of each position.

29.   William J. Kennedy, "The Virgilian Legacies of Petrarch's *Bucolicum Carmen* and Spenser's *Shephardes Calender,* in *The Early Renaisance: Virgil and the Classical Tradition,* ed. Anthony L. Pellegrini, *Acta* IX (Binghamton, NY: The Center for Medieval and Early Renaissance Studies, 1985): 94, singles out *September, October,* and *November* as demonstrating Spenser's understanding of the Virgilian model.

30.   There is interesting new material on this in Kathryn J. Gutzwiller, *Theocritus' Pastoral Analogies: The Formation of a Genre* (Madison, Wis.: University of Wisconsin Press, 1991), Part I.

31.   Cf. e.g., John Van Sickle, *The Design of Virgil's Bucolics,* Filologia e critica, 24 (Rome: Edizioni dell' Ateneo & Bizzari, 1978), 66–68.

32.   And not necessarily to their moral detriment: an important ancestor of the pastoral shepherd is Homer's Eumaeus. See David M. Halperin, *Before Pastoral: Theocritus and the Ancient Tradition of Bucolic Poetry* (New Haven: Yale University Press, 1983), e.g., 224–26, and Griffiths, 44, 49. Gutzwiller is also relevant.

33.   Cf. Shore, 50–52.

34.   See Lynn Staley Johnson, *Shepherdes Calender: An Introduction* (University Park: Pennsylvania State University Press, 1990), 76, and Hume, 38–39, who reads the debate as "essentially about the claims of limited versus unlimited clerical commitment." Hoffman, on the other hand (117–18), is sympathetic to Hobbinol.

35.   Berger nevertheless calls Diggon's answer "one of the more incomprehensible moments in the history of English poetry and speech" (p. 310).

36.   Alpers, 97: "As opposed to words like 'resolve,' 'reconcile,' or 'transcend,' 'suspend' implies no permanently achieved new relation."

37.   The implication of line 172 — "Say it out Diggon, what ever it hight," concerning Roffy's story — is that Hobbinol is more brave in his support for the good than he is willing to attack injustice, just the position one would expect in a classical shepherd.

38.   Gutzwiller traces the history of the position back to the archaic period.

39.   Hume (gently) 39; Johnson (not so gently) 74–77.

40.   See Hallett Smith, *Elizabethan Poetry: A Study in Convention, Meaning and Expression* (Cambridge: Harvard University Press, 1952), 45n, on Hobbinol's expressing "the central doctrine of pastoral," and S. K. Heninger, Jr., "Spenser and Sidney at Leicester House," *Spenser Studies* VIII (1987), on the *Shepherdes Calender* as a common project of Harvey and Spenser; he speaks (on p. 242) of the deference paid to Harvey as Hobbinol.

LESLIE T. WHIPP

Weep for Dido:
Spenser's November Eclogue

*I*N THE NOVEMBER Eclogue of Edmund Spenser's *Shepherdes
Calender*, Immerito includes a lament for Dido; in effect he shows
Colin Clout weeping for Dido, and exhorting shepherds and
nymphs to weep for Dido. I want here to look a bit more closely
at the associations of the name "Dido," and at the significance of
the character of Dido and of her lay in our understanding of Colin Clout and his year, and of the *Shepherdes Calender* as a whole.

The figure of Dido invites such attention for a number of reasons. Spenser nowhere else refers to Dido, only here, and here
she appears to be unnecessarily complex in her associations. That
is, for the ostensible purposes of the lament, any pastoral female
name would do, but the one Spenser chooses to use is not a pastoral figure, and is not a simple figure, but is instead a well-
known epic figure with a considerable history of ambivalent and
contradictory associations. In the "Argument" prefaced to the
November eclogue, E. K., the author's designated mediator between us and the poem, directs our attention to Dido, further
underlining her importance: "In this x. Aeglogue he bewayleth
the death of some mayden of greate bloud, whom he calleth Dido.
The personage is secrete, and to me altogether unknowne, albe of
him selfe I often required the same."[1] E. K.'s note is all the more

17

forceful if, as several recent scholars have argued, E. K. is a mask for Spenser himself, Edmund of Kent, as Schleiner would have it, or "Edmundus Kedemon," as Waldman maintains.[2]

Dido thus invites our attention to her, and to the way she prepares for and constrains the conclusion of the *Shepherdes Calender* in the next eclogue. Yet published criticism has paid little attention to Dido until recently, and a good bit of that has in fact followed the direction E. K. pointed out.[3] Most notably, the work of Paul McLane, seeking to explicate the details of the historical allegory, argues that Dido is a figure for Elizabeth, who by her flirtation with a French marriage, seemed to be dead to the Protestant cause.[4] The bases for identifying Elizabeth and Dido are quite literal, Virgil's Dido having also been named Elissa, and Elissa of "April" having been identified as the daughter of Pan, whom E. K. has explicated as Henry VIII. As Maren-Sofie Røstvig has observed, though, if the value of this poem is primarily topical, and thus so limited to a moment in time, and so little regarding of human experience before and after that moment, then the poem has very little value.[5]

It has also been argued recently that Spenser's Dido has no necessary relationship with Virgil's: In fact, there is nothing in "November" beyond the name of Dido (and the presumed pun on Elissa in the Elisian fields) to confirm our assumption that this is either Virgil's Dido or the chaste "widow Dido" of the alternative tradition.[6] Yet the occurrences of Dido in Renaissance literature prior to Spenser are clearly not independent of the traditional Dido; see for example Petrarch's Dido in *The Triumph of Chastity* (ll. 229–36), George Turberville's "Of Dido and the truth of her death" (ll. 1–15), or Christopher Marlowe's play, *Dido Queene of Carthage.* Further, as a general rule Spenser's practice in using names is not to ignore the associations provided by tradition; certainly other names in *Shepherdes Calender* are richly associative, resonating from the pastoral poems of Theocritus, Virgil, and Marot to the Elizabethan court. So I wish to try to explore a bit more carefully the associations of the name "Dido."

To do so, I find it useful to speak of three different Dido poems in Spenser's November eclogue—the Dido poem which Colin offers us, the Dido poem which E. K. offers us, and the Dido poem which Spenser offers us.

"The Lament for Dido" which Colin offers us is the simplest and most directly accessible of the three. Thenot seeks to elicit a song as a sort of therapy for Colin, because, as he says to Colin,

Thy Muse to long slombreth in sorrowing,
Lulled a sleepe through loves misgovernaunce.

(3–4)

To that end, Thenot advises him that "To sadder times thou mayst attune thy quill," and invites him to sing of "Dido, dead alas and drent" (37), whose death Thenot does in fact claim personally to grieve. Colin acquiesces, "*Thenot* to that I choose, thou doest me tempt," and delivers perhaps the finest elegy in the language.

Despite his compliance and success, Colin nowhere claims to voice his individual grief at the death of Dido in the poem; Colin does have an interest in Dido, does seek to associate himself with Dido, but the grief he expresses is a grief of others, one to which he can give expression because he is independently made miserable by rejection in love, by winter. "Thilke sollein season" (18).

Curiously, Colin refers to the invitation to write the lament as a temptation: "*Thenot* to that I choose, thou doest me tempt." Thenot as tempter? How are we to understand that? Thenot occurs previously in the February eclogue, where he is an Old Man almost in the Pauline sense.[7] That is, as Lynn Johnson has argued, the Thenot of February is a spiteful, self-serving old man who cloaks his hostility in ostensible charity and wisdom.[8] Perhaps this is the Old Man who here tempts Colin to indulge his emotion by composing a lament for Dido and to whom Colin acquiesces.

But in what sense is Colin's lament self-indulgent? Lynn Johnson has argued that the lament for Dido contrasts with his love songs in not being self-indulgent: "Colin in 'Nouember' takes his subject from Thenot's suggestion, sings for someone else, and uses the world as a means of transcending the world's sorrows" (129). I suggest instead that Colin is much more mechanically conventional than that: he has constructed an elegiac consolation beautifully suited to assuage the grief of a Thenot, one illustrating well the consoling conventions of the genre, but not one in which his own sorrow at the wintering of the year and the frustration of his love is in any way transcended: it is not clear from the lay itself, or from any other part of the eclogue, that Colin himself grieves for Dido. Further, the figures and locale in the lay, Lobbin, Dido, and Kent, so far as we are aware, exist without allegorical dimensions for Colin: Colin delivers a literal, not an allegorical poem. Indeed Colin's participation in the situation is quite clearly motivated: when Colin would not sing, Thenot had made him a better offer:

And if thou wilt bewayle my wofull tene:
I shall thee give yond Cosset for thy payne:
And if thy rymes as rownd and rufull bene,
As those that did thy Rosalind complayne,
Much greater gyfts for guerdon thou shalt gayne,
Then Kidde or Cosset, which I the bynempt:
                                         (41–46)

When he ends, Colin gets the "Cossette" and (in what I take to be the author's joke) a natural world which heeds Colin's careful verse by letting "streaming teares be poured out": Thenot ends the eclogue by saying he does not know whether to laugh or cry, but he observes, "Now gynnes to mizzle, hye we homeward fast." (203–8) The day answers his question by crying itself. After that splendid elegy, Immerito ends the eclogue with a joke.

The joke undercuts recent arguments that Dido's spiritual progress in Colin's lay implies a similar progress for Colin himself. The argument is further weakened though if one finds the identification of Spenser and Colin unwarranted, as I do. As Patrick Cullen has observed, "It is Immeritó, not Colin, who 'equals' Spenser" (79). It is reasonable to ascribe the possibility of spiritual growth to the poet, to Immeritó-Spenser, but all the evidence we have concerning Colin suggests that he does not grow at all: "Colin's obsessive love leads to the tragedy of his self-destruction";[9] Colin goes from despair in January to suicide in December, which for Spenser's readers then and now can scarcely be construed as progress. Colin does not seem to be privy to the allegorical dimension of the song he sings.

What about E. K.'s Dido poem? E. K., unlike Colin, may understand the allegory, but refuses to assume responsibility for doing so. He admires the lay and the eclogue very much indeed, he strongly underlines their importance for other readers, he understands the lay and the eclogue more fully than Colin did, he understands that the lay is indeed both literal and allegorical; in the "Argument" for November, he says, "In this xi. AEglogue he bewayleth the death of some mayden of great bloud, whome he calleth Dido. The personage is secrete, and to me altogether unknowne, albe of him selfe I often required the same." E. K. does not want to be thought to understand the allegory, implying instead that the allegory is probably not what it looks like since he with all his insider's knowledge could not figure it out. Such elaborate defensiveness suggests fear of power, and a probable political allegory, particularly if Schleiner and Waldman are correct in arguing that E. K. is a mask for Spenser himself.

To sort that out more clearly, it is useful to turn to Immerito's (Spenser's) perspective on the Dido poem, the November eclogue, and the allegory, and to consider both the allegory E. K. seems to point to by not pointing to it, and another allegory having to do with Colin Clout. In the first allegory, as Paul McLane and many others have argued, Dido works as a figure for Elizabeth, who by her flirtation with a French marriage, seemed to be dead to the Protestant cause. In effect, from the perspective of the persons in the Leicester circle, the flirtation with a French marriage raised the possibility that the Queen might let her satisfaction in her private person overwhelm her responsibilities in her public role, the pleasures of love preempt the royal duty. This topical allegory has been abundantly discussed, and need not be rehearsed here, except for one aspect — the complex appropriateness of the traditions of Dido to that role.

As Don Cameron Allen showed many years ago, and as Barbara J. Bono has more complexly argued more recently, the figure of Dido came to the Renaissance with conflicting associations.[10] Allen laid out two basic traditions — Virgilian and Ovidian. The Virgilian tradition, stemming from the *Aeneid,* is the epic tradition of the queen who places love above her public responsibilities and is abandoned by her lover, who, called by the gods, places his public responsibilities above his love for her; in this version, Dido gives herself over to her emotions, and kills herself, abandoning her people and her public responsibilities. The Ovidian tradition, stemming from the *Heroides,* speaks of Aeneas' departure from the perspective of Dido herself or of Dido's sister, and is sympathetic to Dido, representing Aeneas' actions as selfish rather than heroic, and representing Dido as virtuous and heroic, a woman who kills herself rather than submit to the lust of another man. The traditions thus are at the outset conflicting — Dido the lover who ignores her public responsibilities, and Dido the heroine who values her chastity more than her life. By the thirteenth century, the Ovidian Dido was rather more frequent than the Virgilian.[11] Barbara Bono has recently demonstrated yet more subtlety and complexity in the tradition of "Dido" as Spenser inherited it, a tradition of the malleability of the Dido material and the way it lent itself to appropriate expression of the values of each new age.[12] As tidily messy as this representation of the traditional associations of Dido is, clearly the conflicting implications within it make it a very effective set of associations for use in veiling a comment about the Queen.

Such a tidy sense of the tradition, however, oversimplifies the experience of writers like Spenser, as Boccaccio's treatment of the figure of Dido illustrates. Boccaccio's Dido is various. His early Dido, in his Italian works, is morally ambiguous, often a sympathetic love figure, "an example of suffering in love." After Boccaccio's meeting with Petrarch, though, he began work on his humanistic, Latin writings, working within the tradition of rhetorical criticism deriving from Fulgentius and Donatus, and interpreting Virgil in terms of the praise he seems to give virtue, and the blame he seems to give vice. This led him to speak of Dido in two clear but quite different ways. One derived from Virgil, and interpreted Virgil as showing Dido's concupiscence in order to demonstrate Aeneas's great virtue. The other derived from "historians," writers whom Boccaccio held to be more historically correct, and who stressed the faithfulness and chastity of the life of Dido, explaining that Virgil did not tell the literal truth about Dido. In both cases, the epideictic impulse dominates — of praising virtue and blaming vice. This approach, consistent with the theoretical approach Boccaccio lays out in books 14–15 of his *Geneology of the Gods,* i.e., rhetorical and moral, remained popular in criticism for many generations. Again, one sees how precisely appropriate was Spenser's selection of the name "Dido," how richly suggestive for covertly pressuring the Queen and the courtly circle to regard the French dalliance less favorably. With regard to the first allegory, then, the gloss by E. K. provides the author deniability, while allowing the author covertly to make his first allegorical case.

There is yet another strand to the associations of "Dido," however, and this has to do with the second allegory, with the allegorical implications for Colin and the role of the poet which Spenser builds into the elegy for Dido. As I have already indicated, we are asked to distinguish Immerito and Colin, and to see Immerito, that is Spenser, not Colin, as the new English poet, to see Colin as a negative foil for the brilliant new poet, Edmund Spenser. In that context, Spenser writes a poem for Colin which has implications beyond those which Colin himself could see, and some of those implications derive from this additional tradition of associations for the name "Dido."

That additional tradition is the Augustinian tradition, stemming from Augustine's *Confessions.* This concerns the attitude that a Christian ought to take to Dido's story as represented in the *Aeneid;* Augustine, reviewing his attitude toward classical literature and languages, and puzzling over his early and abiding dislike of Greek, contrasts it with his keen interest in Latin language and literature.

In other subjects, however, I was compelled to learn about the wanderings of a certain Aeneas, oblivious of my own wanderings, and to weep for Dido dead, who slew herself for love. And all this while I bore with dry eyes my own wretched self dying to thee, O God, my life, in the midst of these things.

The essential theme in this Augustinian tradition has just been sounded, the blindness of a man who would weep for Dido dead and know not to weep for his own dying to God, and Augustine goes on to emphasize it:

21. For what can be more wretched than the wretch who has no pity upon himself, who sheds tears over Dido, dead for the love of Aeneas, but who sheds no tears for is own death in not loving thee, O God.

Augustine perceives as well that one is sustained in this blindness by the approbation of those who admire our knowledge, our "conning":

Those around me, also sinning, thus cried out: "Well done! Well done!" The friendship of this world is fornication against thee; and "Well done! Well done!" is cried until one feels ashamed not to show himself a man in this way. For my own condition I shed no tears, though I wept for Dido, who "sought death at the sword's point," (*Aeneid,* VI, 457) while I myself was seeking the lowest rung of thy creation, having forsaken thee, earth sinking back to earth again.

As Augustine thinks of Dido, he sees a similarity between himself and Dido, in that both are dead lovers, Dido the lover of Aeneas and Augustine the lover of God, and he is struck by the enormity of the "madness" which leads him to weep for Dido's death, and not for his own "death" in his relationship with God, a madness for which the world applauds him.

Before I try to state the allegorical implications of this Augustinian tradition for our understanding of the figure of Colin, I wish to underscore the connections between the Augustinian and the Spenserian texts: First, Colin, like Augustine, is "compelled . . . to weep for Dido dead, who slew herself for love," and that clause applies even if Colin is unaware of the political allegory implicit in the character whom he is lamenting. With overtones of Petrarchan exaggeration, Spenser has Colin dwell with Petrarchan exaggeration on the weeping, "Let streaming teares be poured out in store" (61), "Waile ye" (64), "Waile ye" (65), "Waile ye" (66). Yet Colin, too, "bore with dry eyes . . . (his) own wretched self dying to . . . God . . . ," not just in the November eclogue, but throughout the *Shepherdes Calender,* and in the next and final eclogue, we will see him "seeking the lowest rung of . . . creation. . . . , earth sinking back to earth again."

There is yet another turn, for Colin is himself like Dido in having failed to resolve the conflict between the demands of his responsibilities as a poet-shepherd, and the demands of his love, the conflict which provides the slender, central narrative skeleton of the *Calender* as a whole. We are made aware of this conflict in the January eclogue, and explicitly reminded of it in April, June, October, and November and in the December eclogue, the conflict leads to Colin's "self-destruction;" Colin, like Dido, is a victim of his own "obsessive love."[13]

The connections between the text of the *Shepherdes Calender* and Augustine's *Confessions* are scarcely coincidental. Augustine's works had for the most part been continuously available during the medieval period, and were revived with much the same reverence and scholarly attention and reinterpretation by Renaissance humanists as the classical texts were.[14] Perhaps the most significant and influential of the humanists in this connection was Petrarch, who for many years carried on his person a pocket-sized copy of *The Confessions,* and who wrote his own version of that book in his *Secretum.* "It is not too much to conclude," Albert Rabil has written, "that the encounter between Petrarch and Augustine, though in some respects unique among the humanists, brought into being the idea of a Christian classical antiquity, an idea that, on the one side, enlarged humanism and, on the other, subjected the Christian tradition to the same kind of critical analysis that was applied to the pagan tradition."[15] In reading Spenser's *Shepherdes Calender,* I find it useful to think of it as shaped throughout by this Petrarchan-Augustinian merging of Christian and Classical associations, nowhere more so than in the implications of the name "Dido."

The name "Dido" is chosen partly to characterize Colin as one who sheds no tears for the death of his relationship with God. Colin, like Petrarch in the *Secretum,* insists on dwelling in the morbid pleasure and wretchedness of tears and sighs and sleepless nights and solitude of his obsessive love for Rosalind. He does not have enough self-perception to see and to say to God as Augustine did, "I did not love thee," and he does not have, as Petrarch did in the *Secretum* an Augustine to serve as a conscience "who uncovers the secret thoughts which Petrarch tries to hide from himself."[16]

Colin succumbs to the temptation of Thenot, instead, who clearly corresponds to those of whom Augustine had said, 'Those around me, also sinning, thus cried out: "Well done! Well done!"' But Colin cannot see — as Augustine did — that "The friendship of this world is fornication against" God. Colin cannot see or say of himself, as Augustine did, "I myself was seeking the lowest rung of thy creation, having forsaken thee, earth sinking back to earth again;" he will commit suicide instead, but the reader should see Colin in that Augustinian light. Colin is a negative exemplum precisely in his indulgence "in Petrarch's *dissido* or sadness of soul."[17] Like Dido, he gives himself over to his emotions, and kills himself, abandoning his people and his public responsibilities.

What are the implications of this reading of the lament for Dido in our understanding of the structure and meaning of the *Shepherdes Calender* as a whole?

One implication concerns the identification of Colin as a Petrarchan lover-poet, and Spenser's rejection of that way of being a poet. We must distinguish Spenser and Colin, and see Spenser, not Colin, as the new English poet, to see Colin as a negative foil for the brilliant new poet, Immerito-Spenser. This is why the poem which Spenser writes for Colin has implications Colin cannot see. When we see the Dido elegy in its Augustinian tradition, we can also see that Spenser in announcing his poetic vocation sought to distinguish it from the Petrarchan poet: Spenser, unlike Colin, will not be a poet who weeps for Dido.

A second implication of this reading concerns the importance of November to a reading of the *Shepherdes Calender* as a whole: Some recent criticism has viewed the November eclogue as an optimistic interruption of the wintry gloom with which the poem ends, an optimism based upon a transcendence of earthly limitations and the fulfillment of spiritual longing even for Colin.[18] But, in fact, the lament turns around and fiercely undercuts that possibility by contrasting the destiny he sees for Dido with the destiny that he insists on for himself: the point of the lament is that Colin cannot weep for himself, cannot transcend his earthly chains, can only seek the lowest rung of creation. Thus the November eclogue is of a piece with the December eclogue: Colin, unlike Immerito, is hopelessly bound in earth and time, and plods out his gloomy year month by month.

Third, the consonance of November and December lends some support to the argument that there are three different and conflicting patterns of organization in the *Shepherdes Calender* overall, one in which Colin participates, two in which Spenser participates. That involving Colin is a straightforward twelve-month calendar and convicts Colin as an inadequate poet; the second is the cyclical organization of the twelve months by which Colin's linear experience is transcended though yet in time.[19] The third, Spenser's organization, uses E. K.'s taxonomy of eclogues to transcend time, and shows how a proper poet builds a reflection of the spiritual nature of the cosmos into the merely temporal. This structural scheme derives from the sequence of kinds of E. K.'s "ranckes" of eclogues — Plaintive, Moral, and Recreative, and merges contiguous examples of a single "rancke," as follows:

---------P	January
------M	February
---R	March-April
------M	May
---------P	June
------M	July
---R	August
------M	September-October
---------P	November-December

Such analysis yields the spatially palindromic structure P-M-R-M-P-M-R-M-P first described by Marianne Brown.[20] Where the organization associated with Colin is based on twelve units, i.e., can be factored into 3×4, the organization associated with Immerito or Spenser himself is based on nine units, a number based on the three of the Trinity. The significance of the numbers derives from conventional numerological associations, four as the number of temporal things — the seasons, the winds, the elements, the qualities, the divisions of the zodiac, for example, and three as a number of the spiritual things, the Trinity, or the Image of God in Man — Reason, Memory and Will and the ranks of the angels. Concerning the numbers four and twelve, Røstvig observes: "It is a Renaissance commonplace that the world of Time (the twelve months) and Space (the twelve signs of the zodiac) is based on conjunctions between groups of four and three"[21] and cites Augustine's commentary on Psalm 6:

Now it is obvious that the number four refers to the body, from the four elements of which it consists, and the four qualities, dry, wet, hot, and cold. Hence it is regulated by the four seasons, spring, summer, autumn and winter. All this is familiar to you. . . . The number three, however, refers to the soul, as we learn from the precept to love God in a threefold manner. . . .[22]

Røstvig might have cited Augustine's *On Christian Doctrine*, XVI, 25, to the same purpose. And Pietro Bongo attests to the continued vitality of this tradition in the Renaissance.[23] In a sermon, John Donne illustrates well conventions associated with the number 3 at a still later point in time:

> Let us therefore, with S. Bernard, consider *Trinitatem Crea-tricem*, and *Trinitatem Creatam*, A Creating, and a Created Trinity; A Trinity, which the Trinity in Heaven, Father, Son, and Holy Ghost, hath created in our soules, Reason, Memory, and Will; and that we have super-created, added another Trinity, suggestion, and Consent, and Delight in Sin; And that God, after all this infuses another Trinity, Faith, Hope, and Charity, by which we returne to our first. . . .[24]

S. K. Heninger has called attention to a double structure in *The Shep-herdes Calender*, the linear structure of the story of the love-lorn Colin, and the cyclical structure of the year, which, however symbolic it may be of the zodiac and of the circling care of the Christian redemption,[25] must remain in and of itself "for short time an endlesse moniment." What is curiously missing from this analysis of this very obviously religious poem is the representation of the heavenly aspect of the Christian cosmos, the object of the positive love which the earth-mired and time-mired Colin Clout fails to perceive and present in his own life. As Kate Gartner Frost has observed with regard to John Donne's *Devotions*,

> The world of the Renaissance artist was ordered by reason, one that demanded a like aesthetic response. It was not for the artist to impose an individual and thus particular and to some degree irrational order on his creation but rather to reveal to his audience the inherently logical order of the cosmos, thus both turning their gaze to the Creator and eliciting admiration for the skill with which the poet's framework was constructed.[26]

If that applies to Donne, as Frost demonstrates that it indeed does, so much the more it applies a posteriori to the poetry of Edmund Spenser.

Spenser-Immerito, in constructing *The Shepherdes Calender,* and in asking us to see the twelve eclogues as concealing nine, built in not two
structures, but three—the linear structure of the time-bound Colin
Clout, the pastoral earthly structure of the cycle of the twelve-month
year, and the heavenly structure of the trinity of trinities, divinely
ordered, precisely palindromic.

Thus, when one looks at the associations of the name "Dido," and
asks what association of the name might have led the young Edmund
Spenser to select it from among the many, many classical names available to him, one finds a rich tradition that allows Spenser to achieve an
astonishing multivalence in Colin's lament for Dido: while veiling the
implication that the queen might be tempted to let her passion overcome her reason, to let her private satisfaction diminish her exercise of
her public responsibilities, and dangling the implication that the queen
might indeed be the heroic woman who would rather sacrifice her life
than her chastity, the name also allows this brilliant new poet to advertise himself and fashion his own claim to be the new English poet by
convicting his foil, Colin, of being so mired in earth and time that he
cannot see, as the real poet can, that God is the light of his heart, and
the bread of the inner mouth of his soul.

University of Nebraska-Lincoln

NOTES

1.   References from Spenser are to William A. Oram, Einar Bjorvand, Ronald
Bond, Thomas H. Cain, Alexander Dunlop, and Richard Schell, eds. *The Yale Edition
of the Shorter Poems of Edmund Spenser* (New Haven: Yale University Press, 1989).

2.   See Bruce R. Smith, "On Reading *The Shepherdes Calender*," *Spenser Studies: A
Renaissance Poetry Annual,* I (1980): 69–73; Louise Schleiner, "Spenser's 'E. K.' as Edmund Kent (Kenned/of Kent): Kyth (Couth), Kissed, and Kunning-Conning,"
ELR (Autumn 1990): 374–407; and Louis Waldman, "Spenser's Pseudonym 'E. K.'
and Humanist Self-Naming," *Spenser Studies: A Renaissance Poetry Annual,* IX (1991):
21–32. Waldman argues that Renaissance humanists often took literary pseudonyms
made by hellenizing the literal meanings of surnames; since "Spenser" also means
"steward," Spenser would probably have translated it as "Edmundus Kedemon,"
which, abbreviated, would be "E. K."

3.   See, for example, G. C. Moore Smith, "Spenser, 'Shepherd's Calender,'
'November,'" *Modern Language Review* 2 (1907): 346–47; Maren-Sofie Røstvig, "*The
Shepheardes Calender*—A Structural Analysis," *Renaissance and Modern Studies* 13
(1969): 49–75.

4.   Paul McLane, *Spenser's Shepheardes Calender: A Study in Elizabethan Allegory.*
(Notre Dame, Indiana: University of Notre Dame Press, 1961).

5.   Maren-Sofie Røstvig,"*The Shepherdes Calender*— A Structural Analysis," *Renaissance and Modern Studies* 13 (1969): 49–75; Røstvig does develop an argument for a spiritual rather than historical significance for the figure of Dido: "Both the placing and the structure of the Lay of Dido indicate that Spenser uses her death on a funeral pyre as a symbol of the ascent of the mind from earth to heaven" (69).

6.   Donald Cheney, "The Circular Argument of *The Shepherdes Calender*," in *Unfolded Tales: Essays on Renaissance Romance,* ed. George M. Logan and Gordon Teskey (Ithaca: Cornell University Press, 1989): 137–161.

7.   In which the old man "is corrupt according to the deceitful lusts" (Ephesians 4:22).

8.   Lynn Staley Johnson, *The Shepherdes Calender: An Introduction* (University Park: Pennsylvania State University Press, 1990).

9.   Cullen, p. 98.

10.   Don Cameron Allen, "Marlowe's Dido and the Tradition," in *Essays on Shakespeare and Elizabethan Drama in Honor of Hardin Craig,* edited by Richard Hosley (Columbia: University of Missouri Press, 1962); Barbara J. Bono, *Literary Transvaluation: From Vergilian Epic to Shakespearean Tragicomedy* (Berkeley: University of California Press, 1984).

11.   Judith Miller Ortiz, "The Two Faces of Dido: Classical Images and Medieval Reinterpretation," *Romance Quarterly* 33 (1986): 421–29.

12.   Barbara Bono, *Literary Transvaluation: From Vergilian Epic to Shakespearean Tragicomedy* (Berkeley: University of California Press, 1984).

13.   Cullen, p. 98.

14.   Eugene F. Rice, "The Renaissance Idea of Christian Antiquity: Humanist Patristic Scholarship," in *Renaissance Humanism: Foundations, Forms, and Legacy, Volume 1, Humanism in Italy,* ed. Albert Rabil, Jr. (Philadelphia University of Pennsylvania Press, 1988), 17–28.

15.   Albert Rabil, Jr., Petrarch, Augustine, and the Classical Christian Tradition," in *Renaissance Humanism,* I:97.

16.   Hans Baron, *Petrarch's* Secretum; *Its Making and Its Meaning* (Cambridge: The Medieval Academy of America, 1985), 222.

17.   Albert Rabil, Jr., "Petrarch, Augustine, and the Classical Christian Tradition," in *Renaissance Humanism:* I:97.

18.   See, for example, John D. Bernard, "'June' and the Structure of Spenser's *Shepherdes Calender,*" *Philological Quarterly* 60 (1981): 305, or Donald Cheney, op. cit.

19.   S. K. Heninger, The Implications of Form for the *"Shepherdes Calender," Studies in the Renaissance,* 9 (1962): 309–21.

20.   Marianne Brown, "Finely Framed, and Strongly Trussed Up Together: A Structural Approach to Edmund Spenser's *The Shepherdes Calender,* Diss., University of Oslo, 1978; cited in H. Neville Davies, "Spenser's *Shepherdes Calender:* The Importance of November," *Cahiers Elisabethains,* 20 (1981), 35–48.

21.   Røstvig, op. cit.

22.   St. Augustine, *On the Psalms* (1960), i. 63 ff.

23.   Petri Bongi Bergomatis, *Numerorum mysteria, Opvs maximarvm rervm doctrina, et copia refertvm, in quo mirus in primis, idemq perpetuus arithmeticae Pythagoricae cum diuinae paginae nvmeris consensus, multiplici ratione probatur,* (Bergomi: Typis Comini Venturae,

1599), v. p. 108 ff. and pp. 143–44 on the number 3; 201 ff. on the number 4, and p. 388 ff. on the number twelve and its factors 3 and 4.

24.   *The Sermons of John Donne,* eds. George R. Potter and Evelyn M. Simpson, 10 vols. (Berkeley: University of California Press, 1952–63), Vol. III, No. 5, 144–45.

25.   Maren-Sophie Røstvig, "Structure as prophecy: the influence of Biblical exegesis upon theories of literary structure," *Silent Poetry,* ed. Alastair Fowler, (London: Routledge and Kegan Paul, 1970), 63.

26.   Kate Gartner Frost, *Holy Delight: Typology, Numerology, and Autobiography in Donne's* Devotions Upon Emergent Occasions (Princeton, N.J.: Princeton University Press, 1990), 93.

ANTHONY ESOLEN

Spenserian Chaos:
Lucretius in *The Faerie Queene*

S PENSER'S FASCINATION with allegorical multiplicity — with what can resemble sheer disorder — is reflected in his treatment in *The Faerie Queene* of images of chaos and confusion. In particular, Spenser enjoys a rapprochement with Lucretius, the great poet of atomic randomness and physical law.[1] This rapprochement was unusual in Spenser's day. For Calvin, the Roman was "the filthy Lucretius," whose Epicurean school set up a shadow-deity so as to undermine all belief in God. Hooker pities Lucretians and "English Sadduccees" who deny the soul's immortality; Sidney's Pamela duels with the wicked queen Cecropia over whether the universe is guided by Providence or is produced by random atomic collision; DuBartas makes unacknowledged use of Lucretius' explanations of natural phenomena such as lightning, but in general wages constant war against Epicureans and Lucretians; Davies scoffs at atomism in *Orchestra,* his poem of cosmological and political order. The tag "Epicurean" was applied indiscriminately to various sorts of social rebels, from libertines to atheists to rabble-rousing Anabaptists.[2] Yet despite what would seem very good reasons for leaving Lucretius out of his poem entirely, Spenser alludes to *De Rerum Natura* during some of *The Faerie Queene's* most cosmologically important moments, and, in the episode at the Temple of Venus, translates Lucretius' invocation to Venus in toto. In addition, the goddesses with whom Lucretius' *alma Venus* is allied—Isis and the great mother Cybele—are critical to interpretation of Spenser's views of creation, sexuality, and civilization.

What is the final principle of nature: government or chance? Lucretius embeds this question in his oxymoronic phrases "natura creatrix" (1.629, 2.1117, 5.1362) and "fortuna gubernans" (5.107). Each phrase may be read in two ways, depending upon which word one stresses, or which idea one subordinates. The Latin compression leaves the subordination or coordination unclear. Nature and fortune may be the non-principles of a godless universe, or they may *govern,* that is, steer, destine, order. Lucretius opts against teleology. Fortune governs the world—meaning that the world is not governed at all, except insofar as certain things naturally happen given the characteristics of atoms and their laws of motion. And yet what in Lucretius is ambiguous phrasing becomes metaphysical profundity in Spenser. The gods of the pacifist Roman enjoyed a static tranquillity, unable to touch or to be touched; Spenser's Providence not only creates and orders human history but seems at times to burst into it in the most flagrant and joyous ways. Spenser insists upon creation and order, but that creation and order uses as its *materia informis* something wild and wanton which is itself a worthy creation of the generative God and which must never be eliminated. Such a capacious embrace of order and freedom is thoroughly in accord with Spenser's linkage of human sexuality with action on behalf of God and queen. This paper will examine a few of the more cosmologically, psychologically, and politically interesting moments of Spenserian chaos, attending to Spenser's allusions to Lucretius and finally to Spenser's adaptation of the hymn to Venus.

The odd harmony between Spenser and materialism often arises when he presents a goddess as a controlling principle for the physical and moral universe. Take, for example, Cambina.

Spenser's iconography makes it clear that when Cambina halts the fight between Triamond and Cambello (4.3.37f.) she acts as Cybele, the Mater Magna, the Phrygian goddess of generation and civilization. This turreted, lion-yoking goddess appears everywhere in classical literature. Ovid's *Fasti* 4.179–372 gives a most engaging account. Cybele is identified with Rhea, the wife of Saturn (Chronos), the god of time who devours his children. Cybele spirits Jupiter away to Crete and tricks her husband by giving him a blanketed stone to swallow; meanwhile her Corybantes and Curetes clash their kettledrums and cymbals so that Saturn will not hear the infant's cries (197–214). She is also the mother of Rome, as the Romans traced their ancestry to the Trojans and the Phrygians, and she makes a grand entrance into the mouth of the Tiber centuries after the city has been founded (247–348). She is a civilizing goddess, having tamed the lions and having been the first to give towers to cities (215–21). She punishes her follower Attis, who had taken an oath of celibacy, by causing him to go mad and castrate himself (221–46); she encourages the visiting of neighbors, being herself a peregrine deity (354–56); she likes white cheese and pounded herbs, because they remind her of her old home on Mount Ida (367–72). In the *Metamorphoses* she turns Hippomenes and Atalanta into the two lions who draw her chariot, after an annoyed Venus has induced them to copulate in the great mother's temple (10.681–707). She is also the tutelary deity of Aeneas' ships and therefore of Rome itself (14.533–65)—her main role throughout Vergil (*Aen.* 6.781–787; 9.77–122; 10.215–259). Catullus ends his poem 63, primarily a monologue in which Attis bemoans his impulsive emasculation, with a prayer that the goddess and her fury stay far from his home (91–93). As Peter Hawkins and Thomas P. Roche, Jr., have shown, these aspects of the Cybele myth were known to Spenser through the classical texts themselves and through the interpretations of them given by such mythographers as Boccaccio, Cartari, and Conti, who in Renaissance fashion emphasized her civilizing over her chaotic side.[3]

Yet none of the poets above provides the fully cosmic-civic Cybele which Spenser needs. Catullus stresses her fury and unreason, but has no other use for her. Vergil tames Cybele by making her the mother of Rome, referring in passing to the wild drumming and clashing of her followers. She is not felt to be *the* physical force which makes all things grow. Ovid is mainly interested in the origins of endearing myths and rituals. Though he does associate Cybele with Rhea, he never treats her as the goddess of nature, nor does he bring into stark relief the contradiction of a goddess who inspires both natural chaos and civic order. For the latter one requires a poet who has a religious sense of the power of nature, and a skeptical respect for the uses which this religious sense can be put to. Such a poet was Lucretius.

In *De Rerum Natura,* the cult of Cybele arises out of a man's consideration of the earth's generative powers (2.598–645). Cybele sits calmly in her chariot, wielding her unifying power to tame the wildest beasts (604–5) and to teach her devotees to apply their worship of her to love for their mothers and their motherland. Thus natural and political allegory merge. Yet she has more than a trace of the demonic about her, with her frenzied, self-flagellating eunuchs and their terrifying music. "Raucisonoque minantur cornua cantu," "They thrust forth their horns with a hoarse bray," says Lucretius, who then describes how these priests wield ("praeportant") their weapons, "signs of violent furor," in order to strike terror into impious and ungrateful souls. The impiety and ingratitude are sins against the above-mentioned parents. Lucretius recognizes the utility to the Roman state of this patriotism-inspiring myth. Yet, true to his Epicurean quietism, he recoils from the scene, dismissing Cybele in cursory fashion: "quae bene et eximie quamuis disposta ferantur, / longe sunt tamen a uera ratione repulsa " ("which things, no matter how ingeniously presented, true reason must emphatically reject")(644–45).

How can a Christian adapt this Cybele, presented by a poet who is alive to the power of nature and the virtues of civilization but who shrinks from patriotism and religious fervor? Spenser could have omitted the images of human suffering, erasing the political from his natural allegory. He does not. Spenser's Cambina is mild compared with Lucretius' Cybele, being but a concerned sister of Cambello and a learned magician with potions for concord and friendship. Yet Spenser admits the demonic: Cambina enters the fray not with a peaceful, orderly pageant, but with a barely restrained riot:

> All suddenly they heard a troublous noyes,
> That seemd some perilous tumult to desine,
> Confusd with womens cries, and shouts of boyes,
> Such as the troubled Theaters oftimes annoyes.
> (4.3.37.6–9)

Women and boys—no men—follow Cambina. Such too are the followers of the egalitarian giant ("fooles, women, and boys," 5.2.30.9) and of Acrasia in her Bower. The rhyming "boyes" suggests an undesirable state: the followers have not matured sexually, or, like Cybele's *galli,* they have made fulfillment impossible, or, like the boys Marlowe praises and, perhaps, like the lewd boys in Acrasia's Bower, they are more interested in each other than in the women they accompany.[4] In any case, having read Lucretius' account of Cybele and her violent cult, we cannot interpret these lines naively. Lucretius probes the benighted minds of the worshippers, for he does not believe in the goddess; Spenser, finding the disorder similarly distasteful, still incorporates it into Cambina: it is in her nature to be introduced by shrieking women and boys.

Nor is the violence accidental. As Cambina proceeds to the arena where Cambello and Triamond fight, her chariot is thronged by a "rude rout" of lower-class onlookers. She rides through their midst, her supposedly tame lions breaking free and trampling them:

> And as she passed through th'vnruly preace
> Of people, thronging thicke her to behold,
> Her angrie teame breaking thir bonds of peace,
> Great heapes of them, like sheepe in narrow fold,
> For hast did ouer-runne, in dust enrould,
> That thorough rude confusion of the rout,
> Some fearing shriekt, some being harmed hould,
> Some laught for sport, some did for wonder shout,,
> And some that would seeme wise, their wonder turnd to dout.
>
> (41)

This belittling of a few menials is one of Spenser's least attractive motifs. He uses it in Guyon's battle against the notably lower-class sense-simulacra which attack Alma's fortress (2.9.13-17); in Artegall's and Talus' scattering of the giant's partisans (5.2.51-54); even in the humorous scene in which the commoners of Eden, including "one that would wiser seeme," measure the length of the monster on the highway (1.12.9-12). Yet the device is philosophically and politically important. Cambina has entered among the confused cries of women; but now it is surely *her* team which causes confusion while she looks on, regally. Confusion must accompany Cambina, because she is the principle that reconciles opposites. No concord without discord—and a discord which ever threatens to break loose. In essence she too is an emblem of confusion, that very word suggesting her opposing qualities of reconciliation (con-fundere, to pour together, to fuse) and chaos. Like the conjugal snakes wound about Mercury's caduceus, those snakes "entrayled mutually in louely lore" about Cambina's "rod of peace" use their power to "confound" the "hellish fiends," her enemies (4.4.42.3-7; see also 2.12.29-31, in which the Palmer uses his caduceus to subdue the Circean beasts incited by "Venus sting").[5] This confusion of lower elements is her guarantor of power, or is indeed her power. From above, reconciliation and harmony; from below, subjugation. As Hawkins says, Spenser "draws our attention to the wildness of nature that can never be tamed, and perhaps also to the violence that is built into civilization itself."[6]

What makes Spenser's allusion to Lucretius' Cybele still more probable and significant is that in Lucretius the goddess is, as in Spenser, an allegory of a physical force. For Lucretius, this force is the recombinant inclination of atoms. Atomic strife and conjuction are inseparable and produce the universe. Everything, says Lucretius immediately before the Cybele episode, is a mixture of seeds. The greater the number of properties or faculties a thing possesses, the greater the number and kinds of atoms that compose it (584–88); of this the ever-fruitful earth is proof. Spenser's names for the brother and sister (Cambello, Cambina) suggest that he too had in mind a universal combining force, for him that providential force which unites the pairs of elements (see the double marriage of brothers and sisters at the end of the canto). The emblem of the calm ruler weathering the storm beneath her, or channeling its power, is written into the laws of the physical world. Lucretius may turn in disgust from the wild worship of Cybele, but of course the Epicurean ideal was a life of utter tranquillity, free from political entanglement. Spenser's militant Protestantism requires boldness and action. For those a little wildness is not a bad thing.

Courtship too requires a dash of chaos. In Lucretius, sexual passion is a warfare in which both fighters wound each other (4.1049–57), vainly attempting to possess the other entirely, biting and bruising and hungering (1105–11). The best thing for a man to do is to dissipate his passion by cultivating fickleness. That way, like Spenser's doughty Blandamour, he can jump from one brief furor to another, depositing his sperm "in corpora quaequae" (1065), into any old body! But Spenser wishes rather to concentrate *amor,* directing it towards the loved one alone. If this love is friendship (which can only be based on virtue), it will kindle "zealous fire," producing "braue thoughts and noble deedes" (4.10.26.8–9). If it is sexual love, it will help raise a "large posterity . . . Of blessed Saints for to increase the count" (*Epith.* 417, 423). In any case it will be about and doing.

And so when Scudamour enters the Temple of Venus, his task is not to walk a mean between the rapes which frequent Book Four and the useless frigidity of Spenser's "Stoicke censours" (Proem 3.9). Instead he must concentrate the violence of his young passion into winning the loved one. As John C. Bean argues, "the tension between spontaneity and law is central to Spenser's concept of chastity." Bean points out that this tension involves no compromise or dilution of passion, but a celebration of passion's virtuous release.[7] Just as Britomart *ought to* fall hopelessly in love, Scudamour ought to be bold: he must "vse his blis" (10.8.8), not yielding to Doubt or Delay or Daunger, which cause the lover to fall into diffidence, the ultimate Spenserian sin.

At the temple gates, Scudamour meets the porter, Concord, who resembles Cambina in her cosmic power to reconcile opposites. That is appropriate, since for Spenser sexual love is but one manifestation of a love which unites the elements with each other and the spiritual world with the earthly. Cambina puts an end to a single battle; Concord must make peace perpetually between Love and Hate, the two opposing forces in the cosmos. Love is the stronger, of course, and yet it is odd that Spenser should present Love as one of the two forces to be reconciled, rather than as the reconciling force itself. Moreover, Hate, though restrained, is a necessary component of the reconciliation. Their relationship suggests not so much Ovid's discussion of how Love combined the four elements warring in chaos (*Met.* 1.5–31; cf. *Fowre Hymnes,* "Love," 57–91), as it does Empedocles' assertion that two forces, Love and Strife, compose the universe. In refuting Empedocles, Lucretius praises his materialist and poetic predecessor but ignores his attribution of purpose to the atoms, which combine and fall apart without any prompting (1.716–829). By contrast, Spenser elevates these two elemental tendencies to the *means* by which the true Love, the divine Wisdom alluded to in 35.1–4, creates and sustains everything. Hate is the principle of dissolution and violence: his "yron tuskes" (33.9) and the club with which he threatens to brain Scudamour (36.5) link him with the various boars and savages of unbridled male sexuality that run wild in Faery Land. Yet that same sexual force, if it will but submit to the "louely band" of Concord (33.5), can be productive indeed. Says Alastair Fowler, "it is only by the help of Concord, or, as we might put it, through the integration of aggressive and erotic impulses, that Scudamour can enter the Temple of *Venus Hermaphroditos.*"[8]

Only after we see Hate and Love holding hands — Hate biting his lips like a surly child — does Spenser introduce us to Concord's daughters Peace and Friendship, "they both her twins, both born of heauenly seed" (34.3). Now Spenser's phrase, "born of Heauenly seed," echoes the same section of *De Rerum Natura* in which we find the discussion of the Mater Magna. Lucretius, after asserting the indivisibility and the basic quality-lessness of the atoms — they possess shape and size, but not, for instance, color — concludes we are all made up of the same universal stuff that rains from heaven and forms in its various conjunctions plants, animals, and human beings: "Denique caelesti sumus omnes semine oriundi," "Therefore we are all born of heavenly seed" (2.991). "Semina" is Lucretius' happiest epithet for the atoms. It links his probabilistic atomism with the earth's exuberant sexuality, which he so feelingly celebrates:

> omnibus ille idem pater est. unde alma liquentis
> umoris guttas mater cum terra recepit,
> feta parit nitidas fruges arbustaque laeta
> et genus humanum, parit omnia saecla ferarum,
> pabula cum praebet, quibus omnes corpora pascunt
> et dulcem ducunt uitam prolemque propagent.
> quapropter merito maternum nomen adepta est.
>
> (2.992–997)

> For all have this very same father; whence, when the
> nourishing mother earth receives the sweet drops of rain, she
> gives birth to the glossy fruit, the thriving groves, the
> human race; she gives birth to all generations of beasts,
> providing for them the food with which they feed their bodies
> and enjoy sweet life and propagate their young. Therefore she
> rightly assumes the name of mother.)

In just such language Lucretius has already described the fecundity of the earth. Because the earth contains all the elements necessary to sustain our lives, we call her "magna deum mater" and "nostri genetrix" (598–99; the Cybele passage is introduced immediately after the following):

> tum porro nitidas fruges arbustaque laeta
> gentibus humanis habet unde extollere possit,
> unde etiam fluuios frondes et pabula laeta
> montiuago generi possit praebere ferarum.   (594–7)

> (Then too [the earth] possesses [the elements] from which it
> can raise glossy fruit and thriving groves for the human race,
> and supply streams and leaves and abundant food for the race
> of mountain-wandering beasts.)

The marriage of heavenly and earthly seeds—in Lucretius a random union of atoms from above with atoms from below—impregnates the earth; "therefore she rightly assumes the name of mother" (998; cf. 5.795–76). Interestingly, when Spenser introduces us to Genius, the god of generation, he echoes Lucretius' line: "Therefore a God him sage Antiquity / Did rightly make, and good *Agdistes* call" (2.12.48.1– 2). Spenser weaves this net of allusions to adopt the surging power of the Lucretian vision for the purposes of Christian allegory. The moments in *De Rerum Natura* when the poet, carried away by the infinite supply and resourcefulness of his atoms, verges upon the furor of a worship of Nature, are the moments which Spenser seizes on, preserving the excitement but insisting upon its government by God and not by chance. In Spenser, Peace is not exactly a tranquil thing.

But "preserving" is the wrong word above; "amplifying" is closer to the truth. For when Spenser adapts Lucretius he increases both the wantonness of the chaos and the control to which it is subject, resulting in greater action than in the Roman poet. Mother of both the peaceful and the violent, Concord spurs Scudamour on, entertaining him "in gentle wise" (10.36.2) when he loses heart, and befriending the bold church-robber when he leaves with his captive Amoret (57.8–9). Between his entrance and his exit Scudamour hears the violent complaints of those who have not won their loves. Among these is one who "through loues constrayning, / Tormented sore, could not containe it still, / But thus brake forth, that all the temple it did fill" (43.7–9). In this song Spenser paraphrases, and appropriates, Lucretius' glorious invocation. I present the passages in full, so that the reader may note carefully where Spenser diverges from the original:

> Aeneadvm genetrix, hominum diuomque uoluptas,
> alma Venus, caeli subter labentia signa
> quae mare nauigerum, quae terras frugiferentis
> concelebras—per te quoniam genus omne animantum
> concipitur uisitque exortum lumina solis—
> te, dea, te fugiunt uenti, te nubila caeli
> aduentumque tuum, tibi suauis daedala tellus
> summittit flores, tibi rident aequora ponti
> placatumque nitet diffuso lumine caelum.
> nam simul ac species patefactast uerna diei
> et reserata uiget genitabilis aura Fauoni,
> aeriae primum uolucris te, diua, tuumque
> significant initum, perculsae corda tua ui;
> inde ferae pecudes persultant pabula laeta

et rapidos tranant amnis (ita capta lepore
te sequitur cupide quo quamque inducere pergis);
denique per maria ac montis fluuiosque rapacis
frondiferasque domos auium camposque uirentis,
omnibus incutiens blandum per pectora amorem,
efficis ut cupide generatim saecla propagent.
quae quoniam rerum naturam sola gubernas
nec sine te quicquam dias in luminis oras
exoritur neque fit laetem neque amabile quicquam,
te sociam studeo scribendis uersibus esse,
quos ego de rerum natura pangere conor
Memmiadae nostro, quem tu, dea, tempore in omni
omnibus ornatum uoluisti excellere rebus.
quo magis aeternum da dictis, diua, leporem!

(1.1–28)

(Mother of the race of Aeneas, pleasure of gods and men, sweet
Venus, you who under the wheeling stars cause the ship-bearing
sea and the fruitful earth to teem with life—for it is
through you that every kind of living thing is formed and,
arising, first sees the light of the sun—from you, goddess,
from you and your approach the winds and the clouds of heaven
fly; for you the daedal earth sends up its sweet flowers, for
you smile the level stretches of the sea, and the peaceful sky
glows in a bath of light. For as soon as the vernal face of
day is revealed, and the engendering west wind, now unloosed,
blows strong, then straightaway the birds of the air, pricked
in their hearts by your power, signal you and your entrance;
then the cattle, wild with desire, lope through the thriving
pastures and swim across swift rivers (so seized by your charm
any one of them willingly follows you wherever you wish to
lead it); then through the seas and the rapacious mountain
streams and the leafy dwellings of birds and the greening
fields, instilling in the hearts of all an alluring love, you
cause them to propagate their generations, each according to
its kind. And because you alone govern the nature of things,
and because without you nothing can rise to the bright shores
of light, nor thrive, nor be worthy of love, I implore you to
bind yourself in friendship to these verses on the nature of
things which I am attempting to compose for our splendid

Memmius, whom you, goddess, have always wished to excel in all
things. All the more for his sake, goddess, lend timeless
charm to my song!

Great *Venus,* Queene of beautie and of grace,
The ioy of Gods and men, that vnder skie
Doest fayrest shine, and most adorne thy place,
That with thy smyling looke doest pacifie
The raging seas, and makst the stormes to flie;
Thee goddesse, thee the winds, the clouds doe feare,
And when thou spredst thy mantle forth on hie,
The waters play and pleasant lands appeare,
And heauens laugh, and al the world shews ioyous cheare.

Then doth the daedale earth throw forth to thee
Out of her fruitfull lap aboundant flowres,
And then all liuing wights, soone as they see
The spring breake forth out of his lusty bowres,
They all doe learne to play the Paramours;
First doe the merry birds, thy prety pages
Priuily pricked with thy lustfull powres,
Chirpe loud to thee out of their leauy cages,
And thee their mother call to coole their kindly rages.

Then doe the saluage beasts begin to play
Their pleasant friskes, and loath their wonted food;
The Lyons rore, the Tygres loudly bray,
The raging Buls rebellow through the wood,
And breaking forth, date tempt the deepest flood,
To come where thou doest draw them with desire:
So all things else, that nourish vitall blood,
Soone as with fury thou doest them inspire,
In generation seeke to quench their inward fire.

So all the world by thee at first was made,
And dayly yet thou doest the same repayre:
Ne ought on earth that merry is and glad,
Ne ought on earth that louely is and fayre,
But thou the same for pleasure didst prepayre.
Thou art the root of all that ioyous is,

Great God of men and women, queene of th'ayre,
Mother of laughter, and welspring of blisse,
O graunt that of my loue at last I may not misse.

                                                4.10.44–47)

At virtually every opportunity Spenser overgoes Lucretius in celebrating the wildness of love's power. For Lucretius' adjective "naui-
gerum", ship-bearing (out of place in Spenser's Temple), Spenser substitutes "raging". When Lucretius' Venus arrives, the seas "laugh" and
the heavens, made peaceful, "shine in a bath of light." But for Spenser
the pathetic fallacy implied in "laugh" is an opportunity to lend the
world greater will to fall in love: the waters do not laugh but "play,"
the heavens do not shine but "laugh," "and all the world shews ioyous
cheare," Spenser adds, to universalize the delight. Lucretius' "sweet
flowers" become "abundant flowers," and Spenser uses an extra half-
line to stress the earth's prolific sexuality—for these flowers are thrown
forth from the earth's "fruitfull lap." In Lucretius the west wind is
"reserata," "unbarred" or "set free." Spenser alters the sense from
passive to active, attributing this setting free to the spring itself, which
is said not merely to be "genitabilis" but to "breake forth out of
his lusty bowres." These "lusty bowres," unlike the Bower of Bliss, bring
about a refreshing, muscular action, and in fact seem to turn the world
into one great lusty bower, as all living things "learne to play the Paramours," a stupendously cheerful line which is entirely Spenser's. Lucretius' birds are pricked in the heart—actually, goaded—by the power of
love: Spenser picks up the bawdy verb "prick" from Chaucer and so has
his birds "priuily pricked with [Venus'] lustfull powres." Lucretius'
birds inhabit leafy houses; Spenser restrains them to "leavy cages," so
that their loud chirping—again Spenser's addition—sounds all the more
insistent: "And thee their mother call to coole their kindly rages."
Spenser increases the number and sorts of animals incited, not, as in
Lucretius, by "blandum amorem," but by "fury," to roaring, braying,
rebellowing, and the heroic "breaking forth." Finally, while Lucretius
applies the action of Venus to his own poem, entreating a goddess in
whom he does not really believe to endow his verses with eternal
charm, Spenser remains on the level of the sexual, or rather he elevates
pleasure itself to the *telos* of all beautiful living things:

> Ne ought on earth that merry is and glad,
> Ne ought on earth that louely is and fayre,
> But thou the same for pleasure didst prepayre.

Two images of confusion in Spenser's paraphrase deserve special mention. First, Spenser does not bother to outdo Lucretius' fine epithet for the earth, "daedala tellus." That is not surprising, considering the importance for Spenser of the image of the labyrinth. The word "daedal" — from the ingenious Daedalus who made the Cretan labyrinth — is perfect for meshing ideas of ingenious harmony and wild wandering. Second, Hamilton notes that Spenser derives his rebellowing bulls from Vergil's third Georgic (215-23, 253-54; compare also to *FQ* 1.2.16). But even here Spenser is being consistently Lucretian. Macrobius, at pains throughout the sixth book of the *Saturnalia* to enumerate instances of Vergil's indebtedness to earlier poets, especially Ennius, Lucretius, and Homer, points out that Vergil's line, "reboant siluae et longus Olympus," "the woods and tall Olympus echo back," adapts Lucretius 2.28. The key word is "reboant," "rebellow, echo". That wild sylvan resounding is a favorite with Spenser. He uses it in scenes which are highly charged sexually and which dance on the brink of chaos; besides *Epithalamion*'s refrain, see the satyrs who capture the civilizing Una, pounding the earth with their feet (1.6.14.3-4; compare Lucr. 1.14) as if they had been made mad by "Cybeles franticke rites" (15.3), or the nymphs chasing the mischievous Faunus (7.6.52.6-9) who brings about both chaos and marriage (53,55).

Yet many of Spenser's alterations show his commitment to the un-Lucretian principle of divine control. Before the hymn even begins Venus' Temple is compared, favorably, to the one framed by Solomon for the Old Testament God (30.6-7). Venus' hermaphroditism, hidden by a veil, resembles that of Dame Nature, who is explicitly associated with the Son by Whom all things are made (7.7.7). The singer calls Venus "Queene of beautie and of grace," and it is hard to imagine that the word "grace," uttered in a temple, could be free of theological significance. This is an active, grace-granting Venus, one who may intercede in one's amours, as the singer prays at the end of his song. Scudamour himself prays inwardly for her "gratious help" (48.5); true to his character and to Spenser's predilection for active virtue, Scudamour helps himself by taking Amoret by the hand, whereupon the goddess helps him by laughing with "amiable grace" (56.3). In Lucretius the winds and clouds flee at Venus' approach; Spenser alters the verb to "feare," suggesting obedience and awe. In fact Venus is cast — for a moment — in the role of creator, since at her bidding the "pleasant lands appeare," a development found in Genesis 1:9. Lucretius remarks that the whole world is governed by Venus, "tu sola gubernas." Now government is an orderly notion and would have served Spenser's plan, but Spenser raises the stakes: his Venus has "made" the world "at first" and repairs it daily.

The result of this twofold pressure on Lucretius' language is to alter the purpose of the hymn. In *De Rerum Natura* the hymn ends with a prayer that Venus pour sweet nothings into the ears of Mars, so that Rome will enjoy the peace needed for free philosophical speculation. The study of the universe, for Lucretius, is geared toward attaining the ease of the Epicurean gods, who are removed from human cares and toil. But when one of Gloriana's knights allows his Mars to be disarmed, he enjoys not ease but stasis, sluggishness. Thus in the Bower of Bliss (linked to the Temple episode by, among other things, the interruption by an anonymous singer),[9] Spenser reworks the Venus-Mars tableau in Lucretius to give us a knight drained of vigor, sexual or otherwise.[10] In love as in faith and politics, Spenser favors the brave, those who direct their energies into "derring-do".

The trouble with Epicureans is that they are not Epicurean enough. They do not have a divine conception of pleasure, and they do not know how to achieve that pleasure. They languish like the lovers at the foot of Venus' altar. Spenser's readers may have recalled Lucian's description in *Dea Syria* of the temple of the goddess Astarte, whom Lucian identifies with both Venus and Cybele. In this temple castrated priests take such sexual liberties as they can with devotees of the goddess—and take them eagerly and often (see *Dea Syria* 22). But for Spenser such pleasure, beginning and ending in itself, is trivial, is as frustrating and dull as what the timid lovers suffer in the Temple of Venus. Action, guided by faith, is necessary: whether Guyon's destruction of the stultifying Bower (echoing Josiah's razing of, among other abominations, the groves of Astarte, 2 Kings 23), or Scudamour's procreative church-robbing and abduction.

And so for Spenser chaos is not the guiding principle of nature, but it has its place. Like undifferentiated sexual energy, chaos is created and restrained and used by God so that despite itself it becomes an agent of God's plan. Over and over in *The Faerie Queene* we see order wrought out of (and not simply replacing) confusion. Mutabilitie is a bold usurper but she is also a beautiful woman, "tall as any there / Of all the gods" (7.6.28.3–4), and Nature—mutably flickering between Christ and the hermaphroditic Venus—calls her "daughter" (7.7.59.1), implying at once subordination and kinship and affection. The chaos to which Agape, a "bold fay" (4.2.49.6) descends to lengthen the lives of her sons, is "hideous" (47.9); yet there sit the Fates who make possible both the union of the sons' three souls and the resulting double marriage of siblings Cambello and Cambina to siblings Canacee and Triamond. Proteus is a changeable and wanton old lecher, yet his chaos is of a freezing, imprisoning variety: he wishes not so much to stir love in Florimell as to kill it by misdirecting it (see 3.35.1–4, 41–42). By contrast, the seas themselves unite for the marriage of the Medway and the Thames, and it is only this boisterous event—held at Proteus' house—which brings Florimell and her beloved Marinell together. At that wedding the bridegroom, the Thames, is said to be decked out like Cybele, that civilizing "mother of the Gods" (11.28.1), "arayd with pompous pride" (28.4), thus cross-sexually becoming himself an emblem of *concordia discors,* of the productive uses of chaos.[11]

Perhaps the most noxious figure of chaos in the central books of *The Faerie Queene* is Argante, the epitome of female lust. Yet even she has an *alter ego* in Isis. At first it seems that Spenser has omitted from his poem most of the heady sexuality with which the Isis myth is imbued. Britomart, after all, does not gather up and refit the scattered limbs of Artegall, nor does she raise a pillar in memory of his lost phallus. Plutarch informs us that Isis and Osiris copulated *in utero*—a lusty expression of unity in multeity if there ever was one.[12] Now nothing so drastic happens with Britomart and Artegall. Yet their essential twinning is made manifest by Britomart's dream at Isis Church, and by the icon of Isis herself. Holding a "long white sclender wand" (5.7.7.5), Isis sets her foot upon a crocodile "that with her wreathed taile her middle did enfold" (5.7.6.9). The masculinity of the goddess is suggested both by the wand she holds—perhaps reminiscent of Osiris' lost member—and by the crocodile's tail, which replaces her own middle. Meanwhile the crocodile is referred to by a feminine pronoun: "her taile." The effect is one of cross-sexuality and hermaphroditism, as it is too in Britomart's dream, in which the union of Isis and Osiris is preceded by his swelling with pride (is this tumescence or pregnancy?) and her beating him back with her rod. It is difficult to determine who is the greater aggressor. Perhaps that is as it should be. For if Isis is the principle of equity, as Spenser explains (5.7.3), she needs occasionally to intrude upon the law, to wrest it to her will. Justice itself must be ravished now and again.

If Isis and Osiris create order from disorder, Argante and her twin brother Ollyphant give us an infernal parody of that order. Their ancestry suggests both Mutabilitie's project to disenthrone Jove and return everything to chaos, and the raw power of the Mater Magna. Argante is

A daughter of the Titans which did make
Warre against heauen, and heaped hils on hight,
To scale the skyes, and put *Ioue* from his right:
Her sire *Typhoeus* was, who mad through merth,
And drunke with bloud of men, slaine by his might,
Through incest, her of his owne mother Earth
Whilome begot, being but halfe twin of that berth.

                                        (3.7.47.3–9)

She and her other half, Ollyphant, bring many knights to "foule coon-fusion" (48.4). Argante's is the confusion of rampant and random promiscuity, mingling not only brother with sister but human being with beast, abrogating any sense of propriety or even generation:

These twinnes, men say, (a thing far passing thought)
Whiles in their mothers wombe enclosd they were,
Ere they into the lightsome world were brought,
In fleshly lust were mingled both yfere   (48.5–8)

But greatest shame was to that maiden twin,
Who not content so fowly to deuoure
Her natiue flesh, and staine her brothers bowre,
Did wallow in all other fleshly myre,
And suffered beasts her body to deflowre.   (49.3–7)

Clearly Argante is a perversion of the Cybele-Venus-Isis goddess of natural order and the disorder with which it is bound. She must "feed her fancy with delightfull change" (50.3), and so whenever she can overcome a young man she conveys him, as Venus conveys Adonis, to a "secret place / Where in eternall bondage dye he must, / Or be the vassall of her pleasures vile" (50.6–8). Appropriately, she is described by the Squire of Dames, who resembles Scudamour in his aggressiveness but Argante in his lack of principle and his utterly unmoored sexual behavior.

    No discussion of Spenserian chaos should omit the Garden of Adonis, Spenser's allegory of physical generation. Here Venus enjoys eternal pleasure with her lover Adonis, but she can only do so by incorporating him into the world as the "Father of all formes" (3.6.47.8), a being who lives by the life he gives to other beings. Matter, Spenser's unalterable "substance," cannot fade, but can be altered to and fro by means of the forms or shapes it assumes. Form, then, is "eterne in mutabilitie," that is, eternally mutable, for all things change continually, are eternal by virtue of mutability, the sole universal constant. Thus, woven into the order suggested by Venus' and Adonis' continual copulation is the disorder suggested both by Adonis' flux of forms and by the matter upon which he acts, namely the unformed stuff provided by Venus, the earth:

> For in the wide wombe of the world there lyes,
> In hatefull darknesse and in deepe horrore,
> An huge eternall *Chaos,* which supplyes
> The substaunces of natures fruitfull progenyes.
>
> (36.6–9)

Similarly, the boar that slew Adonis is chained beneath the mount where the god is now hidden, suggesting that he too is eternal, ever restrained, like Chaos, but also ever the violent enabler of the now perpetual bliss which Venus and Adonis enjoy.[13] The site of that "strong rocky Caue" in which he is imprisoned "for ay"—if Adonis' "stately Mount" is taken to represent the *mons Veneris*—links the boar with the "wide wombe of the world" above. Chaos is eternal, the boar never dies; meanwhile Adonis is continually slain, only "by succession made perpetuall," living in constant change and therefore constant death, which is also constant copulation with Venus and therefore constant procreation of new things.

One is reminded here of Milton's Chaos, "the womb of Nature and perhaps her grave" (*PL* 2.911), translating Lucretius' description of the earth, "omniparens, eadem rerum commune sepulcrum" (5.259). The womb-grave union is essential to Lucretius' materialism; if certain configurations of atoms were immortal, or if matter itself could be reduced to nothing, nature would lack the necessary food for the creation and maintenance of air, stars, wheat, rivers. Nature recreates ("reficit", by way of elemental refection) one thing from another, nor does she allow anything to be born unless it is aided by a death (1.263–64). Death too is a part of procreation. Worn out age must yield to the newness of things, says Lucretius, "et ex aliis aliud reparare necessest," "and it is necessary that [age] fashion anew something else out of other things"(3.964–65).

But the Lucretian "reparare" above, picked up by Spenser in the hymn to Venus, "so all the world by thee at first was made, / And dayly yet thou doest the same repayre," signals at once how similar and yet how critically different our poets are in their attitudes towards Nature. For Lucretius the repair of the earth is but a holding action, a temporary replenishing of life. Eventually, like an old man who loses atoms faster than he can supply them through food, the earth will die; Nature herself is already, compared with her former fertility, "effeta" (2.1150), weary from too much birthing. The cosmos as a whole will live on, atoms and void, creating other earths which will die in turn. Atoms and void are perpetual, always conserved; what they create is always mortal. But if we place "repair" in a Christian context, it acquires a theological connotation, since the fact that things fall apart is linked with, though not identical to, sin. Since sin necessitates Christ's redemption, the tendency of the world towards dissolution is linked also with an apparently opposite longing for culmination in the Heavenly Jerusalem. To "repair" the world, then, may mean both to supply the means by which the physical world continues, *and* to redeem the moral world, which can achieve perfection only when the physical world (at least as we know it) ceases to be. Thus to repair means to fix in such a way that decay will coincide with God's providential plan to end the world and replace it with a new heaven and a new earth. In Lucretius the earth is only partly repaired, and so dwindles to nothing; in Spenser the incompleteness of the repair is what will lead to the eschaton.

In conclusion, appreciation of the uses of chaos can teach us with what attitude we should read *The Faerie Queene*. Discussing creation in *Confessions* 13.24, Augustine asks why God repeated the command "increase and multiply," directed first at the animals and then at human beings. He concludes that more than reproduction is intended. Guided by faith, we are to hear God's word in a creative way, resulting in a vast variety of interpretation and action. For Augustine, allegory and multiplicity go hand in hand. The Bible is overdetermined and underdetermined: one truth may be expressed in many images, and one image may express many truths. This multiplicity reflects the power of the Spirit and the richness of creation in a mutable world. As for mutability itself, it comes into being only after God has created things which can experience the changes of time; the chaotic matter which God created before time exhibits the paradox that boundless mutability is not mutability at all, but stasis. So Nature puts it when she advises Mutabilitie to control herself: "Thy decay thou seek'st by thy desire" (7.7.59.3). As with the physical, so with the semantic: to know what God meant by the first line of Genesis, one would have to see Him face to face; meanwhile, one can marvel, like Augustine, at the plenitude of possibilities.

Spenser's reader, too, should not be dismayed by many-ply allegory. "Add faith unto your force and be not faint," Una calls to the Red Cross Knight as he lies half-strangled in the coils of Errour (1.1.19.3). Like Venus, this beast is spontaneously procreative, needing nothing beyond herself for impregnation; her spawn is as abundant and as disorderly as that of "old father Nilus" (21.1). Yet if we conclude that Spenser wants us to strangle whatever wanderings there are in his own poem, choking them with the iron grip of faith, then we show the very faintheartedness Una warns against, for we will see evil lurking in every passing pleasure. We should remember that Spenser's "Force" admits of more than a little wildness in the service of God. We are to have a hearty encounter with the poem, emerging victorious not by means of rigid rule but by means of a faith-directed passion, such as Scudamour uses to bring Amoret away. Una is one, as truth is always one — yet after the victory over the dragon even she is called "the Errant damozell" (2.1.19.8). There is something endearing about a unitary Truth who can be found in the by-ways of Faery Land pursuing her love and her quest.

Notes

1. My texts are *Edmund Spenser: The Faerie Queene,* ed. A. C. Hamilton (London and New York: Longman, 1977), and Lucretius, *De Rervm Natvra,* eds. William Allery Leonard and Stanley Barney Smith (Madison, Wis.: University of Wisconsin Press, 1942).

Decades ago a small war was waged over the question of Lucretian influence on Spenser. The main proponent was Edwin P. Greenlaw, in "Spenser and Lucretius," *SP* 17 (1920): 455–84; "Spenser's Influence on Paradise Lost," *SP* 17 (1920): 320–59; "Some Old Religious Cults in Spenser," *SP* 20 (1923): 216–43; "Spenser's Mutabilitie," *PMLA* 47 (1932): 46–78. Greenlaw's position was not extreme. He merely wished to assert that among other influences on Spenser's cosmology one should recognize that of the Roman materialist. J. W. Bennett, "Spenser's Garden of Adonis," *PMLA* 47 (1932): 46–78, gives the most cogent attack, revealing the dubiety of some of Greenlaw's connections and placing Spenser squarely in a Neoplatonist camp. Others joined the fray, including Brents Stirling, "The Philosophy of Spenser's Garden of Adonis," *PMLA* 49 (1934): 501–38; William P. Cummings, "The Influence of Ovid's *Metamorphoses* on Spenser's 'Mutabilitie Cantos,'" *SP* 28 (1931): 241–56, and Evelyn Albright, "Spenser's Cosmic Philosophy and his Religion," *PMLA* 44 (1929): 715–59. All were determined to save Spenser from heresy. Later critics who address the issue include John E. Hankins, *Source and Meaning in Spenser's Allegory: A Study of The Faerie Queene* (London: Oxford University Press, 1971), and Robert

Ellrodt, *Neoplatonism in the Poetry of Edmund Spenser* (Geneva: Droz, 1960); both deny materialism in Spenser. For William Nelson, Lucretius' "alma Venus" was a form of the ordering nature-deity Spenser adored; *The Poetry of Edmund Spenser* (New York: Columbia University Press, 1963), 106, 199, 305. Yet for Nelson that fact is of minor significance. I believe Nelson's view has prevailed: most critics accept that Spenser alludes to Lucretius here and there, as a scatter-shot eclectic poet will, and do not bother to probe the allusions or to ask whether Lucretius and Epicureanism had any special social or political significance for Spenser's contemporaries.

2.   See Calvin's *Institutes of the Christian Religion* 1.5. Trans. John Allen (Philadelphia: Presbyterian Board of Publication, 1844), vol. 1 of 2, 62. For Sidney, see *The Countess of Pembroke's Arcadia,* 3.10, and the study by Edwin P. Greenlaw, "The Captivity Episode in Sidney's *Arcadia,"* *Manly Anniversary Studies* (Chicago, 1925): 54–63. For Hooker, see *Of the Laws of Ecclesiastical Polity* (London, 1597), 5.2. Du Bartas is an example of a poet whose relationship with Lucretian materialism was highly ambivalent. In week 1, day 1 of *Divine Weeks,* tr. Joshuah Sylvester (London, 1608), Du Bartas assails such Epicurean tenets as randomness (38–61), the plurality of worlds (346–73), and the infinity of the cosmos (374–91). His attack on atomism persists through week one. But according to Victor Harris, Du Bartas "accepts both the mutability of the forms and the permanence of matter, and the physical composition of his universe seems to be taken directly out of Epicurean philosophy." See *All Coherence Gone* (Chicago: The Open Court, 1949). V. H. Whitaker, "Du Bartas' Use of Lucretius," *SP* 33 (1936): 134–46, notes Du Bartas' slavish rendering of Lucr. 1.150–264 for his discussion of matter and the mutability of forms, 1.2.164–206. Perhaps Du Bartas' fierce attacks were spurred by the fear that Lucretius was right about more than naturalistic details.

Epicureans have always been accused of sloth and licentiousness. References could be multiplied endlessly. In Cicero, *Academica* 1.2, Varro says that Epicurus identifies the good of man with that of cattle. Robert Burton, *Anatomy of Melancholy* 3.4.2.1, accuses Epicureans, Libertines, and atheists of worshipping their bellies. According to Christopher Hill, *The World Turned Upside Down: Radical Ideas During the English Revolution* (London: Maurice Temple Smith, 1972), 326, "under Elizabeth the view was attributed to the Libertines that 'a man ought not to weary his body in travail and labor; for they said that the Holy Ghost would not tarry in a body that was weary and irksome'." (The citation is of John Strype, *Annals of the Reformation* 2.2.288–89.) Hill relates materialist positions to those of lower-class sectarians, Anabaptists in particular.

3.   See Hawkins, "From Mythography to Mythmaking: Spenser and the *Magna Mater* Cybele," *Sixteenth Century Journal* 12.3 (1981): 51–64, and Roche, *The Kindly Flame: A Study of the Third and Fourth Books of Spenser's Faerie Queene* (Princeton: Princeton University Press, 1964), 23–28. Hawkins's article is a fine discussion of the various ancient sources for Spenser's Cambina, Isis, Agdistes, Mutabilitie, Nature, and the hermaphroditic Venus.

4.   Note Marlowe's alleged usage in the Baines Note: "All they that loved not tobacco & boyes were fools" (J. B. Steane, *Marlowe: A Critical Study* [Cambridge: Cambridge University Press, 1964], 364). According to the *OED,* in the Elizabethan era the word "boy" might mean "a male child below the age of puberty," "a young man," "a servant, slave," "a camp-follower," a "knave, varlet, rogue," and, most curi-

ous for the association with disorder, "a member of a fraternity or band, as in *Peep of Day Boys,* a secret organization in Ireland; *Roaring Boys,* riotous fellows of the time of Elizabeth and James I."

5.   Alastair Fowler, *Spenser and the Numbers of Time* (London: Routledge and Kegan Paul, 1964), 155–64, discusses the caduceus as a rod of peace and of fate. He also notes that the entwined serpents were seen as symbols of sexual generation, if not of the male and female genitals themselves. He cites the *Collectanea* appended to Valerianus' *Hieroglyphica, sive de sacris Aegyptiorum, aliarumque gentium litteris* (Frankfort, 1613), 187–88.

6.   Hawkins, p. 61.

7.   "Cosmic Order in *The Faerie Queene:* From Temperance to Chastity," *SEL* 17 (1977): 67–79.

8.   *Spenser and the Numbers of Time,* p. 166.

9.   Isabel MacCaffrey, *Spenser's Allegory: The Anatomy of Imagination* (Princeton: Princeton University Press, 1976), 323–24, notes that in ignoring Delay's wiles (4.10.14) Scudamour uses his fleeting time well and thus provides us with "the obverse of the *carpe diem* song in the Bower of Bliss."

10.   I have discussed the intertextual relationships between the Bower of Bliss and the Lucretian hymn in "Spenser's 'Alma Venus': Energy and Economics in the Bower of Bliss," forthcoming in *ELR.*

11.   Hawkins, p. 58, argues that "there is even in the identification of the male Thamis with Cybele a suggestion of the bisexual Agdistes."

12.   Classical commentators consider Isis the Egyptian avatar of Venus. Macrobius, *Saturnalia* 1.20, calls the earth Isis and the sun Osiris or Adonis; so does Diodorus Siculus, 1.11.1–6, who, like Plutarch in *Isis and Osiris* 363D–64A, interprets Isis as matter impregnated by the sun. Macrobius, 1.21, links Venus and Isis with the Mater Magna and her doomed lover, Attis. For Osiris' dismemberment and his phallic rites see Plutarch, 351F–55E; in this vein see the Cybele-Attis relationship presentend in Catullus 63. The legend of the copulation *in utero* can be found in Plutarch, 356A.

13.   In *Spenser's Image of Nature: Wild Man and Shepherd in The Faerie Queene* (New Haven: Yale University Press, 1966), 137, Donald Cheney argues that "with [his] death and metamorphosis [Adonis] is translated into a state in which the Boar roams no longer and enjoyment is perfect and continual, without the intervention of death — either sexual or literal." I picture a more active garden, one full of little else but living and dying and sexual intercourse, with the Boar of headstrong aggression restrained, not simply gotten out of the way.

JEFFREY P. FRUEN

The Faery Queen Unveiled?
Five Glimpses of Gloriana

*I*N A PREVIOUS ESSAY I argued that Gloriana, despite appearances to the contrary, is indeed to be regarded as the unifying "argument" (I.Pr.4) of Spenser's narrative, her pivotal importance being obscured only by the "couert vele" (II.Pr.5) of an autonomous but quasi-biblical typology.[1] The question of her allegorical significance I left at that time for later consideration, and a comprehensive treatment I must still postpone, but the preliminary observations that follow point clearly, I think, to a decisive answer. For in what little Spenser does tell us about his elusive heroine we get at least five glimpses of an allegorical characterization that well befits both the poem's "generall end" of "fashion[ing] a gentleman or noble person in vertuous and gentle discipline" ("Letter to Raleigh") and the scripture-like manner in which its title character is presented.

I. GLORIANA, WISDOM,
AND THE ZURICH LATIN BIBLE

Naseeb Shaheen has all but exhaustively cataloged the wealth of biblical allusions in *The Faerie Queene* through comparisons with the various sixteenth-century English Bibles and the Vulgate.[2] Yet further research might serve to identify references to the various sixteenth-century Protestant Latin Bibles as well; certainly there is one twice-repeated allusion, bearing on the interpretation of the faery queen herself, that depends on such a text. For both of Spenser's accounts of the vision that inspired Arthur's quest for Gloriana seem distinctly reminiscent of a single verse from the Apocrypha of the Zurich Latin Bible of 1543, and so imply that she is to be associated with the personified Wisdom celebrated there.

Spenser mentions Arthur's vision in two places. In the "Letter to Raleigh" he writes:

> ... Arthure ... I conceiue ... to haue seene in a dream or vision the Faery Queen, with whose excellent beauty rauished, he awaking resolued to seeke her out. . . .

The poem itself is slightly more expansive:

> But whether dreames delude, or true it were,
> Was neuer hart so rauisht with delight. . . .
>
> * * *
>
> From that day forth I lou'd that face diuine;
> From that day forth I cast in carefull mind,
> To seeke her out with labour, and long tyne,
> And neuer vow to rest, till I her find. . . .
> (I.ix.14–15)

Both of these texts are related to the apocryphal book the Wisdom of Solomon.[3] In Wisdom 8:2, as part of an allegorical expansion of the vision described in 1 Kings 3, Solomon is presented as recounting how he came to go in quest of Wisdom, here personified as a visionary mistress. The Zurich version translates:

> Hanc ego dilexi & a iuuentute mea quaesiui:
> Hanc studui sponsam adiungere mihi,
> & pulchritudinis eius amore captus sum.[4]

(Her I loved and from my youth sought out:
I bent my mind to make her my bride,
and with love of her beauty I was ravished.)

Before comparing the Latin text to Spenser's, we may seek to avoid ten-
dentiousness by noting some of the definitions of its key words in
Thomas Cooper's Latin dictionary of 1565, a work Spenser would have
used extensively at the Merchant Taylors' School.[5]

quaesiui:	from *quaero* "to desire to haue: to seeke for . . . to labour or trauayle to gette"
studui:	from *studeo* "to applie the minde, or care for a thinge"; cf. *studiosus* "that setteth his minde to a thinge"; *studium* "An ear-nest bending of the minde to any thinge," "care and studie"
pulchritudinis:	from *pulcher* "beautifull . . . excellent"
captus:	"Rauished . . . Delighted"

In the case of *dilexi,* on the other hand, Cooper's "To . . . loue meanely"
does not give a very good idea of the intensity of feeling expressed by
diligo in biblical Latin. When we are commanded to love God with all
our heart, soul, and mind (Matt. 22:37), for example, the verb in the
Vulgate, Zurich, and Tremellius-Junius versions is *Diliges,* and the
bride's "welbeloued" in the Song of Songs is her *dilecte;* while in the
Vulgate the love of bride and bridegroom that is "strong as death" (8:6)
is not *amor* but *dilectio.*[6] The word is thus well suited to suggest both
profound moral commitment and passionate sexual love.

With these definitions in mind, we can observe the following instances in which Spenser's diction seems to reflect the Latin:

"Letter to Raleigh":

with whose *excellent beauty rauished,*	[*pulchritudinis, captus*]
he . . . *resolued* to *seeke her out* . . .	[*studui, quaesiui*]

I.ix.14.6, 15.5–7:

Was neuer hart so *rauisht with delight.* . . .	[*captus*]
From that day forth *I lou'd* that face diuine;	[*ego dilexi . . . a*]

From that day forth *I cast in carefull mind,*   [*a . . . studui*]
To *seeke her out with labour, and long tyne* . . .   [*Hanc . . . quaesiui*]

The close configuration of "excellent beauty" with "rauished," "re-
solued," and "seeke her out" in the "Letter to Raleigh," or of "rauist
with delight" with "cast in carefull mind" and "seeke her out with labour
and . . . tyne" in the poem itself, would certainly seem to bespeak a connection with the expressions of the Bible text (*pulchritudinis, captus,
studui, quaesiui*) as one who had learned Latin using Cooper's dictionary
would translate them.

And there is ample reason to regard these parallels as more than a
matter of coincidence. For one thing, the poet's invocation of Elizabeth
as a "Mirrour of grace and Maiestie diuine" (I.Pr.4) has already been
shown to establish her "true glorious type" as a counterpart of Wisdom, herself a "mirroure of the maiestie of God" (Wis.7:26).[7] And
other, more general parallels with the account in I.ix.14–15 are at hand
in other biblical Wisdom-quests:

> Mine heart reioyced in her . . . & from my youth vp soght
> I after her.
> (Ecclus. 51.15)

> Seke after her, and searche her. . . .
> For at the last thou shalt finde rest in her. . . .
> (Ecclus. 6:28–29)[8]

In addition to the direct parallels between Gloriana and scriptural Wisdom, we may also adduce the strong and long-noted resemblance between
Gloriana and the Sapience of *An Hymne of Heauenly Beautie,* a figure herself
known to be derived largely from biblical Wisdom allegories.[9] Since Sapience recalls both biblical Wisdom and Gloriana, we should hardly be
surprised to find that Gloriana herself is presented as a sapiential figure,
even if two of the most striking allusions linking the faery queen to
Wisdom do depend on expressions peculiar to the Zurich Latin Bible.

For Spenser was not the only Elizabethan on whose mind the Zurich
reading of Wis. 8:2 left its imprint. Cicero had quoted Plato as saying
that, if only we could behold the face of Virtue, "it would excite a won-
derful love of Wisdom" ("*mirabiles amores . . . excitaret sapientiae*").[10] But
Sidney in the *Apologie,* as we now can see, has conflated Cicero's famil-

iar phrasing with Solomon's "*pulchritudinis eius amore captus,*" leaving us
with his own memorable formulation of "the saying of *Plato* and
Tullie": "who could see Vertue would be wonderfully *rauished with the
loue of her beauty.*"[11] However neglected its readings may be in our day,
Spenser apparently had good reason to think that his first readers would
recognize an allusion to at least this one verse of the Zurich Latin Bible.

II. WISDOM AS THE LIGHT OF NATURE
IN CALVIN AND MELANCHTHON

The primary objection to a simple identification of Gloriana's allegorical significance with that of Sapience in *An Hymne of Heauenly Beautie*
has always been that Sapience is a heavenly figure whom "Both heauen
and earth obey" (*HHB* 197), while Spenser's emphatic contrast of Gloriana's city Cleopolis with the New Jerusalem (*FQ* I.x.55–63) shows
that, while Gloriana herself is "heauenly borne" (59), the scope of her
rule and the values that she sponsors are earthly and secular.[12] Yet it is
not so difficult as it may seem to reconcile this secular characterization
of Gloriana's rule with the biblical allusions that characterize her as a sapiential figure; for biblical Wisdom also had a secular significance.
    We can begin by clarifying the contrast of Cleopolis with the New Jeru-
salem, which would seem to be that drawn by A. S. P. Woodhouse between the orders of Nature and Grace,[13] or by Calvin between "earthly"
and "heavenly things":

> I call "earthly things" those which do not pertain to God or His
> Kingdom, to true justice, or to the blessedness of the future
> life; but which have their significance and relationship with
> regard to the present life and are, in a sense, confined within its
> bounds. I call "heavenly things" the pure knowledge of God,
> the nature of true righteousness, and the mysteries of the Heav-
> enly Kingdom.
>
> (*Institutes* II.ii.13)[14]

Concerning "the present life," as Calvin goes on to say, "[t]here is
nothing more common than for a man to be sufficiently instructed in a
right standard of conduct by natural law" (ii.22), so that "[i]n every age
there have been persons who, guided by nature, have striven toward
virtue throughout life" (iii.3):

> Indeed, I admit that the endowments resplendent in [such per-
> sons] were gifts of God and seem rightly commendable if judged
> in themselves. . . .
>
> . . . [Yet] anything in profane men that appears praiseworthy
> must be considered worthless. . . . As for the virtues that
> deceive us with their vain show, they shall have their praise in
> the political assembly and in common renown among men; but
> before the heavenly judgment seat they shall be of no value to
> acquire salvation.   (iii.4)

Most Christians had long agreed that merely to follow "a right standard of conduct by natural law" was "of no value to acquire salvation,"
and that to rest confident in natural virtues as if they had such value was
positively damnable. But it was also widely agreed that, in Hooker's
words, "[w]hen supernatural duties are . . . exacted, natural are not rejected as needless"; on the contrary, "Scripture [itself] is fraught even
with laws of Nature" (*Laws* I.xii.1).[15] Thus even for Calvin the values we
can discover through "the light of reason" have their place, and a place ordained by God, in "civic . . . order" and "the arrangement of this life" (*Inst.*
II.ii.13); but if considered as either a means or an alternative to "acquir[ing]
salvation," they must be repudiated with vehement contempt.

This relation between "earthly" and "heavenly" values accounts for
the way Spenser's Hermit seems to endorse the values of Cleopolis
heartily in their own right, while dismissing or even condemning them
from the perspective of the New Jerusalem.[16] What remains to be seen
is why the same biblical figure who is the basis for Spenser's emphatically
heavenly Sapience should also be reflected in his portrayal of Gloriana,
whose reign is limited to the decidedly "earthly" Cleopolis.

That personified Wisdom in the Bible was commonly understood by
Spenser's contemporaries to image the Logos or "eternal Sonne of God"
(Geneva gloss on Prov. 8:22) has long been recognized;[17] less familiar is the
fact that other interpretations of the figure were also well-established. Of
these, the Wisdom who presides over the "natural" values of "civil life" is
presented with particular clarity by one of Gabriel Harvey's favorite
theologians, Philip Melanchthon.[18] In the 1555 vernacular edition of his
Loci Communes, Melanchthon elucidates the authority of those laws of
nature with which, as Hooker says, even the Scripture is "fraught":

> Many ask, what is natural law? The answer is that it is precisely
> the eternal unchangeable wisdom in God which he proclaimed in

the Ten Commandments. . . . God planted the glory of this, his
own unchangeable wisdom, in men in the first creation. . . .

. . . External civil life is to be regulated according to this
natural light, and note well that this natural light and the Ten
Commandments, when truly understood, are one single wisdom, doctrine, and law.   (Art. VII, p. 128)

"External civil life is to be regulated according to this natural light" or
"law," which is also "wisdom." As we will see, Melanchthon was not
alone in treating the "law" and "light" of nature as synonymous. More
to the point here is that his "wisdom" is recognizably the personified
Wisdom of the Apocrypha. For Melanchthon's identification of Wisdom with the Ten Commandments unmistakably derives from Ecclus.
24:26 and Bar. 4:1 (these will be quoted in due course); and that he is
consciously thinking of Wisdom as personified there is confirmed by a
number of less emphatic parallels, such as the imperative to "love . . .
this very beautiful wisdom," which is given as our "light" (*Loci*
127–28; cf. Wis. 8:2, 7:29, 7:10).

Melanchthon's explicit identification of biblical Wisdom with the
natural light might seem to be exceptional, but the same idea can be
traced in Aquinas (*ST* I–II.91.2 is a fitting gloss on Ecclus. 1:10), and
in Calvin, who, after referring "the light of men" in John 1:4 to "the
light of understanding," goes on to draw a further connection:

And since this light, of which *the Speech* [i.e., the Logos] was
the source, has been conveyed from him to us, it ought to serve
as a mirror, in which we may clearly behold the divine power
of *the Speech.*
        (*Commentary on the Gospel According to John*)[19]

This is to say that, as Aquinas puts it, "the intellectual light itself which
is in us is nothing other than a participated likeness of the uncreated
light" (I.84.5), "wisdom created [being] a kind of participation of the
uncreated Wisdom" which is the Logos (41.3). But what is most striking from our point of view is that Calvin's image of the light of understanding as a mirror of divine power derives from the same verse in the
Wisdom of Solomon to which Spenser alludes in making Gloriana the
"type" of Elizabeth as a "Mirror of . . . Maiestie diuine" (I.Pr.4)—though
to be sure Calvin adopts the reading later reflected in the Authorized
Version and takes Wisdom to mirror not the majesty but the "power"

(Zurich *"virtutis"*) of God (Wis. 7:26). And, curiously enough, Calvin and Melanchthon may well have been correct in identifying this goddess-like figure from the Wisdom of Solomon with the light of understanding or agent intellect.[20] For one thing, the *energeias* which the English translators render as "maiestie" or "power" corresponds to the *energeia* "activity" which Aristotle characterizes as the "essential nature" of the agent intellect or *nous poietikos* (*De Anima* III.5).[21] Even more striking, the philosopher explains that the agent intellect "is what it is by virtue of making all things" in that it recreates them in the possible intellect; and so, as we learn from *A Discourse of Ciuill Life* by Spenser's friend Lodowick Bryskett, "some haue said this . . . agent vnderstanding to be the worker of all things" (p. 124).[22] What makes this striking is that exactly the same phrase is used apropos of Wisdom:

> And all things bothe secret and knowen do I knowe: for wisdome the worker of all things, hathe taught me it.
>
> (Wis. 7:21)

> If riches be a possession to be desired in this life, what is richer then wisdome, that worketh all things?   (8:5)

It is with some justification, then, that Calvin, like Melanchthon, recognizes in the Wisdom of the Apocrypha a symbol of the natural light; and he, like Melanchthon, finds that "civic . . . order" and "the arrangement of this life" are to be "regulated" in accordance with that very "light of reason" (*Inst.* II.ii.13), since by it human beings discern "the distinction between good and evil" and are "endued with prudence for regulating their lives" (*Comm. John* 1:5).

Here, then, is a scriptural Wisdom whose influence is emphatically limited to "earthly things." Though represented as "the brightnes of the euerlasting light" and "mirroure of the maiestie of God" (Wis. 7:26), though "conveyed from [the Logos] to us" and serving as the "mirror" of his "power" (*Comm. John* 1:4), still it is only "[e]xternal civil life [that] is to be regulated according to this natural light" (*Loci* 128), which can avail us nothing with respect to "the mysteries of the Heavenly Kingdom" (*Inst.* II.ii.13). The Gloriana who not only resembles heavenly Sapience but in her own right recalls the Wisdom of the Zurich Latin Bible, the Gloriana who is the "type" of Elizabeth as "Mirrour of . . . Maiestie diuine" (I.Pr.4), who is "heauenly borne," and yet who is "soueraigne" only in the "earthly frame" of Cleopolis

(I.x.59) and sponsors only that "suit of earthly conquest" which the seeker of heaven must learn to "shonne" (60) — this Gloriana may very fittingly be seen as alluding to a Wisdom so conceived. And it may also readily be seen, given that this Wisdom is the "mirror" and "likeness" of the Logos, why her embodiment in Spenser's poem should be made the focus of an "earthly" typology both distinct from and yet analogous to that which culminates in the Incarnate Logos, Christ.

III. The Light of Nature
and the Quest for Wisdom

Yet, however fitting it might be in these respects for Gloriana to recall Wisdom as an image of the light of understanding, is it really plausible that a light which was, after all, understood to be a universal endowment, one integral to every human soul, should be imaged in a figure characterized predominantly by *absence*? For in the poem even her own knights can enjoy her "royall presence" (II.ii.44) only in memory and expectation, while for Arthur she is merely a tantalizing apparition "Whom that most most noble Briton Prince so long / Sought through the world, and suffered so much ill" (I.Pr.2), "Yet no where can her find" (II.ix.7, 38). Can this be an image of the light of nature as personified by Wisdom?

Yes; for the light personified by Wisdom, the "*vndefiled* mirroure of the maiestie of God" (Wis. 7:26), is not merely the light of nature as men and women commonly experience it. It is, more characteristically, an unusually pristine and radiant illumination, "aroused and . . . fortified," one by no means to be enjoyed universally or without intermission.

To a great extent this conception is reflected in the theologians. According to Melanchthon, it will be remembered, "God planted the glory of this, his own unchangeable wisdom, in men in the first creation"; yet "[i]n the wake of sin," as he goes on to say, "the light in human reason was not as clear and bright as before" (*Loci* 128), and so it must be "strongly aroused and the sense of it fortified" by our own strivings (xxix).[23] Calvin, as might be expected, lays a greater emphasis on both the severity of its impairment and the necessity of grace for its restoration: "to begin with, God's image was visible in the light of the mind" and "in some part . . . now is manifest in the elect, in so far as they have been reborn in the spirit" (*Inst.* I.xv.4); but for humankind in general, "in this corrupted and degenerate nature *light* has been turned into *darkness*," albeit "not wholly extinguished" (*Comm. John* 1:5; cf.

Wis. 7:10, 29–30). Yet Calvin would also seem to allow that the light of nature can shine with more than usual brightness even in those not "reborn." For it is not only in the arts that the "impious" sometimes reveal an exceptional clarity of reason that serves "to display in common nature God's special grace" (*Inst.* II.ii.14, 17):

> [Other] examples . . . seem to warn us against adjudging man's nature wholly corrupted, because some men have by its prompting not only excelled in remarkable deeds, but conducted themselves most honorably throughout life. . . .
>
> . . . For either we must make Camillus equal to Cataline, or we shall have in Camillus an example proving that nature, if carefully cultivated, is not utterly devoid of goodness. . . .
>
> Here, however, is the surest and easiest solution to this question: these are not common gifts of nature, but special graces of God, which he bestows variously and in a certain measure upon men otherwise wicked.   (II.iii.3–4)

By clear implication, then, a light of the mind which exceeds the "common gifts of nature," which goes beyond the "universal reason and understanding by nature implanted in men" (II.ii.14), would nonetheless seem to be available even to "men otherwise wicked." And it is noteworthy that, between the "special grace" of Calvin and the personal striving called for by Melanchthon (Calvin's "nature . . . carefully cultivated"), we have precisely the means by which Arthur takes Guyon to have won Gloriana's favor: "gracious lot, and they great valiaunce / Haue made thee soldier of that Princesse bright" (II.ix.5). Not that we are intended to see Gloriana or those who serve her as excluded from salvation: if the pathway to the New Jerusalem "neuer yet was seene of Faeries sonne" (I.x.52), that is simply because no one, insofar as he or she is "borne of the flesh" and not of the spirit, can "se the kingdome of God," much less "enter into" it (John 3:6, 3, 5).[24] Yet the fact that those who seek the New Jerusalem must come to "shonne" the "earthly conquest" she upholds (I.x.60) shows that the service of the faery queen has nothing to do with salvation as such, so that the natural light as she seems to image it, while it may be enhanced by God's "special grace," cannot be that which Calvin finds only in the elect.

With these distinctions in mind we can more readily identify the similar ones in the Bible's Wisdom allegories, which likewise sometimes specify a "universal" and natural endowment — though, indeed, one so proportioned as to display "God's special grace" in "common nature" — and sometimes one peculiar to the "pious" and "elect":

> He hathe powred her out vpon all his workes, and vpon all flesh, according to his gift, and giueth her abundantly vnto them that loue him. . . .
> . . . [She] was made with the faithful in the wombe. . . .
> (Ecclus. 1:10, 15)

Most commonly, however, Wisdom — particularly the Wisdom of those texts in which Calvin and Melanchthon recognize her as a symbol of the light of nature — is imagined as the all-but-unattainable object of an effort which takes the form of an erotic quest, a quest in which her prospective lover must undergo the discipline and tribulation of living up to the moral law. For though she may take the initiative in making herself known, to find her again and win "possession" of her "light" (Ecclus. 4:16, Bar. 4:2) is not an easy matter:

> For she goeth about, seking suche as are mete for her, and sheweth her self cherefully vnto them. . . .
> For the most true desire of discipline is her beginning: and the care of discipline is loue;
> And loue is the keping of her lawes. . . .
> (Wis. 6:16–18)

> For first she wil walke with him by croked waies, and bring him vnto feare, and drede, and torment him with her discipline vntil she haue tryed his soule, and haue proued him by her judgements.
> Then she wil returne the straight way vnto him, and comfort him, and shewe him her secrets, <and heape vpon him the treasures of knowledge, and understanding of righteousnes.>
> (Ecclus. 4:17–18)

> Seke after her, and searche her, & she shal be shewed thee; and when thou hast gotten her, forsake her not. . . .
> Let thy minde be vpon the ordinances of the Lord, and be continually occupied in his commandements: so shal he stablish thine heart, and giue thee wisdome at thine owne desire.
> (6:28, 38)

Who hathe gone ouer the sea, to finde her, and hathe broght
her, rather than fine golde? . . .

This is the boke of the commandements of God, and the Law
that endureth for euer . . .

(Bar. 3:30, 4:1)

In this "unchangeable wisdom" which God "proclaimed in the Ten
Commandments," Melanchthon recognized the natural light (for "this
natural light and the Ten Commandments . . . are one single wisdom,
doctrine, and law") (*Loci* 127–28). Yet, while the scripture tells us that
Wisdom has been "powred . . . vpon all flesh," it also specifies that
God, as Calvin says, "bestows [it] variously" (*Inst.* II.iii.4), "according
to his gift" (Ecclus. 1:10). And certainly it is clear that the Wisdom of
the passages we have just quoted is not effectively present in every person or at all times. Though she "may first shewe her self vnto . . . such
as are mete for her" (Wis. 6:13, 16), she will also abandon the man
would follow her and leave him to wander in "feare, and drede, . . . tor-
ment[ing] him with her discipline," until she "returne[s] the straight
way vnto him" (Ecclus. 4:17–18).[25]

Such a Wisdom, who appears before her chosen lover long enough to
let him know that "desire of discipline is her beginning" and "loue the
keping of her lawes" (Wis. 6:17–18), then vanishes "vntil she haue
tryed his soule" (Ecclus. 4:17), is scarcely less characterized by her
absence from those who would serve her than is Gloriana. In effect, as
our quotations from Calvin and Melanchthon suggest, her disciples
receive an intimation of what the sin-darkened light of nature was
before the Fall, and what in some measure it can be again if enhanced by
"special grace" or "aroused and . . . fortified" by arduous discipline; but
they are then left in humanity's accustomed "*light* [that] has been turned
into *darkness*" to undertake precisely such discipline in the hope of en-
joying her resplendent clarity again.[26] If the "vndefiled mirroure" that
is the most characteristic sapiential version of the light of nature is so
nearly inaccessible as this, the very fact that Gloriana's crusading
knights do know her presence only in memory and expectation makes
her a more fitting image of it. The fact that she appears to Arthur only
long enough to entice him to wander "through the world" in quest of
her serves not to cast doubt on her association with this sapiential light,
but to confirm it. And the fact that Spenser's typology results in her
near-total exclusion from his narrative proves to be even more in keeping with her allegorical significance.

IV. THE "IMPERIALL POWRE" OF THE
AGENT INTELLECT

Gloriana is thus, with respect to those who have seen and hope to see again "the person of her Maiestie" (II.ii.41), the image of a sapiential light more resplendent than the norm. To Arthur she is

> that Princesse bright,
> Which with her bounty and glad countenance
> Doth blesse her seruaunts, and them high aduaunce,
> (ix.5)

and as such recalls the Wisdom whose reward to her disciple is, in Coverdale's version, to "make him a glad man, . . . and heape vpon him the treasures of knowledge" (Ecclus. 4:18),[27] or who in the Vulgate "*[j]ucunditatem et exultationem thesaurizabit super illum*" (Douay "shall heap upon him a treasure of joy and gladness") (15:6). For Guyon, moreover, it would appear that the faery queen's "bountie," in which he finds "the beautie of her mind," is all but identical with her "imperiall powre" (II.ix.3); and this recognition of "imperiall powre" as a faculty of *mind* points us to three particular prerogatives of the intellectual light or agent intellect which Gloriana, like Wisdom, seems to exercise par excellence.[28]

The role of the agent intellect in human understanding is conveniently explained by Bryskett. From sense impressions the common sense and fantasy abstract the immaterial species of things, which are then received by the conscious or "possible" intellect; but those species would there remain "blind and obscure" if not for the light of the agent intellect, which "worketh the same effect towards things intelligible that the Sun doth towards things visible":

> . . . for it illumineth those kinds or formes which lie hidden in that part possible, dark and confused, deuoyde of place, time, and matter. . . . And hence it commeth that some haue said this possible vnderstanding (as we may terme it) to be such a thing, as out of it all things should be made, as if it were in stead of matter; and the other agent vnderstanding to be the worker of all things. . . . [For by its power] the [possible] vnderstanding, and things vnderstood, become . . . properly and truly one selfe same thing. . . .   (pp. 123–25)

In this respect, as Aristotle himself says, "the soul is in a way all existing things" (*De Anima* III.8): as we think of the world or any part of it, the agent intellect by its sun-like radiance "illumineth" and in that sense recreates it in our minds.[29]

What does all this have to do with Gloriana or with Wisdom? We have already seen that such "work[ing]" is apparently the source of Wisdom's intellectual bounty:

> If riches be a possession to be desired in this life, what is
> richer then wisdome, that worketh all things?   (Wis. 8:5)

And the fact that Wisdom's illuminating power encompasses the shaping of the entire world shows clearly how it might be taken as imperial:

> She also reacheth from one end to another mightely, and
> comely doeth she order all things.   (8:1)

In each of these respects, accordingly, the imperial sway of the agent intellect over "all things" is reflected in the portrayal of Gloriana. The "Great guerdon" (II.ix.6) she bestows on her servants we have already seen. Spenser does not, of course, make her the creator of his world; she is, after all (or so I take it), not a mere personification but a feigned person, one who figures forth the light of the mind even as the historical Moses was held to figure forth the Law (2 Cor. 3:13 and gloss). The poet does contrive, however, through rapturous hyperbole to make her the *illuminator* of her world, and even to make her "soueraigne power" that which "sustene[s]" all faery land, just as the agent intellect presumably sustains the world which it creates:

> Sunne of the world, great glory of the sky,
>   That all the earth doest lighten with thy rayes,
>   Great *Gloriana*, greatest Maiesty, . . .
>
>   (VI.x.28)

> Whose glory shineth as the morning starre,
>   And with her light the earth enlumines cleare; . . .
>
>   (II.ix.4)

> Great and most glorious virgin Queene aliue,
>   That with her soueraigne powre, and scepter shene
>   All Faery lond does peaceably sustene.
>
>   (ii.40)

In our first two quotations here, he has even described her in terms belonging more properly to the "euerlasting light" of which Wisdom is the "brightness" (Wis. 7:26):

> And beholde, the glorie of the God of Israel came from out of the East, . . . and the earth was made light with his glorie.
>
> (Ezek. 43:2)

> I Iesus . . . am . . . the bright morning starre [gloss: "that giueth light to euerie one that commeth into this worlde" (John 1:9)].   (Rev. 22:16)

As to the third quotation, Calvin reminds us that the Logos himself, by whom "*all things were created,*" is also "said to uphold all things" (Heb. 1:3)—and that the light of understanding is, as we have seen, the "mirror" in which we may behold his "divine power" (*Comm. John* 1:4).

It is thus the world-making capacity of the agent intellect, essential to all human understanding, which Spenser can most immediately be seen to hint at in the radiance and "imperiall powre" of his heroine, particularly if we identify the latter with her "bountie." But this is not the only sense in which a capacity of the light of understanding could be called imperial, and certainly not the one most obviously relevant to our poet's "vertuous and gentle discipline." "External civil life," as we saw earlier, "is to be regulated according to this natural light" (*Loci* 128), and so the contrast between Gloriana's capital and the New Jerusalem points up the distinction between the values appertaining to "the arrangement of this life" and those belonging to "the mysteries of the Heavenly Kingdom" (*Inst.* II.ii.13). In heeding these respective value-systems, we may now go on to observe, our objective was to be the attainment of "two distinct felicities" or "end[s]" (*Discourse* 22, *ST* I–II.62.1), both ordained by God;[30] and within human society, as Dante explains, "to direct the human race to temporal felicity" is particularly the function of the emperor:

> [God's] unutterable providence, then, has set two ends before man to be contemplated by him: the blessedness, to wit, of this life, . . . and the blessedness of eternal life. . . .
>   . . . [T]o the first we attain by the teachings of philosophy, following them by acting in accordance with the moral and intellectual virtues. . . .

Wherefore man had need of a twofold directive power according to his twofold end, to wit, the supreme pontiff, to lead
the human race, in accordance with things revealed, to eternal
life; and the emperor, to direct the human race to temporal
felicity in accordance with the teachings of philosophy.

(*De Monarchia* III.16)[31]

For the supreme pontiff, of course, Spenser had little use. But Dante
was an authority of some standing in Elizabethan imperial theory,[32] and
his words make doubly clear another sense in which that light which is
within us the "directive power" to "temporal felicity" can be called
"imperiall": it is both a faculty of mind which a succesful emperor must
possess in eminence, and one which serves within every individual as a
microcosmic emperor, dictating how "civil life is to be regulated." Presumably it is to this function of the agent intellect that Guyon is literally referring when he specifies of Gloriana that "the beautie of her
mind" lies not only in her "bountie," but in her "imperiall powre."

The "imperiall powre" of the agent intellect therefore extends to the
faculty by which an emperor is able to propose the laws which enligh-
ten his subjects and hold his polity together ("By me, Kings reigne, and
princes decree iustice," as Wisdom tells us in Prov. 8:15); and in this
respect, no less than in creating the world anew within our minds, it
could no doubt be said, like Gloriana, "all the earth [to] lighten" and
"Faery lond [to] peaceably sustene." But it is not enough to say that this
power enables an emperor to reign, or even that it holds an imperial
position within each individual. Rather, just as Gloriana purports to be
the "type" or original (I.Pr.4) of that "most royall Queene or
Empresse" Elizabeth ("L.R."), so the "imperiall powre" which ought
to reign within each of us could be seen as in its own right "the first and
originall mistris" of the world, the prototype of all lawgivers in history.
On this view the directives of actual emperors are called for only because,
as we have already seen, the light of the mind is for most of us all but "extinguished" (*Comm. John* 1:4) until it has been "aroused and . . .
fortified" (*Loci* xxix). As Pierre Charron explains (*Of Wisdom,* 1601):

[T]his law and light is naturall in vs, and therefore it is called Nature, and the law of nature. . . . The law of *Moses* in his deca-
logue, is an outward and publicke copie, the law of the twelue
tables, and the Romane law, the morall instructions of diuines
and Philosophers, the aduisements and counsels of lawyers, the

edits and ordinances of Princes are no other but petie and particular pourtrai[t]es thereof. . . . [Of this] first and originall
mistris . . . all the lawes of the world, are not other but copies
and abstracts[;] . . . [thou] holdest hidden the original, and
makest as if thou knewest it not, extinguishing as much as in
thee lieth this light, which enlighteneth thee within. . . .

(II.iii.6)[33]

Doubtlesse, Nature in euery one of vs is sufficient, and a
sweet Mistris and rule to all things, if we will hearken vnto her,
employ and awaken her. . . .
But we doe not only not hearken vnto it, . . . we endeauour
to auoid it, . . . louing better . . . to runne to studie and arte. . . .
[W]e esteeme only that which is bought, which is costly, and is
brought from farre. . . .   (8–9)

In this "sweet Mistris" (evidently she is both prince and paramour),
then, we have a "law and light" of nature whose sway is in one sense
universal—from her all lesser princes derive all their authority—but
which is nonetheless, in its most effectual form, for all practical purposes absent; indeed, due to our suffocating neglect, it is now she who
seemingly must be endeavored after and "brought from farre." Wisdom, too, appears as such a mistress, frankly claiming to be rightful
ruler of the world, yet now requiring to be sought out:

My dwelling is aboue in the height, and my throne is in the
piller of the cloude. . . .
I possessed the waues of the sea, and all the earth, and all people, and nacion, <and with my power haue I troden downe the
hearts of all, bothe High and low.> . . .
Come vnto me all ye that be desirous of me . . .

(Ecclus. 24:7, 9, 22)

This Wisdom is a mistress, moreover, of whome we find a "copie" in
the Law of Moses:

All these things are . . . the Law that Moyses <in the
precepts of righteousnes> commanded. . . .   (26)

This is one of the texts that led Melanchthon, as we have seen, to recognize "this natural light and the Ten Commandments . . . [as] one single

wisdom, doctrine, and law" (*Loci* 128). Its significance for us, like that of the first passage from Charron, is more particular. Both serve to emphasize that, even though the agent intellect as a faculty of the soul exercises its world-making and life-directing powers within each of us individually, there was nonetheless a very cogent sense in which it could be regarded (in its most pristine form at least) as "the first and originall mistris" not of the individual microcosm, but of the external world at large.[34]

In presenting Gloriana as a "soueraine Queene" and "mightie Emperesse" whose concern is with righting wrongs (V.i.4), as a monarch who "all the earth doe[s] lighten" (VI.x.28) and "Faery lond does peaceably sustene" (II.ii.40), and as one of whom "the beautie of her mind" lies in "her bountie, and imperiall powre" (ix.4), therefore, Spenser is merely reinforcing what we have already seen: the faery queen images the light of nature as it is portrayed in the Wisdom of the Bible. She represents an intellectual splendor which is "the worker of all things," "[b]y [whom] Kings reigne," and who once from her throne "possessed . . . all the earth, and all people, and nacion."

V. The Compass of Spenserian Glory

Gloriana as we have seen her thus far seems eminently suitable as the focal character of a work whose "generall end" is "to fashion a gentleman or noble person in vertuous and gentle discipline"; but much less clear is the basis on which the poet can claim that "In that Faery Queene I meane glory" ("Letter to Raleigh"). In this essay, accordingly, we need to elucidate Spenser's overall conception of glory as one which the light of nature is by rights pre-eminent and pivotal. In many respects his conception simply reflects (and presumably derives from) that of Calvin, as a cluster of verbal echoes suggests; but in others he reverts to a view that helps to mark a sharp divergence from Calvin's viewpoint.

Before proceeding to Calvin's own conception of glory, therefore, we need to have some notion of three much earlier (indeed, ancient) developments which it presupposes. The first of these is the impact of the application of the word *glory* itself to God by the Bible's major prophets; for their usage led to a shift in the semantic ground covered by the word generally. Hebrew *kabod* had originally denoted "weight," as Greek *doxa* had "opinion," and Latin *gloria*, "fame"; but with the appearance of the Septuagint and Old Latin versions of scripture, the recurring prophetic conception of God's *kabod* as a dazzling theophanic splendor carried over to *doxa* and *gloria* as the words by which *kabod* was ordinarily translated. Each word came to have "light" or "splendor" as a key part of its meaning; and this connotation of radiance prevailed even outside of theophanic contexts.[35] Thus Paul uses *doxa* both of the insupportable radiance that manifests the power of God (e.g., 2 Cor. 3:7) and of the purely material splendor of the sun, moon, and stars (1 Cor. 15:41); while by the time of Aquinas "radiance" had come to seem the root meaning of *gloria* in every sense, including fame:

> Glory means a kind of radiance, so that in Augustine's words *being the recipient of glory is the same as being radiant with light.* Now radiance implies both a certain beauty and its manifestation. So the term *glory* strictly connotes the manifestation by someone of a thing which in our eyes seems beautiful, whether it is a physical or a spiritual good.   (II–II.132.1)[36]

"Glory" in the sense of a self-revelatory splendor, though initially attributed only to God himself, thus became the characteristic of any "physical or . . . spiritual good" whose "beauty" is widely manifested by (or as if by) an inherent radiance. And, as a glance at the relevant entries in Osgood's *Concordance* will show, this conception was still very much alive in Spenser's time.[37]

A second key development came with the recognition that examples of this kind of "glory" or splendor among created things could themselves be seen as theophanic: "For by the greatnesse & beutye of the creature, the maker therof maye playnely be knowne" (Wis. 13:5 [Cov.]). This doctrine is most explicitly developed in terms of glory by Sirach, who makes it the theme of several consecutive chapters of Ecclesiasticus. His initial emphasis is on the splendor of the heavenly bodies and other wonders of nature, but even fame is included among those glories of creation which he takes to manifest the glory of God:

> The sunne that shineth, loketh vpon all things, and the worke thereof is ful of the glorie of the Lord. . . .
>
> Oh, how delectable are all his workes . . .
>
> The one commendeth the goodnes of the other, & who can be satisfied with beholding Gods glorie?
>
> This high ornament the cleare firmament, the beautie of the heauen so glorious to beholde. . . .

> . . . [T]he Lord hathe made all things, and giuen wisdome to
> such as feare God.
>   Let us now commend the famous [Vulg., Trem. *"gloriosos"*]
> men. . . .
>   The Lorde hathe gotten great glorie by them, and that by his
> great powre from the beginning. . . .
>   (Ecclus. 42:16, 22, 25; 43:1, 33; 44:1–2)

In short, because the workmanship of all things is "ful of the glorie of
the Lord," to gaze upon "the beautie of the heauen so glorious to
beholde" is in its own right a way of "beholding Gods glorie"; and even
mere earthly fame, like the gift of "wisdome" that secures it, is one of
the workings of his "great powre."

The final development we need to consider before turning to Calvin
also takes the splendors of creation to be revelatory of the creator, but
emphasizes as specifically moral the content of their theophany. This
view is glanced at as early as the Psalms:

> The heauens declare his righteousness, and all the people
> se his glorie.   (97:6)

But it is most conspicuously argued, though without explicit reference to
glory, in Paul's Epistle to the Romans. Where Sirach had cited both the visible creation and the "wisdome" bestowed on the pious as revealing God's
glory, the apostle instead names both the visible creation and the sense of
right and wrong found even among Gentiles as revealing God's *law:*

> For the inuisible things of him, that is, his eternal power and
> Godhead, are sene by the creation of the worlde, being consid-
> ered in *his* workes. . . .
>   . . . [Thus even the Gentiles] knewe the Law [gloss: "*Or,
> righteousnes*"] of God. . . . [Gloss: "Which Law God writ in
> their consciences, and the Philosophers called it the Law of
> nature. . . ."]
>   (Rom. 1:20, 31)

Thus, as Melanchthon was later to explain, all of nature is replete with
"traces of God" ("*vestigia Dei*"), so that "everything in the universe testifies that there is a God, that there is wisdom, goodness, and justice";
yet the clearest such testimony is to be found in the human mind and in

the knowledge of good and evil imprinted on it.[38] If this emphatically moral theophany-via-creation were to be put back into Sirachian terms (as theophany via created *glory*), we would clearly have a conception of glory which not only included the law or light of nature "written in [our] hearts" (Rom. 2:15), but actually recognized a moral force in all created splendors.

Calvin comes very close to formulating this conception. Usually, it is true, he reserves the word *glory* for the glory of God, declining to apply it directly to God's works. Yet his argument in *Institutes* I.v. is precisely that the glory of God *is* splendor, that in beholding created splendors we behold that glory, and that such splendors thereby promulgate the moral law. The emphasis on glory as light in the opening of the chapter is unrelenting:

> [U]pon his individual works [God] has engraved unmistakable marks of his glory, so clear and so prominent . . . [that] the prophet very aptly exclaims that he is "clad with light as with a garment" [Psalm 104:2]. It is as if he said: Thereafter the Lord began to show himself in the visible splendor of his apparel, ever since in the creation of the universe he brought forth those insignia whereby he shows his glory to us, whenever and wherever we turn our gaze. . . . And since the glory of his power and wisdom shine more brightly above, heaven is often called his palace <Ps. 11:4>. Yet, in the first place, wherever you cast your eyes, there is no spot in the universe wherein you cannot discern at least some sparks of his glory. You cannot in one glance survey this most vast and beautiful system of the universe, in its wide expanse, without being completely overwhelmed by the boundless force of its brightness.
>
> (*Inst.* I.v.l)

And what we see "shining in heaven and earth," as he explains elsewhere, extends even to God's "virtues" (Lat. *virtutes,* Fr. *vertus*): "kindness, goodness, justice, judgment, and truth" (x.2; cf. v.10).[40] Of course, this is not to say that creation's visible splendors afford moral guidance sufficient to direct our lives, since we know that "all mortals 'became vain in their reasonings' <Rom. 1:2> after the majesty of the Creator had been disclosed to them in the fashioning of the universe" (v.13):

> It is therefore in vain that so many burning lamps shine for us in the workmanship of the universe to show forth the glory

of its Author. Although they bathe us wholly in their radiance,
yet they can of themselves in no way lead us into the right path.

(14)

Calvin thus makes the point that the moral law is somehow implicit in
the visible splendors of creation only to dismiss it as of little practical
importance. On the other hand, as we have already seen, he recognizes
that the natural light, in earthly matters, often does suffice to "lead us into
the right path": "There is nothing more common than for a man to be
sufficiently instructed in a standard of right conduct by natural law"
(II.ii.22), so that "[i]n every age there have been persons who, guided by
nature, have striven toward virtue throughout life" (iii.3). We need
hardly be surprised, then, to find that the natural light holds for Calvin a
place of rare distinction among created manifestations of God's glory.

That both the physical and mental attributes of humanity manifest
God's glory with unusual clarity is something Calvin more than once is
at pains to emphasize. If the most impressive way "to look upon
[God's] glory" is to consider the "innumerable and yet distinct and
well-ordered variety of the heavenly host" (I.v.2), he maintains, still
man is the single work of God in which his glory shines most brightly,
being in his own right a "microcosm" and "a rare example of God's
power, goodness, and wisdom" (3). Indeed, "each one [of us] undoubt-
edly feels within the heavenly grace that quickens him," so that the
Psalmist, in praising "the admirable name and glory of God which shine
everywhere," emphasizes especially that "a clear mirror of God's works
is in humankind," while Paul stresses that "by adorning us with such
great excellence [God] testifies that he is our father" (3, citing Psalm
8:2 and Acts 17:28). The obvious traces of divinity in man are even
cited as evidence for the divine governance of the universe:

> [Human beings] have within themselves a workshop graced
> with God's unnumbered works and, at the same time, a store-
> house overflowing with inestimable riches. . . . Do all the
> treasures of heavenly wisdom concur in ruling a five-foot
> worm while the whole universe lacks this privilege?
>
> (4)

In short, as Calvin never tires of repeating, "in forming man and in
adorning him with such goodly beauty, and with such great and numerous gifts, [God] put him forth as the most excellent example of his
works" (xiv.20).

Yet the part of man in which Calvin finds glory to be most resplendent is precisely that which Spenser images in Gloriana. For while "the
likeness of God extends to the whole excellence by which man's nature
towers over all the kinds of living creatures." so that "God's glory
shines forth in the outer man," nevertheless from the time of Adam's
creation "the primary seat of the divine image was in the mind and
heart, or in the soul and its powers" (xv.2–3). And of "those faculties
in which man excels, and in which he ought to be thought the reflection of God's glory," the light of understanding is pre-eminent:

> [T]o begin with, God's image was visible in the light of the
> mind, in the uprightness of the heart, and in the soundness of
> all the parts. . . . [Of these John singles out] ". . . the light of
> men" <John 1:4> . . . [so as] to praise God's singular grace,
> wherein man excels the remaining living creatures, . . . because
> he attained no common life, but one joined with the light of
> understanding. [In this] he shows at the same time how man
> was created in God's image. [For] God's image is the perfect ex-
> cellence of human nature which shone in Adam before his
> defection. . . .   (4)

Prior to the Fall, at least, "the light of the mind" — the same light
which Scripture images in Wisdom, and Spenser in Gloriana — was thus
for Calvin the single most striking "reflection of God's glory" in all creation. And even though it has been darkened by the Fall, that light remains such a resplendent gift that for once even Calvin is willing to des-
ignate a mere created splendor by the name of "glory":

> . . . God's wonderful goodness is displayed the more brightly in
> that so glorious a Creator, whose majesty shines resplendently
> in the heavens, graciously condescends to adorn a creature so
> miserable and so vile as man is with the greatest glory, and to
> enrich him with numerous blessings. . . .
>   . . . [For the Psalmist] represents [men] as adorned with so
> many honours as to render their condition not far inferior to
> divine and celestial glory . . . , [chief among them] the disting-
> uished endowments which clearly manifest that men were
> formed after the image of God. . . . The reason with which
> they are endued, and by which they can distinguish between
> good and evil; the principle of religion which is planted in them;

their intercourse with each other, which is preserved from being broken up by certain sacred bonds; the regard to what is
becoming, and the sense of shame which guilt awakens in
them, as well as their continuing to be governed by laws; all
these things are clear indications of pre-eminent and celestial
wisdom. David, therefore, not without good reason, exclaims
that mankind are adorned with glory and honor. *To be crowned*
[Psalm 8:5], is here taken metaphorically, as if David had said,
he is clothed and adorned with marks of honour, which are not
far removed from the splendour of the divine majesty.

> (*Comm. Ps.* 8:4–5)[41]

Obviously, "all these things" — these "indications of . . . celestial wisdom" which are also the marks of that "greatest glory" with which
humanity has been "adorned" — are the fruits or functions of the natural
light, essential as it is to "the arrangement of this life" (*Inst.* II.ii.13).
And if what Calvin takes to be the Psalmist's glorification of this light
with its "sacred bonds" seems extravagant with regard to the darkened
illumination most of us experience, it would surely have seemed fitting
for the restored splendor to be enjoyed by one who has succeeded in the
quest for Wisdom:

> Then shal her fetters be a strong defence for thee, . . . &
> her chaines a glorious raiment. . . .
> Thou shalt put her on as a robe of honour [Vulg., Trem.
> "*gloriae*"], & shalt put her vpon thee, as a crowne of ioye.
> (Ecclus. 6:30, 32)

Thus Calvin has taken the ancient recognition of created splendors as
theophanic "glories" and, while declining to describe most of them as
"glorious" in their own right, has both singled out the intellectual light
as supreme among such splendors and explicitly recognized in all of
them a certain moral force. In so doing, he has prepared the way for
Spenser to reintegrate these conceptions and so arrive at a generalized
notion of glory which has the light of nature at its core.

For we are now clearly in a position to account for the fact that the
faery queen, while said to represent glory, so forcefully recalls Wisdom
as a symbol of the light of nature. Like Aquinas, it would appear, Spenser accepts any literal or figurative radiance as being "glorious"; like
Sirach, he accepts all created glories as implicit theophanies; and like

Paul or Melanchthon or Calvin, he understands the main thrust of such natural theophanies to be the inculcation of the moral law. But the most resplendent of created glories, as Calvin makes clear, and by far the most efficacious in making plain to us the demands of a "vertuous and gentle discipline," is the light of understanding. The glory imaged in the faery queen is thus simply glory in its most general sense as radiance or splendor, for any God-created splendor tends to promulgate the natural law;[42] but the *ne plus ultra* of such glory is the natural light.

In Spenser's allegory, therefore, that quintessence of glory which is imaged in the very person of the faery queen seems to consist entirely of the light of understanding, while the lesser splendors encompassed by the term are presented as her garments. The scope of his conception is articulated in a single stanza:

> In her the richesse of all heauenly grace
>   In chiefe degree are heaped vp on hye:
>   And all that else this worlds enclosure bace
>   Hath great or glorious in mortall eye,
>   Adornes the person of her Maiestie;
>   That men beholding so great excellence,
>   And rare perfection in mortalitie,
>   Do her adore with sacred reuerence,
> As th'Idole of her makers great magnificence.
>
> (II.ii.41)

This stanza abounds with words or concepts we have seen Calvin use repeatedly in describing the glory manifested in humanity: "riches," "(heavenly) grace," "great," "glory," "adorns," "majesty," "excellence," "rare," "perfection"; so much so that I presume the recollection of Calvin to be deliberate, though Spenser's application is often different.[43] Here, appropriately enough, "the richesse of all heauenly grace" points to the plenitude of the natural light with which God "graciously condescends to adorn a creature so miserable and so vile as man" (*Comm. Ps.* 8:5), bestowing it even more generously on some by "special grace" (*Inst.* II.ii.17). That Gloriana's person is "Adorne[d]" with all *visible* splendors, however, points to the function of that light as "the worker of all things" (Wis. 7:21). According to Calvin, after all, God as creator of the external world is invisible, yet "clad with light" (Ps. 104:2) in the sense that the "visible splendor" of his creation is the "apparel" in which he "show[s] himself" (*Inst.* I.v.l); by the same token, therefore, it might be said that the agent intellect is clad with the splendors of the universe which its radiance creates anew within the mind. (In that sense "this worlds enclosure bace" extends to "these heauens which here we see," for even they are "bounded" and "corrupt" with respect to the supercelestial world [*An Hymne of Heauenly Beautie*, ll. 64–66]). Once it is thus appareled, however, we can see that the intellectual light (especially when enhanced by "special grace") does indeed exhibit a "great excellence, / And rare perfection in mortalitie"; for in it we see not only the "excellence by which man's nature towers over all the kinds of living creatures" (*Inst.* I.xv.3) — itself the result of "God's singular grace" — but an approximation of "the perfect excellence . . . which shone in Adam before his defection" (4). We may even recognize this light as worthy of our "sacred reuerence," and not only for its "rare perfection," nor even because it promulgates God's law, so that Guyon can say "To her I homage and my seruice owe" (II.ii.42). Rather it may also be revered as constituting, in a dual sense, "th'Idole of her makers great magnificence": for it is not merely the single most glorious work of God's "great power" (Ecclus. 44:2; Vulg., Zur. "*magnificentia*"), but is also in its own right a great maker, being the mirror of his "power" or "maiestie" (Wis. 7:26) and so "the worker of all things" (7:21) within the intellect, even as God himself is "the worker of all things" *tout court*.

Of course, Gloriana is also explicitly associated with glory in the sense of fame. Whether Spenser considered this to be a conspicuous part of the glory actually *imaged* in his heroine, however, seems to me uncertain. Sirach, as we have seen, does regard glory even in this sense as theophanic (Ecclus. 44:1–2); but in Spenser such glory is not something which the faery queen can be seen to represent, but something she bestows (I.x.59). In this respect, as in so many others, she has been made to resemble Wisdom:

> Length of daies *is* in her right hand, & in her left hand riches and glorie.
>
> (Prov. 3:16)

> Exalt her, and she shal exalt thee: she shal bring thee to honour, if thou embrace her.   (4:8)

As Spenser's contemporary Peter Muffet says in paraphrasing these verses, "wisdom, as a bountiful queen, giveth to those who obey her, not only long life, but worldly wealth, and earthly glory," so that "if thou shalt exalt and entertain wisdom, she as a queen will make thee honourable, and as it were a knight" (*A Commentary on the Whole Book of Proverbs* [?1596]).[44] Such a figure is less suited to represent fame itself than to image the natural light, which fame is to be sought by heeding.[45]

If the high regard for fame which he shares with Sirach further aligns Spenser with the Bible's Wisdom allegories, however, it no less clearly marks his divergence from the thought of Calvin, whose nod to "common renown among men" is not so much grudging as disdainful (*Inst.* II.iii.4; cf. III.xiii.2, xiv.16). Up till now the reader may have felt that Calvin as he appears in this essay sounds suspiciously like Hooker in the respect he seemingly accords to the autonomy and dignity of human reason in the wake of the Fall. This is partly because the differences between Calvin and Hooker on this point are more a matter of emphasis than is always recognized (least of all by Calvin's Elizabethan followers, who often seem determined to out-Herod Herod, as Hooker himself points out [*Laws* V.app.i.6]). Mostly, though, it is because I have been using Calvin to elucidate Spenser's thinking rather than his own. Spenser limits the denigration of Gloriana's values to a few stanzas (I.x.58–62) in a poem which is designed to celebrate them, and makes her the presiding spirit of all the "priuate morall vertues" ("Letter to Raleigh") while relegating "Holinesse" to a single (albeit pivotal) book; in Calvin the proportions are reversed. While Spenser may have relished the opportunity to turn Calvin's eloquence to his own purpose, then, he generally prefers to go like Melanchthon or Hooker on his own more or less Thomistic way.[46] "When supernatural laws are . . . exacted," Hooker tells us, "natural are not rejected as needless" (I.xii.1), but rather "laws of nature . . . are . . . necessary also even in themselves" (V.app.i.7); and thus "when we extol the complete sufficiency of . . . the Scripture, . . . the benefit of nature's light [must] not be thought excluded as unnecessary" (I.xiv.4). In his exaltation of Gloriana, Spenser does more than merely anticipate Hooker's characteristic emphasis on the authority of reason. By making her the focus of a Bible-like typology, he in effect puts his poem forward as a complementary scripture in its own right, one dedicated to "the benefit of nature's light" just as the Bible is dedicated to "salvation through Christ" (ibid.). That nature's light is itself a "mirror" of the power of the Logos (*Comm. John* 1:4) would scarcely have seemed to Calvin to justify such huge audacity.

Even for Calvin, of course, the natural light and created splendor in general have their role in "the arrangement of this life." But not even Aquinas, Melanchthon, and Hooker, not even the Cambridge Platonists, go so far as Spenser in magnifying the autonomy and prestige of the light of nature and its attendant glories. What even the Bible's Wisdom allegories exult in over the space of only some dozen scattered pages, Spenser makes the "argument" of a vast heroic poem intended to rival Homer. What Charron aggrandizes in a few short chapters, what Melanchthon honors in a few short paragraphs, what Calvin enthuses over in the occasional odd sentence, Spenser makes the culmination of a laudatory typology like the biblical typology that culminates in Christ. Yet, if we remember how extraordinary were the prerogatives ascribed to the Bible's (and Melanchthon's) Wisdom, to Charron's "mistris," and even to Calvin's "greatest glory"—and if we remember that for Spenser this quintessential "glory" is enhanced by "special grace," as Gloriana's very name suggests[47]—we may come to the view that his "generall intention" in the faery queen was not entirely unfitting.[48] We may come to the view that what the poet tells Burleigh concerning the apparently "ydle rimes" of *The Faerie Queene* in general is particularly true of those "rimes" pertaining to its heroine:

> Vnfitly I these ydle rimes present,
> The labor of lost time, and wit vnstayd:
> Yet if their deeper sence be inly wayd,
> And the dim vele, with which from common vew
> Their fairer parts are hid, aside be layd,
> Perhaps not vaine they may appeare to you.
>
> (Ded. Son. to Burleigh)

When the veil is laid aside from his accounts of Gloriana, we find a life-directing glory truly integral, on Spenser's terms, to the poem's "generall end" of "fashion[ing]" its readers "in vertuous and gentle discipline."

St. Paul, Minnesota

NOTES

1. Jeffrey P. Fruen, "'True Glorious Type': The Place of Gloriana in *The Faerie Queene*," *Spenser Studies*, VII (1987), 147–73; on the typological thrust of the "vele" with respect to Gloriana, see pp. 161–64. All quotations from Spenser are from the one-volume *Poetical Works*, ed. J. C. Smith and E. de Selincourt (Oxford: Clarendon Press, 1912). My title also throws a cautionary sidelong glance at the overweening of "C" in "The 'Faerie Queene' Unveiled," *N & Q*, ser. 3, 4 (1863): 21–22, 65–66, 101–103; partially reprinted in *The Works of Edmund Spenser: A Variorum Edition*, ed. Edwin Greenlaw, et al., I (Baltimore: Johns Hopkins University Press, 1932), 451–52.

2.   Naseeb Shaheen, *Biblical References in "The Faerie Queene"* (Memphis: Memphis State University Press, 1976).

3.   All Latin and English Protestant Bibles of the sixteenth century included the Apocrypha. The Geneva Bible of 1560, while of course denying them canonical authority, does refer to them as "'scriptures" (headnote to the Apocrypha) and even "Holy Scriptures" (general title page); and the books of Wisdom and Ecclesiasticus, which chiefly concern us here, are so frequently cross-referenced with the Old and New Testaments that the essential soundness of their theology can hardly have seemed doubtful. See *The Geneva Bible: A Facsimile of the 1560 Edition,* with an introduction by Lloyd E. Berry (Madison: University of Wisconsin Press, 1969). Except where otherwise noted, all of my biblical references are to this edition. (In the Geneva translation of Ecclesiasticus, passages recognized as interpolations are included in square brackets; I change these to pointed brackets to distinguish them from my own alterations or additions.)

4.   The Zurich Latin Bible of 1543 was perhaps the most influential Protestant Latin Bible during Spenser's years at the Merchant Taylors' School and Cambridge (1561–76), being superseded only by the Tremellius-Junius version as it appeared (NT 1569, OT 1575–79). In 1545, Robert Estienne reprinted it, identified only as a "new" version, in parallel columns with his own critically restored text of the Vulgate. See *The Cambridge History of the Bible,* ed. S. L. Greenslade, III (Cambridge: Cambridge University Press, 1963), 65–66, 71; and *The New Catholic Encyclopedia,* 1967, *s.v.* "Bible," II, 455. My quotations are from Estienne's edition: *Biblia. Quid in hac editione praestitum sit, vide in ea quam / opere praeposuimus, ad lectorum epistola. /* Lutetiae / . . . Roberti Stephani . . . / M.D. XLV. In all of my quotations from sixteenth-century texts, contractions are expanded, long-*s* changed to *s,* and ligatures omitted. In this case, for clarity of reference, I have also restored the poetic verse-lineation ascribed to the text by modern scholars.

5.   Thomas Cooper, *Thesaurus Linguae Romanae et Britannicae,* 1565; facsimile reprint (Menston: Scolar Press, 1969). The definitions I cite come not only from Cooper's main entries, but also from the translations given with his contextual quotations. On the use of Cooper at Merchant Taylors', see T. W. Baldwin, *William Shakspere's Small Latine & Less Greeke* (Urbana: University of Illinois Press, 1944), I, 421.

6.   Often-reprinted versions such as the Vulgate I quote variously from whatever editions come first to hand (the Douay and Authorized Versions are also in this category). The Tremellius-Junius version is quoted from the London edition of 1585: *Testamenti Veteris / Biblia Sacra / Sive / Libri Canonici / Prisce Iudaeorum / Ecclesiae a Deo Traditi, / . . . / . . .* Immaneuele / Tremellio & Francisco Junio / . . . / Londini, / Excudebat Henricus Midletonus, / . . . / M.D. LXXXV.

7.   Thomas E. Maresca, *Three English Epics: Studies of "Troilus and Criseyde," "The Faerie Queene," and "Paradise Lost"* (Lincoln: University of Nebraska Press, 1979), p. 62; see also Fruen, p. 158. In the sequence of the poem, Gloriana is the "type" of Elizabeth in the quasi-biblical sense that Elizabeth as addressed in the proems is "the first draught and purtrait" of Gloriana, "the liuelie paterne to come" (gloss on Heb 10:1) — "paterne" here being picked up from the last half of Heb. 8:5, where it translates "*typon*"; see Fruen, pp. 159–61.

8.   While the Wisdom allegories in the first nine chapters of Proverbs are also relevant, those in Wisdom (ch. 6–9) and Ecclesiasticus (ch. 1, 4, 6, 14–15, 24, 51) are par-

ticularly significant here. And Spenser may not have thought himself the first author to use these biblical materials in a faery mistress story. When Arthur of Little Britain tells his friends of the dream in which his own visionary mistress appeared to him in the form of an eagle, his phrasing comes almost as close to that of the biblical texts quoted here as it does to Spenser's:

> And euer syth I woke my herte and loue hath ben so set on that egle that I can not draw my herte fro her. For I loue her so entyerly that as longe as I lyue I shall neuer cease to trauell & labour tyll I haue founde her.

See *Arthur of Brytayn: The hystory of the moost noble and valyaunt knyght Arthur of lytell brytayne,* trans. John Bourchier, Lord Berners (London: Robert Redborne, [ca. 1550]), cap. xvi, fol. xiiiᵛ. The influence of this episode on Spenser was first noted by John Colin Dunlop, *History of Prose Fiction* (1814), rpt. as *History of Fiction* (London: G. Bell & Sons, 1896), I, 260. Perhaps less striking in terms of verbal parallels is the encounter with the faery mistress in *Syr Lamwell,* the form in which Spenser presumably knew Marie de France's *Lanval:* "Lamwell behelde that lady bryght / Her loue hym rauysshed anone ryght." See the appendix of *Bishop Percy's Folio Manuscript: Ballads and Romances,* ed. John W. Hales and Frederick J. Furnivall (London: Trubner, 1867), I, 525. On the other hand, as the poet who treats "Medway" as a form of "Medua" (IV.xi.8, 45), Spenser may well have recognized that "Lamwell" is a form of "Lamuell," a name which in turn reflects the "Lamuel" of Prov. 31:1 in the Vulgate (see A. J. Bliss, "The Hero's Name in the Middle English Versions of *Lanval,*" *MAE,* 27 [1958], 82 and n.); and that regal figure, according to the Geneva gloss, is really Solomon himself, the Bible's pre-eminent quester after Wisdom.

9.   See especially *FQ* II.ii.41, ix.3, 5 and *HHB* 242–48, 253–59. The virtual identification of Gloriana with Sapience was first made by Jefferson B. Fletcher, "A Study in Renaissance Mysticism: Spenser's *Fowre Hymnes,*" *PMLA,* 26 (1911), 474–75, and most recently restated by Douglas Brooks-Davies in his Introduction to Spenser, *The Faerie Queene: A Selection* (London: Dent; New York: Dutton, Everyman's Library, 1976), p. x. Especially intriguing applications of this view are those by Josephine Waters Bennett, "Spenser's Muse," *JEGP,* 31 (1932), 217, and Janet Spens, *Spenser's "Faerie Queene": An Interpretation* (London: Edward Arnold, 1934), pp. 50, 112, 113, 114. The biblical provenance of Sapience was first thoroughly (though not exhaustively) documented by Charles Grosvenor Osgood, "Spenser's Sapience," *SP,* 14 (1917), 167–77.

10.   Latin quoted from Cicero, *De Officiis* I.v, trans. Walter Miller, Loeb Classical Library (Cambridge: Harvard University Press; London: Heinemann, 1913); alluding to Plato, *Phaedrus* 250d.

11.   Sir Philip Sidney, *An Apologie for Poetry* (ca. 1583), in *Elizabethan Critical Essays,* ed. G. Gregory Smith, (Oxford: Clarendon Press, 1904), I, 179; emphasis added to the final phrase. Raleigh, in 1590 a confidante of Spenser's for a relatively short time, may intend this identification of Cicero's Virtue with the Bible's Wisdom in referring to "true vertues face" in his second commendatory poem (Spenser's *Poetical Works,* p. 409). For that matter, Spenser himself may be making the same identification in *FQ* III.iii.1, again reflecting Wis. 8:2, but taking *diligo* in its other sense as synonymous with *deligo* "to choose": "that doth true beautie loue, / And choseth vertue for his dearest dame" (cf. Zurich *pulchritudinis, amore, dilexi, sponsam*).

12.   See Isabel E. Rathborne, *The Meaning of Spenser's Fairyland* (New York: Columbia University Press, 1937), 17–19; and Robert Ellrodt, *Neoplatonism in the Poetry of Spenser* (Geneva: Librairie E. Droz, 1960), 50, 58. Also relevant in establishing the purely secular values of Cleopolis are Thomas P. Roche, Jr., *The Kindly Flame: A Study of the Third and Fourth Books of "The Faerie Queene,"* (Princeton: Princeton University Press, 1964), 38–43; and Carol V. Kaske, "Spenser's Pluralistic Universe: The View from the Mount of Contemplation (*F.Q.* I.x)," in *Contemporary Thought on Edmund Spenser,* ed. Richard C. Frushell and Bernard J. Vondersmith (Carbondale: Southern Illinois University Press, 1975), 130–41.

13.   A. S. P. Woodhouse, "Nature and Grace in *The Faerie Queene,*" *ELH,* 16 (1949): 194–228; "Nature and Grace in Spenser: A Rejoinder," *RES,* n.s. 6 (1955): 284–88; "Spenser, Nature and Grace: Mr. Gang's Mode of Argument Reviewed," *ELH,* 27 (1960): 1–15. I am indebted to the third essay for a number of my citations from Aquinas, Calvin, and Hooker. The unfortunate personal animus of this third essay may be what has kept it from being reprinted, but Woodhouse's impatience seems even more understandable in retrospect, for dismayingly few of the many who have offered to challenge or correct his original argument show much sign of having read it carefully. In her chapter "Nature and Grace Reconsidered," for instance, Anthea Hume is right to insist that Guyon is a Christian and so cannot be a "natural man" as Woodhouse defines the term, but this has virtually nothing to do with Woodhouse's overriding question of whether temperance as Guyon exemplifies it is natural or supernatural in its "motivation and sanction." See Anthea Hume, *Edmund Spenser: Protestant Poet* (Cambridge: Cambridge University Press, 1984), 59–71.

14.   John Calvin, *Institutes of the Christian Religion,* ed. John T. McNeill, tr. Ford Lewis Battles, Library of Christian Classics, vols. 20–21 (London: SCM Press, 1960); henceforth cited in the text as *Inst.* Calvin's distinction (see also II.ii.12) is surprisingly close to that of Aquinas, as in *The "Summa Theologica" of Saint Thomas Aquinas,* trans. Fathers of the English Dominican Province, revised by Daniel J. Sullivan, in *Great Books of the Western World,* vols. 19–20 (Chicago: Encyclopedia Brittanica, 1952), I–II.62.1, 63.4; 109.2; II–II.23.7. Where not otherwise noted, all references to Aquinas are to this selection, cited in the text as *ST.*

15.   Richard Hooker, *Of the Laws of Ecclesiastical Polity,* in *The Works of that Learned and Judicious Divine Mr. Richard Hooker,* arranged by John Keble, revised by R. W. Church and F. Paget, 3 vols. (Oxford: Clarendon Press, 1888), vols. I–II.

16.   Kaske does an especially good job of bringing out this contrast, though it is hardly necessary to conclude that in drawing it Spenser "contradicts not only Christian tradition but himself" (p. 135). On the contrary, such ambivalence was an integral feature of Christian tradition, clearly reflected in the distinction between Nature and Grace which Woodhouse documents in figures ranging from Augustine to Aquinas to Calvin to Hooker ("Spenser, Nature and Grace," 3–6). The tension, indeed, had been built into Christianity by no less a figure than St. Paul. Having established that the moral content of the Mosaic law corresponds to what pagans call the law of nature (Rom. 1:31 and gloss, 2:14–15), the apostle repeatedly denounces trust in that law as a means of seeking salvation: it is merely "the strength of sinne" (1 Cor. 15:56) and serves us only "vnto death" (Rom. 7:10), bringing a spurious righteousness worth no more than "dongue" (Phil. 3:8). Yet, for all this, we must nonetheless strive to adhere to it: "Do we then make the Law of none effect through faith? God

forbid: yea we establish the Law" (Rom. 3:31). (See also Rom. 3:20, 24, 27, 28; 6:14–15; 7:6; 10:3; 1 Cor. 6:9–10; Gal. 2:16, 3:10–11; Eph. 2:8–9; Phil. 3:6). Adherence to the law thus corresponds to Spenser's "earthly conquest," which we are duty-bound to pursue in this life and yet must "shonne" altogether at the end of life when we can turn all our hopes to heaven (I.x.60).

17.   See the Spenser *Variorum,* VII (1943), 561, 564.

18.   On Harvey's esteem for Melanchthon, see Virgil K. Whitaker, *The Religious Basis of Spenser's Thought,* (Stanford: Stanford University Press, 1950), 66. The influence of Melanchthon in Elizabethan England is also noted in H. S. V. Jones, "The *Faerie Queene* and the Mediaeval Aristotelian Tradition," *JEGP,* 25 (1926): 292–98, and in the preface to Philip Melanchthon, *Melanchthon on Christian Doctrine: "Loci Communes" 1555,* trans. Clyde L. Manschreck, introduction by Hans Engelland (New York: Oxford University Press, 1965), xx–xxii. Except where otherwise noted, all quotations from Melanchthon will be from Manschreck's translation, cited in the text as *Loci.*

19.   John Calvin, *Commentary on the Gospel of John,* trans. the Rev. William Pringle, 2 vols. (Edinburgh: Calvin Translation Society, 1847); henceforth cited in the text as *Comm. John.*

20.   Spenser may have thought that Aristotle got the idea from the author of Wisdom, since there were purportedly at least thirty passages in which Plato could be seen to be "imitat[ing]," "paraphras[ing]," and "all but translating" texts from the Hebrew Scriptures; see Eusebius, *Preparation for the Gospel,* trans. Edwin Hamilton Gifford, 2 vols. (Oxford: Clarendon Press, 1903), books XI–XIII, passim.

21.   Aristotle, *De Anima,* trans. J. A. Smith, in *The Basic Works of Aristotle,* ed. Richard McKeon (New York: Random House, 1941); the Greek is quoted from Aristotle, *De Anima,* trans. R. D. Hicks (Amsterdam: Adolf M. Hakkert, 1965).

22.   Lodowick Bryskett, *A Discourse of Ciuill Life* (1606); facsimile reprint in *Literary Works,* ed. J. H. P. Pafford (London: Gregg International Publishers, 1972); henceforth cited in the text as *Discourse.* See also chapter 4, below.

23.   The last phrase quoted is not from the 1555 *Loci,* but from the 1543 version as quoted in Hans Engelland's Introduction.

24.   For a different view, see Kaske, pp. 131–32.

25.   I take it that "the straight way" here means "*by* the straight way," as at 1 Sam. 6:12; cf. the Douay version. Whether Arthur and Gloriana would have been similarly reunited if the poem had been completed is something the Wisdom analogues do not enable us to decide, since many of them leave the love-quest still in progress. My own inclination is to agree with Rathborne (p. 233) that Arthur and Gloriana, like Redcrosse and Una, would have been allowed a brief time together before Arthur was summoned to manage the cares of his own kingdom; but it is certainly possible that our expectation of finally encountering the faery queen in Book XII was to be rewarded only with the recounted memory of her feast, which is all that the "Letter to Raleigh" promises.

26.   Hence the thematic fitness of Arthur's tirade against Night at III.iv.55–60; stanza 58 is based in part on Job 24:13–17, where what the "*rebelles Lumini*" resist, according to Spenser's old schoolfellow Lancelot Andrewes, is the light of nature: see *A Preparation to Prayer* (1611), Sermon 2, p. 15; reprint appended to *The Morall Law Expounded* (London: Sparke, Milbourne, Cotes, and Crooke, 1642). Arthur himself is clearly subject here to the "vnreasonable affections" that "darken the light of reason" (Bryskett,

Discourse, 190), though less so than some critics would have us believe: in an outlaw-infested wilderness where no unarmed person is safe without an armed escort, he is more than justified in trying to catch up to Florimell to offer his protection, as her own servant gratefully attests (v.10–11).

27.   *The Holy Scriptures,* trans. Myles Coverdale (1535; rpt. London: Samuel Bagster, 1838). I have not been able to check the readings of the Great or Bishops versions.

28.   On this "bountie" and "imperiall powre" as a political prerogative of Elizabeth, see David Lee Miller, *The Poem's Two Bodies: The Poetics of the 1590 "Faerie Queene"* (Princeton: Princeton University Press, 1988), pp. 155–57. A fully-rounded critique of Gloriana would of course show how the poet accommodates his overriding "generall intention" in the faery queen to his "particular" intention to "shadow" Elizabeth ("Letter to Raleigh"), and vice versa; but this "generall intention" has been so generally neglected that for the moment it requires our full attention. We might also remember that even those aspects of Gloriana that seem to point directly to Elizabeth ultimately have a different origin:

> [O]n those islands which I have called Fortunate there was a queen of surpassing beauty, adorned with costly garments and ever young, who still remained a virgin, not wishing for a husband, but well contented to be loved and sought. And to those who loved her more she gave a greater reward. . . .

This is not Spenser or Sidney or Lyly currying favor with Elizabeth, but Cardinal Bembo allegorizing the beauty of God. See Pietro Bembo, *Gli Asolani* (1505), trans. Rudolf B. Gottfried (Bloomington: Indiana University Press, 1954), 184–85; the passage is cited in connection with Gloriana by Merritt Y. Hughes, "The Arthurs of *The Faerie Queene,*" *EA,* 6 (1953): 195. Abetted by Leone Ebreo's identification of the divine beauty with Wisdom and the Logos (see Ellrodt, 183–93), Bembo's queen "adorned with costly garments" becomes Spenser's Sapience "Clad like a Queene in royall robes" (*HHB* 185); and since even Scripture is wont "in one text to speak of the Wisdom begotten and wisdom created" (*ST* I.41.3), the same imagery of a "virgin Queene" enthroned "in widest Ocean" (*FQ* II.ii.40) can be applied with equal fitness to the light of nature.

29.   That faery land is "enlumine[d]" (II.ix.4) by the faery queen may therefore suggest a putative etymology of *faery* from Gk. *phaeos* "light" and Fr. *faire* "to make." That Gloriana images a supercelestial Neoplatonic sun of intelligibility is more or less clearly suggested by both Spens, p. 112, and Brooks-Davies, *Spenser's "Faerie Queene": A Critical Commentary on Books I and II* (Totowa, N.J.: Rowman and Littlefield, 1977), 3, 127.

30.   See Roche, pp. 39–43.

31.   In *A Translation of the Latin Works of Dante Alighieri,* trans. A. G. Ferrers Howell and Philip H. Wicksteed (London: Dent, Temple Classics, 1904), 277–78.

32.   See Frances Yates, *Astraea: The Imperial Theme in the Sixteenth Century* (London and Boston: Routledge and Kegan Paul, 1975), pp. 41, 45–47.

33.   Pierre Charron, *De la Sagesse* (1601, 1604); quoted from *Of Wisdome,* trans. Samson Lennard (before 1612); facsimile reprint (Amsterdam and New York: Da Capo Press, 1971).

34.   The faery land Gloriana illumines is thus what Coleridge calls "mental space" only in that it represents the external world as experienced and dealt with by us internally as moral agents; I am not claiming that events in *The Faerie Queene* take place as psychomachia within an individual or typical personality.

35.   Up to but not including the citation from Aquinas, this paragraph is based on A. J. Vermeulen, *The Semantic Development of Gloria in early-Christian Latin* (Nijmegen, Netherlands: Dekker and van de Vegt, 1956), pp. 5, 6, 9, 12–16, 18, 22–23, 26–27.

36.   Quoted from *Summa Theologiae: Latin Text and English Translation,* vol. 41, trans. T. C. O'Brien (New York: Blackfriars with McGraw Hill, 1972).

37.   Charles Grosvenor Osgood, ed., *A Concordance to the Poems of Edmund Spenser* (Washington: Carnegie Institute, 1915). The *OED* and the concordances to other Elizabethan authors tell a similar tale.

38.   From the 1535 *Loci,* in *Corpus Reformatorum* 21:369; I follow the translation and paraphrase in Carl E. Maxcey, *Bona Opera: A Study in the Development of Philip Melanchthon* (Nieuwkoop: B. de Graaf, 1980), 137.

39.   That Spenser knew this chapter and was influenced by it in *An Hymne of Heauenly Beautie* has been recognized since 1914, when it was pointed out by F. M. Padelford; see *Variorum* VII, 555. I have changed the square brackets used by Calvin's editor or translator to pointed brackets in order to distinguish his inserted scriptural references from my own references, additions, and alterations.

40.   In view of the attributes listed, Battle's translation of *"virtutes"* as "powers" seems rather beside the point. For the Latin and French I cite Iannis Calvini, *Institutio Christianae Religionis* (Berolini: Gustaum Eichler, 1834); and Jean Calvin, *Institution de la Religion Chrestienne* (Paris: Librairie Philosophique J. Vrin, 1957), respectively.

41.   John Calvin, *Commentary on the Book of Psalms,* trans. the Rev. James Anderson, 5 vols. (Edinburgh: Calvin Translation Society, 1845–1849). Here "the principle of religion" refers of course to natural religion, not the true "mysteries of the Heavenly Kingdom" (*Inst.* II.ii.13).

42.   The qualification "God-created" is essential, for one of Spenser's recurring themes is the danger presented by fraudulent or disproportionate glories, seen with particular clarity in his accounts of Lucifera (I.iv.8–9) and Philotime (II.vii.44–46). On the other hand, the more vivid among God-created glories can justly be used to figure forth such purely intelligible splendors as might otherwise remain obscure, and the attempt to do so is a hallmark of Spenser's poetic practice. Compare Sidney's agenda for the poet in the *Apologie,* in Smith, I, 165, 179.

43.   Similar language — along with "magnificence" — appears in Calvin's preface to the New Testament, in *Commentaries,* trans. Joseph Haroutunian with Louise Pettibone Smith, Library of Christian Classics, vol. 23 (London: SCM Press, 1958), 58–60. Jan Karel Kouwenhoven, *Apparent Narrative as Thematic Metaphor: The Organization of "The Faerie Queene"* (Oxford: Clarendon Press, 1983), offers a very different interpretation of Spenser's stanza (pp. 22–23) and of his notion of glory (passim), one avowedly Calvinist (p. 27) and yet not remarking any verbal parallels.

44.   Peter Muffet, *A Commentary on the Whole Book of Proverbs* (Edinburgh: James Nichol, 1868), 19, 24. I rely on the *New Cambridge Bibliography of English Literature* for the date of 1596; this reprint purports to be from a second edition of 1594. For Muffet, personified Wisdom includes any of "the means and instruments which th[e] eternal Wisdom useth to lighten men by" (p. 8).

45.   On the other hand, Petrarch's personified Glory in *Rime Sparse* 119 (Canzone 12 *in vita*) is clearly modeled on biblical Wisdom (cf. lines 1–21, 26–28 of the canzone with Wis. 7:29, 8:2, 6:16–17, 8:13, Ecclus. 4:11, 17–18). This Glory (= Fame) makes vivid the nature of her invisible twin sister, Virtue — whom Cicero, as we saw, identifies with Wisdom. And Raleigh, at least, does take pains to evoke the *Rime Sparse* in connection with Gloriana, his commendatory sonnet (Spenser's *Poetical Works,* p. 409) harking back to *RS* 186–87 (Sonnets 153–154 *in vita*).

46.   That "Spenser emerges as the religious fellow of Hooker" is Whitaker's conclusion (p. 69), though it may be noted that to agree with Calvin against Hooker is not *necessarily* to swerve from a basically Thomistic viewpoint. For example, the distinction between natural and supernatural values seen in the contrast between Cleopolis and the New Jerusalem is less close to Hooker's version of that distinction than to that of either Calvin or Aquinas, both of whom explicitly distinguish natural values as those pertaining solely to human society on earth from supernatural as those proportioned to divine society in heaven (see chapter 2, above, and the citations in n. 14). Yet Spenser's emphasis on the *indispensability* of natural values even for those guided by the values of heaven is much closer to either Aquinas or Hooker than to Calvin.

47.   How much Hebrew Spenser remembered from the Merchant Taylors' School is unclear, but the Geneva Bible's "Brief Table of the Interpretation of the Propre Names . . . in the Olde Testament" makes plain that "Hanna" (listed *s.v.* "Anah") means "gratious or mercifull." Since "Tannakin" was a nickname for "Ann" (see the *OED*), Gloriana's other name of Tanaquill may also suggest this secular grace; or *tana-* might be associated with Titan as a name for the sun (see C. Bowie Millican, "Spenser's and Drant's Poetic Names for Elizabeth: Tanaquil, Gloria, and Una," *HLQ,* 2 [1939]: 255), or with Hebrew *tanna* "teaching." Since the meaning of English *quill* "feather" was regularly extended to "wing" in one direction and "pen" in the other, the possible significances for *Tanaquill* become numerous: to name only two, it may point to the natural light as a gracious *sun* with *wings* (mirroring the divine sun of Mal. 4:2), or as the *pen* that inscribes the *teaching* of the law on our hearts (Rom. 2:15).

48.   Harvey, despite initial misgivings, certainly seems to have come around to this view. The Commendatory Verses by H. B. (Spenser's *Poetical Works,* p. 409) show that their author had at least an inkling of Gloriana's sapiential significance, since the reference to "that most princely doome, / In whose sweete brest are all the Muses bredde," recalls *The Teares of the Muses,* where those goddesses "in the bosome of all blis did sit" (308) as "the brood of blessed Sapience" (72), the latter phrase apparently being equivalent to "The golden brood of great *Apolloes* wit" (2). The link between this "Sapience" and Apollo is noteworthy in view of Harvey's complaint in 1579 that *The Faerie Queene* as it existed then was "*Hobgoblin* runne away with the Garland from *Apollo*" (Spenser's *Poetical Works,* p. 628). In his 1590 Commendatory Verses to the poem (p. 409), however, he not only picks up on the relation between Gloriana/"Sapience" and the Muses, but shows himself both knowledgeable and enthusiastic about the significance of her world-illumining "imperiall powre" as we have explored it in chapter 4:

And fare befall that *Faerie Queene* of thine[:]

* * *

Subiect thy dome to her Empyring spright,
From whence thy Muse, and all the world takes light.

Since all identifications of the seemingly well-informed H. B. remain conjec-
tural, a further conjecture may as well be added: that H. B. is either simply a misprint
or a compositor's misreading of L. B., Lodowick Bryskett, *H* and *L* being quite
similar in the secretary hand.

NOTE: Despite the coincidence of our titles, Francesco Perez's *La Beatrice Svelata*
(Palermo, 1865) came to my attention too late to affect this essay. For him, it is
Dante's heroine who recalls, partly by way of apocryphal Wisdom, that "eternal em-
press" the agent intellect; but he means the external, unitary agent intellect of the
Arab Aristotelians.

GREGORY WILKIN

Spenser's Rehabilitation of the Templars

*F*OUR OF *The Faerie Queene*'s dedicatory sonnets are addressed to
Elizabethan Templars: Christopher Hatton, Henry Percy, Walter Raleigh, and Thomas Sackville.[1] Thomas Howard, a Middle
Templar, was the father of Lady Douglas, who inspired the elegy
Daphnaida. Edward Somerset, father of the young women celebrated in the *Prothalamion,* was a Middle Templar.[2] To all of
these, the first glimpse of the title heading for Book One, identifying it as the "Legende of the Knight of the Red Crosse,"
would have suggested the actual knights of the red cross, their
Templar forbears, the Order of the Poor Knights of Christ and
the Temple of Solomon, the largest crusading order, founded in
1128 and abolished in 1328 by the Council of Vienne.[3] The
Templar red cross was distinctive by design; Eugenius' wording
is *ut inter ceteros essent notabiliores* [so that they might be more distinct from the others].[4] That they were the "red cross knights"
was, for at least two centuries, common knowledge. To take
just one example, Nigel de Longchamps has his Burnellus turn
to the Templars right away when he sets about choosing an
order, and it is their red cross that he notes.

> Quia diversas species sunt religionis
>   Nescio praecipue quae sit habenda mihi

89

Si cruce signatus rubeo me confero templo
Trans mare me mittent solvere vota Deo.

[Since there are many kinds of orders, I know
not which I should join: if I sign on with the
Temple, signed with the red cross, they will
send me overseas to fulfill my vow to God.]

We know that Spenser had ready access to chronicles that contain accounts of the Templars;[6] at least one of them has a full account of how the Templars were given the red cross.

> About this time [1118] certain Noble men of the Horsemen being religiously bent, bound themselves in the hands of the Patriarck of Hierusalem, to serve Christ after the manner of the regular Chanons, in chastitie, and obedience, and to renounce their own proper wil for euer. Of which order, the first was the honourable man Hugh Paganus and Gawfride de Saint Andemare; whereat the first, they had no certaine habitation, Baldwine king of Hierusalem graunted them a dwelling place in his pallace by the temple; and the Chanons of the same Temple gaue them the streete thereby to build their house of office in, and the Patriarck, the king, the nobles and Prelates gaue them certain revenues out of their Lordships. Their first profession was for safegarde of the pilgrimes, to keep the waies, against the lying in waite of theeues. About 10 yeeres after, they had a rule appoynted them, and a white habite by Pope Honorius at that time, where they hadde beene nine in number, they beganne to increase into great numbers.

> Afterward in the time of Pope Eugenius, they had crosses of red cloth sowed on their uppermost garments to be knowne from others thereby.[7]

An impressive treasury had been amassed at the Temple in London, partly augmented by their custody of some royal coffers, and as the Templars became arbiters of monetary disputes there began a tradition that would survive in the lawyers' guilds or societies to which Spenser's patrons belonged.[8]

Spenser knew the Temple grounds in London very well. He was often at the home of Essex next door, "where oft," he says, he "gayned giftes and goodly grace," and the nearby Temple buildings inspired a remarkable digression in the *Prothalamion*, in which he shows his familiarity with a truism of Templar history, that their fall was caused by excessive pride.[9]

> those bricky towres
> Which on Themmes brode aged back doe ryde,
> Where now the studious Lawyers have their bowers,
> There whylome wont the Templer knyghts to byde,
> Til they decayed through pride.
>
> (132–36)

Orgoglio, the giant of Pride in Book One, has been seen to be many things. For Mark Rose, the giant's proud, swollen flesh makes him an "ambulatory male member."[10] For Émile Legouis, Orgoglio is Phillip II.[11] For Frank Kermode, "the subjection of Red Cross to Orgoglio is the popish captivity of England from Gregory VII to Wyclif (about 300 years, the three months of viii, 38)".[12] All of this well may be, but when we take Spenser's simplest interpretive invitation, that is, to take the Red Cross Knight as the red-cross knights, the giant of Pride is, quite simply, their gigantic pride, the trait legendarily linked to their undoing.

The story of how they did and how they were undone fits very well into the view of history that Spenser and other Elizabethan anti-Catholics were developing. From their founding in 1118, through a period of early military successes, all the way to the time of their betrayal by the Papacy in 1307, the Templars were the beneficiaries, or, for Spenser, victims of a whole series of papal dispensations and exemptions from local tithes and responsibilities, privileges that reinforced the widespread imputation of pride.

Spenser's Redcross begins his career with the successful disposal of the monster Errour, and, although separated from Una, he enjoys against Sansfoy one of the most clear-cut victories of the entire poem:

> Curses on the Crosse (quoth the Sarazin). . . .
>
> Who thereat wondrous wroth, the sleeping spark
> Of nature gan eftsoones revive,
> And at hishaughtie helmet making mark,
> So hugely stroke that it the steele did rive,
> And cleft his head.
>
> (I, ii, 18–19)

Redcross accompanies Duessa to the House of Pride, where he cannot and does not achieve a clear-cut victory as he did before. Attempting to win a pagan shield, for a lady who does not love him, he undertakes a "doubtfull battle" against Sansjoy, who "no where doth appear, / But vanisht is" (I, v, 13). A dalliance ensues with Duessa (I, vii, 5–7), and then the defeat at the hands of Orgoglio, who then "in a Dongeon deepe him [throws] without remorse" (I, vii, 15). We are witnessing here, among other things, the seduction and betrayal of the Templars by the Roman church.[13]

Historically, Duessa did not love Redcross, or at least not faithfully: Pope Clement V initiated the inquisitions against the Templars in 1307, contriving with Phillip the Fair a systematic harrassment and, finally, dissolution of the order. In France the process was ghastly and traumatic; tortures and executions culminated in the famous martyrdom of the Grand Master, Jacques de Molay. In England the redcross knights were simply imprisoned for a time in "provincial dungeons."[14]

One can see here, and it will be much clearer later in Book One, that Spenser is concentrating on the history of the English branch of the order in his poem. The redemption of Redcross by Arthur is perfectly consonant with the fortunes of the English Templars. Unlike the French king, Edward II came to the defense of the order; when Phillip sent a demand to the English court for stern measures against them, a great council was called at Westminister during which Edward and his peers expressed their disbelief and protest.[15] The English population itself is reported to have responded in a similar way:

> Eighteen months passed before any serious investigations were begun, by which time many prisoners had regained their freedom. Hardly any were recaptured, in spite of the threat of excommunication for giving aid to fugitive Templars.[16]

This is the same kind of magnaminity that Arthur shows in his rescue of Redcross and will exhibit, supposedly, all through the poem. He has, in effect, delivered Redcross from a Catholic torture and execution chamber:

> And there beside of marbel stone was built
> An altare, carv'd with cunning imagery
> On which true Christians blood was often spilt,
> And holy Martyrs often doen to dye,
> With cruell malice and strong tyranny.
>
> (I,viii,36)

Fugitive English Templars were given succour in a number of places; the Order of the Hospital of St. John took many.[17] Accordingly, after Redcross repents his dalliance under the supervision of Penance, it is Mercy that brings him to an installation of charitable men ("seven beadmen" under vows, members of an "order" of which she is a patroness and Charissa is "chiefest founderess" — I, x, 44) who discharge duties to weary travellers in the manner of the Hospitallers.

> Eftsoones unto an holy Hospitall,
> That was fore by the way, she did him bring.[18]
>
> (I, x, 36)

Templars also sought refuge in monasteries,[19] a fact that Spenser may represent in the visit Redcross then makes to the house of Contemplation (I, x, 46).

Spenser's Templar patrons might, at this point in the narrative, have expected the story of Redcross to be done; we have reached the point when the original order of the red cross has been dismantled. But it might have occurred to them, as well, that the red cross lived on: another order was created some thirty years later, that is to say, on St. George's Day, 1344, and its heraldic blazon used the Templar cross, red on a field *argent,* as its base, its background.[20] Half of the men to whom dedicatory sonnets were written were Knights of the Garter: Hatton, Sackville, Cumberland, Essex, Howard, Hunsden, and Grey.

For these, especially for Hatton and Sackville, the combination of the story of the Redcross knight with the legend of St. George connected the Order of the Temple and the Order of the Garter, and thereby maintained, or constructed, a heroic coherence for the history of organized knighthood in England.

There are two things I think we should keep in mind after and about Book One. First, Spenser is reminding us to countenance, indeed to privilege, an historical interpretation. In the fourth stanza of Book Two he calls his poem a "faire mirrhour," and if it is a *mirrour* like the one to which Sackville wrote his *Induction,* it gives us both the lesson of history and a history lesson.[21] Second, he is aware of its flaws as such, at least in conventional terms: he apologizes in the very first five lines of Book Two, for innovating as much as he has; and in this apology he defends himself against those who prefer "just memory." Consider the productive ambiguity of the phrase.

Right well I wote, most mighty Soveraine
That all this famous antique history,
Of some th'abundance of an idle braine
Will judged be, and painted forgery
Rather than matter of just memory.

(II, i, 1–5)

Strictly fair memory would be mere memory. I suggest that, like Milton after him, Spenser wants us to go beyond mere memory. In the story of Redcross he has achieved, among other things, a flattering mythopoeia for his friends, or future friends, the Elizabethan Templars.

This process does not end, necessarily, with Book One. If we consider the poem as a *mirrour* of knighthood, there may be an implicit time-line stretching between Books One and Six. The action of Books One and Two, at least, is in sequence. Guyon, meeting Redcross in Canto One, says: "wretched we, where ye have left your marke, / Must now anew begin, like race to run." (II, i, 32) If the sequence continues, consider this: there may well be a fugitive Templar in Book Two.

Mammon, like Redcross, is a victim of pride (II, vii, 16, 17, 44). He also looks like a Templar, although he does not wear the emblem (understandably, if he is a renegade). The most famous description of the Templars was in St. Bernard's second chapter of *De laude novae militiae:*

They are never combed, seldom washed, but appear rather
with rough neglected hair, begrimed with dust, and with skins
browned by the sun and their coats of mail.[22]

Other Templar trademarks were the untrimmed beard,[23] and tarnished gold armor.[24] Mammon's appearance:

An uncouth, salvage, and uncivile wight,
of griesly hew, and fowle ill favor'd sight;
His face with smoke was tand, and eyes were bleard,
His head and beard with sout were ill bedight,
His cole-blacke hands did seem to have been seard
In smithes fire-splitting forge, and nayles like
claws appeard.

His yron coate all overgrown with rust,
Was underneath enveloped with gold,

> Whose glistering glosse darkned with filthy dust,
> Well yet appeared, to have beene of old
> A worke of rich entayle. . . . (II, vii, 3, 4)

Mammon gives Guyon a tour of a landscape that closely corresponds with that of the Temple of London in Spenser's time. In fact, as Mammon and Guyon make their way down to the riverbank of stanza 56, the landmarks occur in the precise order that they would in a walk from the Round Temple Church through Inner Temple Hall, the grove, and the garden, to the Thames (a popular route that mirrors the walk taken by the wedding procession in the *Prothalamion*). Spenser describes the counterpart to the Inner Temple Hall as "large and wide / As it some Gyeld or solemne Temple weare" (II, vii, 43).

The appearance of a renegade Templar guarding the London Temple and its riches at this point in the poem would make some degree of sense: the order may have been abolished in 1328 but Templar personnel remained at the London Temple for a number of years and it was not until 1337 that the Temple properties devolved to the Hospitallers and the movables to the crown.[25]

If we are meant to make this identification, what of the apparently unflattering association of the Templars with Mammon, the god of money? Sackville, Somerset and the rest would not, I think, have taken it badly: the banking activity carried on in the Temple, corrupt or otherwise, was a particularly incontrovertible fact. Besides, anything negative that he is bringing up in Book Two will be more than counterbalanced by the conspicuously contemporary, that is to say, Elizabethan, style of heroism in Books Five and Six, which present a judicial and commercial ethos for an updated kind of knighthood.[26]

A "mirrour" offers precedents against which to examine present action, and Spenser's may be offering the evolution of the institution of knighthood, an evolution discernible in the successive expectations characters place on knights, building up a cumulative ideal as knightly exemplars take steps toward a fuller integration of virtues. Medina, for example, shows that she simply expects something more than unreflecting brute force, consideration of basic rights:

> Is this the joy or armes? be these the parts
> Of glorious knighthood? after blood to thrust
> And not regard dew right or just desarts?
> (II, ii, 29)

Six cantos later the focus of obligation is just slightly clearer for
Guyon's palmer: "First praise of knighthood is foule outrage to deface"
(II, viii, 25). Glauce's contribution is that love is "the crowne of
knighthood" (IV, vi, 31). This is a large step, and it occurs in the pivotal middle section, Books Three and Four, which in terms of knightly
history can be seen as the courtly love interlude between the crusading
ethos of Books One and Two and the judicial, commercial ethos of the
knighthood of Spenser's time, Books Five and Six. This section, is, of
course, the heart of the poem, where Guyon's destruction of the Bowre
of Blis is answered by the regenerative power of love in the Garden of
Adonis and the Temple of Venus.[27] But in the history of knighthood it
matches a time of seeming misdirection, a time when the growing corpus of chivalric romance, with its increasingly elaborate conventions of
love-service and artifice, changed the perception (at least in that readership) of knightly duty. Accordingly, the knights at Satyrane's tourna-
ment begin to lose their reputation for prowess when Britomart unseats
them all (IV, iv, 44–48). Artegall is found "in womans weedes, that is
to manhood shame, / . . . in stead of Curiets and bases fit for fight" (V,
v, 20). He finds his fellow knights "spinning and carding all in comely
rew" (V, v, 22), but Britomart will finally rescue him and "the liberty
of women . . . repeale" (V, vii, 42). These are simply the temporary in-
equities of the stylized servitude of courtly love. Britomart's contribution of justice and mercy as knightly qualities is the first amendment of
Glauce's statement that love is the crown of the chivalric ideal. Knighthood is continuing to perfect itself.

  The knightly adventures of Book Five are mostly legal cases: a knightly
offense is a "tort" and offenders are "tortious" (v, viii, 30; viii, 51; ix,
12; x, 8). Far from fighting Saracens, Calidore and Calepine oppose the
breakers of the laws of commerce. The cannibals who threaten Serena

>   . . . live
> Of Stealth and spoile, and making nightly rode
> Into their neighbors borders; ne did give
> Them selves to any trade, as for to drive
> The painfull plough, or cattell for to breed
> Or by adventurous marchandize to thrive.
>   (VI, viii, 35)

The Brigants who kill Meliboeus and his wife are "a lawlesse people"
(VI, x, 39). "Rudeness" is also defined as "not yeelding what they

owe" (VI, ii, 1). In terms of the history of knighthood, Books Five and Six show the Elizabethan and Jacobean version, wherein a knight's chief duty is the protection of property rights and the avoidance of scandal, the defense of themselves and others from libel; as Patrick Spurgeon has said. "Leicester, Grey, Raleigh, Essex, and Sidney: all were in disgrace from time to time and most of them died in the rumor-venomed clutches of the Blatant Beast."[28]

His bringing of knighthood up to date in Book Six may give us one more reason to understand why Spenser might have considered the poem done. When we look at the poem, as it stands, as a mirror of knighthood, by the end of Book Six it has done one thing especially well: it has shown us that, like all else in Nature, those famous Templars and knights of the Garter, by "turning to themselves at length again," that is, by paying attention to what they were, "doe worke their own perfection so by fate" (VII, vii, 58).

NOTES

1. See Carol A. Stillman, "Politics, Precedence and the Order of the Dedicatory Sonnets in *The Faerie Queene*," in *Spenser Studies* V, 143–48. H. A. C. Sturgess, *Register of Admission to the Honourable Society of the Middle Temple — From the Fifteenth Century to the Year 1944* (London: 1949), 65 ff.

2. Stillman, *loc. cit.*

3. See Jean Leclercq, "*Un document sur les débuts des Templiers*," in *Recueil d'Études sur S. Bernard et ses Écrits* (Rome: 1960), II, 91 ff; Suzanne-Édith Peuméry, "*La Règle*," in *Historia Spécial*, No. 385 bis (Paris: Jules Tallandier, 1978), p. 19, places the disputed date of the granting of the red cross on April 27, 1147. See, too, Marion Mellville, *Le vie des Templiers* (Paris: Gallimard, 1951), p. 42. The Variorum edition notes that English soldiers in Ireland wore "a cross of St. George;" see *The Works of Edmund Spenser: A Variorum Edition*, ed. Edwin Greenlaw, Charles Grosvenor Osgood, and Frederick Morgan Padelford, nine volumes (Baltimore: Johns Hopkins University Press, 1932–49) I, 177.

4. Leclercq, *op. cit.*, p. 85.

5. Nigel de Longchamps, *Speculum Stultorum*, ed. J. H. Mozley and R. R. Raymo (Berkeley: University of California Press, 1960), pp. 76–77.

6. C. A. Harper, *The Sources of British Chronicle History in Spenser's Faerie Queene* (Philadelphia: Bryn Mawr College Monographs, 1910), No. 7, 27–29: Stow's *Annales*, Nauclerus; *Chronica*, Higden's *Polychronicon*, and Robert Fabyan's *New Chronicles of England and France* contain accounts of the Templars and "may have been consulted by Spenser." See *D. Iohannis Naucleri Praepositi Tubingen Chronica succinctim compraehendentes res memorabiles seculorum omnium ac gentium ab initio mundi usque ad annum Christi nato MCCCCC* (Cologne: Peter Quentel, 1544), 735.

7. John Stow, *The Annales or Generall Chronicle of England, begun first by maister John Stow and after him continued and augmented with matter foregne and domestique, auncient*

and moderne unto the ende of this present yeere 1614 by Edmond Howes, gentleman (London: Thomas Adams, 1615), 139.

8.   J. B. Williamson, *The History of the Temple, London, From the Institution of the Order of the Knights of the Temple to the Close of the Stuart Period* (London: 1924), 83 ff. Exactly when the apprentices of the law arrived Williamson cannot say.

9.   There is anecdotal evidence of the expression "proud as a Templar" in many forms; see Clarence Perkins, "The Knights Templars in the British Isles," in *English Historical Review* XXV (April, 1910), p. 226.

10.   See the account and use of Rose's ideas in D'Orsay Pearson, "Spenser's Labyrinth — Again," in *Spenser and the Middle Ages: Proceedings from a Special Session at the Eleventh Conference on Medieval Studies* (Kalamazoo: 1976), microfiche, p. 62 ff.

11.   "*Orgoglio n'est pas l'orgueil, mais un orgueilleux, le grand orgueilleux, Phillippe II, qui par son mariage avec Marie Tudor, tient un temps l'Angleterre en son pouvoir. Et les oubliettes de château d'Orgoglio où git le pauvre chevalier sont un évocation des prisons et des tortures de l'Inquisition importées en Angleterre sous Marie la Sanglante.* [Orgoglio is not pride, but a proud one, The Great Proud One, Phillip II, who, in marrying Mary Tudor, had England in his power for a time. The oubliettes in Orgoglio's castle, where the poor knight languishes, are an evocation of the inquisitional prisons and tortures introduced into England by Bloody Mary.] *Works,* I, 440–41.

12.   Frank Kermode, "*The Faerie Queene,* I and V," in *Bulletin of the John Rylands Library* XLVII (1965): 150.

13.   In the temporary replacement of Redcross by the satyrs as champions of truth, we may well have a rendering of the primitivist movements of the Waldensians and Albigensians. See Kermode, loc. cit.

14.   Edith Simon, *The Piebald Standard: A Biography of the Knights Templars* (Boston and Toronto: Little Brown, 1959), p. 290 ff.; Thomas Parker, *The Knights Templars in England* (Tucson: University of Arizona Press, 1963), p. 162 ff.

15.   James A. Froude, *The Spanish Story of the Armada and Other Essays* (New York: Charles Scribner and Sons, 1892), p. 252.

16.   Simon, op. cit., p. 300.

17.   F. C. Woodhouse, *The Military Religious Orders of the Middle Ages* (London: 1879), p. 255; Parker, op. cit., p. 163, n. 2: "[By December, 1319] the Hospitallers had already received many Templars into their order."

18.   This reading can easily co-exist with the perception that, on the level of moral allegory, the beadsmen are the Seven Works of Corporal Mercy.

19.   David Knowles and Richard Neville Hadcock, *Medieval Religious Houses in England and Wales* (Bristol: 1971), p. 296.

20.   By the 1340s the association of the red cross with St. George seems to have been overtaking its association with the Order of the Temple. Of the twenty-seven dateable representations of St. George registered at the Princeton Index of Christian Art, fourteen are dated in the fourteenth century and beyond and thirteen earlier. Of the fourteen post-dissolution representations, seven show St. George with a red cross; of fourteen pre-fourteenth-century representations (including one item not registered at Princeton), only three show St. George with a red cross and for two of these there is some doubt.

An enamelled fourteenth-century reliquary in the Valencia Cathedral shows St. George with a cross on a banner and with the "crusader cross," the cross potent with four minor crosses in each quadrant, around the escutcheon. The St. George in the

Luttrell Psalter (c. 1340), folio 39v, shows him holding a shield with a cross; like the cross in the Bodleian Psalter, Auct. D. 4. 4. from the second half of the fourteenth century, the cross is probably meant to be red. The Christ Church Oxford, MS of Walter de Milemete's *De Nobilitate* (1326–27), fol. 3r, shows Edward III being given a shield probably by St. George, unidentified but in a red-cross tunic and with red-cross pouldrons. In the Archiv. Capitolare S. Pietro MS 129 C, (first half of the fourteenth century) a version of the *Historia Georgii,* two of four representations show a red cross. A Coptic textile from Egypt (12th/13th c.) shows St. George on a white horse (Royal Ontario Museum, 978.76.306). MS Lat 8541 of the Bibliotheca Vaticana (first half of the fourteenth century) fol. 54 shows part of a red cross on a white shield. A late fourteenth-century MS from the Biblioteca Estense in Modena (Lat. 842, fol. 240. r) shows an inscribed cross. The church of S. Georgio in Ruballa has a fourteenth-century gradual with a cross-inscribed shield (fol. 193 v). BL Royal MS 19 B XV, a thirteenth-century apocalypse, shows a Christ leading crusaders with red crosses on shields and pennons; B. N. MS Fr. 2630, *Les Histoires d'Outremer,* f. 22v, shows crusaders bombarding Nicaea with the heads of dead enemies; there is a red cross on their banner.

An enamelled cross in the Vyssibrod Monastery dated between the tenth and twelfth centuries shows St. George with a cross in hand, probably red; a *Vitae Sanctorum* from the Hague, Lib. Konink. Bibl. 76 F 5 from the thirteenth century, shows a St. George, identified, with a red cross on his shield and banner on horseback, with others, chasing Saracens beneath a map of the Temple locale, Golgotha, and the Porta David. A church at Fordington, N.B., shows a knight with a red cross aiding two crusaders on horseback; the identification with St. George is not clear.

D'Arcy Jonathan Dacre Boulton makes the claim that the red cross was associated with St. George in the reign of Edward I: "The appeal of the warrior saint George had already been felt by . . . Edward I, who had begun both the practice of displaying the banner of St. George (a red cross on a white field) with those of the English royal saints, Edmund the Martyr and Edward the Confessor, and the practice of displaying the arms of St. George (derived from the banner) on the surcoats of his soldiers," *The Knights of the Crown: The Monarchical Orders of Knighthood in Later Medieval Europe, 1325*–1520 (Woodbridge, Suffolk: Boydell, 1987), 124. His source is, apparently, F. L. Cross and E. D. Livingston, eds., *The Oxford Dictionary of the Christian Church,* Second Edition (London: 1974), 557.

21. See Thomas P. Roche, Jr., "Spenser's Muse" in *Unfolded Tales: Essays on Renaissance Romance,* ed George M. Logan and Gordon Tesky (Ithaca: Cornell University Press, 1989), 162–88. There are times in *The Faerie Queene,* Roche concludes, when "Spenser wanted to emphasize the factual basis of his fiction" (p. 184).

22. Jean Leclercq and H. M. Rochais, eds., *S. Bernardi Opera*(Rome: Editiones Cistercienses, 1963), II, p. 212 ff.

23. Simon, op. cit., p. 299.

24. *Regula Templariorum,* article xxxvi, in *Patrologia latina* CLXVI, ed. J. P. Migne (Paris: 1864), cols. 855–75; subsequent editions are *La Règle du Temple,* ed. Henri de Curzon (Paris: Librairie Renouard, 1886); *Die Ursprügliche Templerregel: kritisch untersucht und herausgegeben,* ed. Gustav Schürer (Freiburg im Breisgau: Herdersche Verlagshandlung, 1903), Volume Three of *Studien und Darstellungen aus dem Gebiete der Geschichte, im Auftrage der Görres-Gesellschaft und in Verbindung mit der Redaktion des Historischen Jahrbuches; La Régle des Templiers,* ed. Laurent Dailliez (Nice: Alpes Méditerranée Éditions-Impres'Sud, 1978).

25. Williamson, op. cit., 75 ff. The actual treasure the Templars left behind at the London Temple was probably far smaller than had been expected. Parker, op. cit., 101: "Instead of great treasures of gold, silver and jewels at the New Temple, the royal officers found only ecclesiastical movables worth 121 pounds and others worth 68 pounds." At other preceptories and manoral centers the finds were more impressive. Parker gives a number of cases of Templars escaping and sequestering Templar wealth, although he decides finally that "it would be unwarrantable to argue that any appreciable number of English Templars escaped or that much Templar wealth was successfully sequestered." See also Clarence Perkins, "The Wealth of the Templars in England," *American Historical Review* XV, p. 254, n. 11.

26. For an account of the contemporary resonances of Books V and VI, see James P. Bednarz, "Raleigh in Spenser's Historical Allegory," in *Spenser Studies* IV (1984), pp. 49–70.

27. Spenser is especially careful how he uses the word "temple" — he brooks no Templar association for the Temple of Venus, distinguishing it from the Temple of Solomon, from which the original Templars got their name: "Not that same famous Temple. . . . which that wise King of Jurie framed" (IV, x, 30).

28. Patrick Spurgeon, *The Poet Historicall: Edmund Spenser, A Study of Renaissance Method and Uses of History* (Dissertation, University of Tennessee, 1963), p. 70.

LAWRENCE F. RHU

Romancing the Word:
Pre-Texts and Contexts
for the Errour Episode

*T*HE INITIAL EPISODE of *The Faerie Queene* culminates in a nightmarish image symptomatic of the Reformation in one of its traditionally definitive features. When Errour vomits a gush of texts,
she seems a grisly revelation of the darkest "consequences of [one
of those] inventions" singled out by Francis Bacon as "[having]
changed the state and appearance of the whole world."[1] Errour, in
her death throes, discloses an unsettling affinity with one of the
enabling technologies of the new epoch, the printing press. Edward Halle's oft-cited account of the bishop of London's futile efforts to contain the circulation of Tyndale's New Testament
details a previous failure in a mission ironically akin to that of the
Redcrosse knight in his first encounter. Cuthbert Tonstall's buy-
ing of books for the purpose of burning them merely provided
Tyndale with revenue for subsequent editions of the offending
volume. In the eyes of this ecclesiastical opponent of innovation a
new monster indeed was at large in the land.[2]

Calling Errour's textual vomit a "nightmare" bespeaks the
realm of dreams when the imagination at rest can fall prey to its
most intimate demons, not the "slomber of delight" induced by
"that sweet verse, with *Nectar* sprinkeled, / In which a gracious
servant pictured / His *Cynthia,* his heavens fairest light."[3] In other

101

words this episode allows a haunting presence to emerge even in the
process of recounting its demise, and shades of this monster return in
various forms hereafter. The threat of demonic recidivism remains in
some minds even beyond the apocalyptic finale of Book I. Among "the
raskall many . . . / Heaped together in rude rablement" who gawk at
the triumphant champion,

> One that would wiser seeme, then all the rest,
> Warnd him not touch, for yet perhaps remayned
> Some lingering life within his hollow brest,
> Or in his wombe might lurk some hidden nest
> Of many dragonets, his fruitfull seed.
>
>   (I.xii. 9–10)

Likewise, Spenser employs an Ovidian simile of spontaneous solar generation in the mudflats along the banks of the Nile to depict the writh-
ing contents of Errour's foul regurgitation (I. i. 21); and then he
returns to exactly this figure in a strikingly different context (III. vi. 8.
7–9), the birth of Belphoebe and prelude to his description of "[s]o faire
a place, as Nature can devize:" the Garden of Adonis.

The dreamlike infusion that we call a "nightmare" is not the divine
afflatus bestowed upon the vatic poet at the behest of a heavenly muse;
rather, it lurks in the margins of consciousness to ambush the unsus-
pecting, who can be misled by (among other things) zeal and overcon-
fidence. While the apocalyptic resonance of Redcrosse's initial encounter only becomes fully audible during his climactic duel in Edenland,
tokens of such significance appear in the opening episode. For example,
Errour's "filthy parbrake" recalls "the three uncleane spirits like frogs"
witnessed by John of Patmos in his vision as they "come out of the
mouth of that dragon, and out of the mouth of that beast, and out of
the mouth of that false prohpet"; and early Protestant expositors of this
passage seem secure in the knowledge of its import. In the Geneva Bible
of 1560, Revelation 16. 13 carries this marginal gloss: "That is a strong
number of this great devil the Popes ambassadours which are ever crying and crocking like frogs and come out of the Antichrists mouth,
because they should speake nothing but lies and use all manere of craftie
deceit to maintaine their rich Euphrates against the true Christians."[4]

Such confident apprehension of the enemy by no means obtained
throughout the nation whose queen Spenser celebrated in his "poem historicall." The sort of frustration experienced by the bishop of London in

his attempts to stem the flow into England of Tyndale's New Testament takes on different forms once that book circulates legally and reaches readers previously more inclined to leave its interpretation to others. For example, in a sermon delivered at Paul's Cross in 1589, Richard Bancroft complains of text-torturing Protestant expositors. Although he clearly opposes what a later age would come to call the magisterium of the Catholic Church (that is, its teaching function, especially in regard to biblical interpretation), Bancroft is also alarmed by unqualified readers of Holy Writ who put strains upon passages from that sacred text and wrest meanings from them that lead to heresy and schism. Thus, Bancroft cites Augustine to the effect that "faithful ignorance is better than rash knowledge" and goes on to invoke Gregory of Nazianzus's assertion, "It falleth not within the compas of everie mans understanding to determine and judge in matters of religion: *Sed exercitatorum:* but of those that are well experienced and exercised in them."[5]

Bancroft's distress at the liberties taken by inexperienced readers participates in the mounting anxiety over Protestant tendencies that seem to be spinning out of control in the Elizabethan '90s. In "Satire III" Donne addresses a command to his readers that sounds exactly like the quest that Redcrosse has undertaken. Donne enjoins them to "seek true religion"; but immediately a question follows: "O where?" Then the poet proceeds to catalogue the throng of rival claims that vie for priority and threaten to distract believers from the unique goal worthy of their sustained efforts. Thomas Nashe's version of the Munster Rebellion in *The Unfortunate Traveler* specificallly relates this problem of theological error to freedom of scriptural interpretation.

> In the days of Nero there was an odd fellow that had found out an exquisite way to make glass as hamerproof as gold. Shall I say that the like experiment he made upon glass, we have practised upon the Gospel? Ay, confidently will I. We have found out a sleight to hammer it to any heresy whatsoever. But those furnaces of falsehood and hammerheads of heresy must be dissolved and broken as his was, or else I fear me the glittering glass of innovation will be better esteemed than the ancient gold of the Gospel.[6]

Given his career as a picaresque trickster, Jack Wilton, the titular hero of Nashe's perversely polymorphous creation, seems an odd sort to decry revolutionary religion in the guise of a defender of the faith. His credibility here ranks with that of Falstaff when he denounces Prince Hal's "damnable iteration" of a passage from Proverbs.[7] If we recall Nashe's conservative participation in the Marprelate controversy, this righteous voice of angry reaction can be traced to a likelier source. But even Jack betrays a sense of the personal incongruity of such pietistic ranting when he describes himself as "duncified betwixt divinity and poetry" (286) in the process of making the transition from this episode to the next in his story.

This feeling of generic indecorum points to a formal issue with thematic consequences that is very much alive in the opening of *The Faerie Queene,* for Spenser's preoccupation with theological error corresponds to the structural feature of romance that particularly concerned Torquato Tasso, the contemporary Italian poet most important to the aspiring Elizabethan laureate. The dizzying proliferation of plot lines in *Orlando furioso* first moved Tasso to enlist the authority of Aristotle to condemn his precursor's seemingly random habits of narration. Subsequently, Tasso employed allegory to thematize, prominently, this potential for chaos in the genre that he sought to incorporate and transcend in his epic. Spenser was certainly acquainted with this symbolic transformation in Tasso's prefatory "Allegoria del poema," where the haunted wood outside Jerusalem becomes a Platonic figure for the "errors of opinion." Cutting down this forest enables the epic action to proceed to its conclusion in a manner far more decisive than any closure that Ariosto brings to bear upon his rambling tale. Just as Redcrosse slays Errour while in the service of Una, Rinaldo's triumph over the enchantments of the forest saves Tasso's poem from the errors of romance and thereby guarantees its unity of plot, a structural accomplishment in terms of neo-Aristotelian poetics which acquires explicit allegorical significance in the preface to the *Liberata.*

A wood of this sort appears at the outset in *The Faerie Queene,* where Spenser represents it via an epic catalogue and thus effects a generic merger of notable originality in what could seem simply a conspicuous reprise of Chaucer. Similar signals of genre and mode abound in this passage, and their shrewd deployment displays a subtlety of poetic craft that was more fully theorized by Spenser's Italian coevals than his Tudor compatriots; for Spenser's inheritance of both his classical and modern precursors sometimes seems retarded by the belated emergence of humanism and literary theory in northern Europe, and the old joke about England's being the place to be when the world ends because everything there happens at least fifty years late seems a fit comment at numerous junctures in *The Faerie Queene*. However, familiar assertions of Spenser's lack of historical discernment, like those made by Thomas Greene and Frank Kermode,[8] warrant interrogation and skepticism when we review the opening of his poem.

For example, much has lately been made of Spenser's fashioning for himself a literary career in the image of Virgil, as the beginning of the proem to Book I clearly illustrates.[9] However, historical philology had not yet decisively demonstrated the spurious (that is, un-Virgilian) origins of the *Aeneid*'s traditional incipit when Spenser rendered those very lines into English at the outset of *The Faerie Queene*. From this perspective, he got off to a pretty bad start for someone who wanted to sound like the Augustan laureate! But he ends up making the very gesture such philologists deem to be their own insight, for he begins Book I proper with his own *arma virumque*: "A Gentle Knight was pricking on the plaine, / Y cladd in mightie armes and silver shielde." Thereby, he laid claim to what a subsequent age might complacently call the "authentic" Virgil, resurrected afresh by the discriminations of historical scholarship.[10]

Imitating the Italians of whatever vintage tests both a poet's reading comprehension and his historical consciousness. But historicism of the latest variety is likely to slight, or overlook, the former, especially when such critics establish their position via a polemic with formalism. Stephen Greenblatt's discussion of the Bower of Bliss omits even the mention of its source in Tasso, while positing romance as the genre of desire, which is then discussed in terms of Freudian psychoanalysis.[11] Jeffrey Knapp's analysis of the Errour episode focuses on two literary kinds, pastoral and epic, while neglecting romance, the very genre that the monster's name encodes.[12] Of course, these fine critics are attending to other priorities; but their ambition to account for the cultural pressures absorbed and refracted in Spenser's text need not suppress the literary history that impinges upon it.

The assimilation of romance's distinctive divagations of plot to ethical errors was a conventional way of moralizing such songs long before the Reformation; but preoccupations with heresy and the vagaries of "freelance" exegesis become especially acute as Protestantism gains ground via print technology, which multiplies such concerns exponentially. Errour is a sort of apocalyptic bookmobile previously unimaginable yet compounded of elements of a familiar literary legacy. She betrays Spenser's anxiety on the brink of a decade of profound religious uncertainty and contestation whose more radical impulses he had formerly defended in their earlier manifestations. But the champion of

Grindal in the age of Whitgift begins to experience more feelingly the differences between idealist and *politique* trends in progressive Protestantism, though such emotions may only emerge indirectly in an episode which seems decisively to eliminate such threats.[13] On the surface, Redcrosse, the designated agent of righteousness, appears to put an end to such dangers once and for all through his ultimatley successful action against Errour.

Spenser read Italian narrative poetry through the lens (or prism?) of its early modern reception insofar as that process had made itself felt in his remote angle of the world. Harington's Englishing of the *Furioso* represents the results of more than a half century of defensive responses to Ariosto's beloved, but increasingly problematic, romance.[14] In setting it forth in 1591, the Tudor poet followed continental precedents and filled its margins with helpful glosses that should have comforted the reader who desired a modern "classic." They point out its frequent references to ancient worthies like Virgil and Ovid; note "invocations," "similes," "sentences" and other such features marking the highest style and sentiments; and guide the reader from the abrupt interruption of an episode to its resumption elsewhere, lest he should feel frustrated or confused by Ariosto's apparently random picking up and dropping of story lines.

The opening of *The Faerie Queene* reveals the incorporation of such classicizing ambitions into the body of the poem itself. Conspicuous allusions promptly lay claim to a Virgilian pedigree for Spenser's poem, and the muse gets her call in good time. Lengthy similes serve as hallmarks of the loftiest genre, and the sensible sound of proverbial wisdom is audible in Una's counsel or in such a dramatically conclusive hexameter as "God helpe the man so wrapt in *Errours* endlesse traine" (I. i. 18. 9). While the poem features its own modest apparatus in the explanatory subtitles to each book and the recurrent quatrains at the head of each canto summarizing the action-to-come, the gist of the most typical marginalia in Harington has been silently absorbed into the poem itself. Spenser has smoothed over transitions and eschews the sometimes violent interruptions that Ariosto willfully perpetrates and for which Harington, like previous publishers on the continent, felt a need to compensate with notices of the story's continuation further ahead. Moreover, Spenser never indulges in the coy teasing that often accompanies such Ariostan routines.

The rigor of Tasso's Aristotelian scruples rendered these sudden shifts less tolerable to him, and the multiplicity of plots thus occasioned aroused a premonitory anxiety in Tasso reminiscent of the nightmarish gush of texts in Errour's last gasp. Listen to his rationale for unity of plot in his *Discorsi dell'arte poetica:*

> [S]uppose the plot is the poet's main purpose, as Aristotle has affirmed and no one has yet denied. If the plot is single, his purpose will be single; if there are many and diverse plots, there will be many and diverse purposes. However, since diverse purposes distract the mind and hinder labor, he who sets himself a single goal will work more effectively than the imitator of a multitude of actions. I add that multiple plots cause confusion, which could go on and on forever if art did not set and prescribe limits. The poet who treats one plot attains his goal when that plot is finished; he who weaves together more may interweave four or six or ten: he is no more obliged to one number than to another. Thus, he can have no sure sense at what point he best stop.[15]

Imagining a distracted poet faced with an unstoppable proliferation of plot lines, Tasso betrays a striking befuddlement in the face of Ariostan habits of composition. Hard-line Aristotelianism, with its insistence upon unity of plot, offered a safe haven from the daunting possibility of such disorder; and initially, it secured Tasso in his opposition to Ariosto's willful appearance of random narration. Platonic allegory subsequently supplied further assurance when Tasso was bringing the *Liberata* to a close in the mid-1570s, and he thus transformed its structural unity into thematic unity via the abstract coherence of sustained symbolic moralization.

Spenser likewise enlists that ancient tradition to provide an orderly rationale for a threatening profusion of substance in the Garden of Adonis. Chaos subsists as the ground of all being in the heart of that "joyous Paradize"; and awareness of this unique source for the multiple forms that come into existence should reassure us of their essential unity despite appearances to the contrary. However, in that sunny locale of benign fecundity, the central presence of Chaos, "[in] hatefull darkness and in deepe horrore" (vi. 36. 7), may belie the consoling claims made in behalf of such a conventionally daunting vortex. Where Whirl is king, we may shudder despite all assertions that everything is under control. Chaos, like the Grim Reaper (of whom we hear shortly thereafter, 39.3), unforgettably qualifies such claims of orderliness and formal decorum and irrepressibly haunts this otherwise amenable locale.

Furthermore, the grim counterpart of this Edenic site may indeed be the dragon, whose last gasp is never quite finally over and done.

University of South Carolina

NOTES

1. *Novum Organum* 1. 129 (p. 118 in *The "New Organon" and Related Writings* ed. Fulton H. Anderson [New York: Macmillan, 1960]).

2. Cited in F. F. Bruce, *History of the Bible in English* (New York: Oxford University Press, 1978), 37–39.

3. Edmund Spenser, *The Faerie Queene* III.proem.iv. 4–9. All citations are taken from the text edited by Thomas P. Roche, Jr. (New York: Penguin, 1987).

4. *The Geneva Bible,* Facsimile of the 1560 edition (Madison: University of Wisconsin Press, 1969).

5. Richard Bancroft, "A Sermon Preached at Paules Cross" (London, 1588/9), University Microfilms 28964, 33–41. Robert Weimann first drew my attention to this text, which is discussed by Millar Maclure in *The Paul's Cross Sermons, 1534–1642* (Toronto: University of Toronto Press, 1958), 72–75. Maclure characterizes this sermon as "the major riposte by the Establishment" to the Marprelate tracts and also makes reference to the anonymous counter-attacks upon Martin by Lodge and Nashe.

6. Thomas Nashe, *The Unfortunate Traveler and Other Works* (New York: Penguin, 1972), ed. J. B. Steane, 282–83.

7. William Shakespeare, 1 *Henry IV* (Arden Edition, A. R. Humphreys, ed.), 1.2.88.

8. "Spenser shares the breadth of Lucretius's metaphysical vision and is able to make the hymn his own. But from the particular perspective of this study, he appears in the hymn as a poet whose loyalty to his own medieval roots limits his room for poetic maneuver, as one unconcerned with the exercise of bridging a rupture and playing with the differences between the separated worlds." Thomas Greene, *The Light in Troy: Imitation and Discovery in Renaissance Poetry* (New Haven: Yale University Press, 1982), 273–74. Again, "We cannot think of Spenser as even trying to achieve a lucid modern historicist view of Virgil, or of antiquity in general." Frank Kermode, *The Classic: Literary Images of Permanence and Change* (Cambridge, MA: Harvard University Press, 1975), 61.

9. Richard Helgerson, "The New Poet Presents Himself: Spenser and the Idea of a Literary Career," (*PMLA* 93 [1978]: 893–911) is the seminal article in this trend. Rpt. in *Self-Crowned Laureates: Spenser, Jonson, Milton, and the Literary System* (Berkeley: University of California Press, 1983).

10. See William Nelson, *The Poetry of Edmund Spenser A Study* (New York: Columbia University Press, 1963), 117.

11. *Renaissance Self-Fashioning: From More to Shakespeare* (Chicago: University of Chicago Press, 1983).

12. "Error as a Means of Empire in *The Faerie Queene* I," *ELH* 54 (1987). Rpt. in *An Empire Nowhere: England, America, and Literature from "Utopia" to "The Tempest"* (Berkeley: University of California Press, 1992). On the other hand, Patricia Parker's reading of Spenser in *Inescapable Romance: Studies in the Poetics of a Mode* (Princeton: Princeton University Press, 1979) is suggestively akin to my approach here.

13. I allude here to John N. King's label for Spenser and his circle as "progressive Protestants" in "Was Spenser a Puritan?" (*Spenser Studies* 6 [1986]) and to Wallace MacCaffrey's distinction between *politiques* and idealists in *Queen Elizabeth and the Making of Policy, 1572–1588* (Princeton: Princeton University Press, 1981).

14. See Simon Cauchi, "The 'Setting Forth' of Harrington's Ariosto." *Studies in Bibliography* 36 (1983): 137–69; and Daniel Javitch, *Proclaiming a Classic: The Canonization of "Orlando Furioso"* (Princeton: Princeton University Press, 1991).

15. *Discorsi dell'arte poetica* a cura di Luigi Poma (Bari, Italy: Laterza, 1964), 24. My translation, which appears in full in *The Genesis of Tasso's Narrative Theory: English Translations of the Early Poetics and a Comparative Study of Their Significance* (Detroit: Wayne State University Press, 1993). An expanded version of this essay appars therein on pp. 57–76.

WENDY RAUDENBUSH OLMSTED

Deconstruction
and Spenser's Allegory

*D*ECONSTRUCTIONIST understandings of language challenge
basic premises of traditional allegorical readings of such texts as
Spenser's *Faerie Queene.*[1] Paul de Man's famous article, "The Rhetoric of Temporality," celebrates a notion of allegory as a purely
artificial sign that disdains recourse to the analogical and anagog-
ical interpretations often appropriate to pre-romantic allegory and
that renounces application to the phenomenal world.[2] Elsewhere,
de Man attacks a basic premise of traditional allegorical reading
when he argues that there is no connection between a text and the
natural or phenomenal cognition in terms of which persons
understand psychological, moral, and cosmological phenomena
outside of the text.[3] He questions the authority of language as a
model for non-linguistic forms of cognition:

> In a genuine semiology as well as in other linguistically
> oriented theories, the referential function is not being
> denied—far from it; what is in question is its authority as a
> model for natural or phenomenal cognition. Literature is
> fiction not because it somehow refuses to acknowledge
> "reality," but because it is not *a priori* certain that language
> functions according to principles which are those, or

111

which are *like* those, of the phenomenal world. It is therefore
not *a priori* certain that literature is a reliable source of information about anything but its own language.

It would be unfortunate, for example, to confuse the materiality of the signifier with the materiality of what it signifies. This
may seem obvious enough on the level of light and sound, but it
is less so with regard to the more general phenomenality of
space, time or especially of the self; no one in his right mind will
try to grow grapes by the luminosity of the word, "day," but it is
very difficult not to conceive the pattern of one's past and future
existence as in accordance with temporal and spatial schemes that
belong to fictional narratives and not to the world.

From this point of view, the use of a text as a model for an analogous
phenomenon in the world is problematic. De Man challenges the tendency to understand the world in terms of patterns that belong to fictional narrative; yet Spenser's *Faerie Queene* invites its reader to do exactly that. How might readers of Spenser's poem as a Renaissance
allegory reply to de Man's skepticism?

Foucault has shown that the Renaissance understood the cosmos as a
system of signs; the Renaissance did not make a strong distinction between signs and the phenomenal world.[4] The Renaissance had no concept of a purely experiential, immediate relation to phenomena and thus
did not ask itself whether language could be adequate to that experience. Things could be signs and psychology, history, and the cosmos
were understood as signs for one another and for philosophical and
theological ideas. Though readers read allegorical texts as analogous to
cosmological, psychological and philosophical meanings, they did not
therefore suppose that they had attained an experience of an absolute
referent or divine center. The divinity of Renaissance allegory was a
god of mystery never fully encompassed in any of the open-ended
readings of texts.[5]

Yet, readers from the romantic period on have been prone to take
allegorical reading as a method for reducing a text to some external
system of meaning. Some argue that traditional allegorical interpretations too frequently ignore the signifying power of the sign and refer
directly to a meaning outside the text. For example, Jonathan Goldberg
objects to readings of Spenser that refer to external systems that contain
supposedly stable meanings. He argues that Spenser's characters cannot
be explained by referring to them as versions of ideas:

. . . characters, who are 'placed' in the text to express aspects of its theme, are not, obviously, characters in the sense of persons; but they are not explained by referring to them as versions of ideas that somehow exist somewhere other than in the textual space they are allotted. To succumb to such interpretive moves, and Spenser criticism has often done so—when, for instance, Britomart becomes the embodiment of the concept of married love in some reader's interpretation—is reductive in the extreme because the actuality of the textual space in which characters move in is ignored and replaced by something supposedly outside it. The need for this external system of meaning can be understood. Spenserian narration generated it, for, as narrative, the poem undoes itself; it creates characters who are also undone. One response to this is to look elsewhere for what the text denies. But characters are not salvaged by being taken out of the text and referred to some other system of supposedly stable and finally reductive set of meanings. Rather, we must see that what generates and undoes the characters in Spenser's poem establishes them in a world of discourse which is so fully responsive to such 'external' systems of meaning that it has already taken them into the text and subjected them to the very narrative strategies that determine the action of the poem. Once again, there is no 'outside' to this text. Characters independent of the text are not being created here, ideas outside the text are not being exemplified.[6]

Goldberg rightly objects to readings that take characters out of the text and refer them to some supposedly stable, reductive meaning, and he observes that Spenserian narration takes systems of meaning into the text and subjects them to its narrative strategies. Yet, allegorical reading does not imply the reduction of the text to an exernal system of meanings, and it does not involve a fallacious extension of fictional schemes into the natural or phenomenal world in the way that Paul de Man finds so troubling.[7]

In order to understand how the reading of allegory relates text to analogue and why this reading is not reductive and why it does not reduce the textual to the phenomenal, I compare a simplified version of an aspect of Goldberg's reading of The Temple of Venus with Renaissance understandings of allegory and riddle. Then I compare Elizabeth Bellamy's deconstructionist reading of the text's attempt to name Queen Elizabeth with a traditional allegorical reading of Spenser's figuration of the Queen. We will find that, in an allegorical reading, Spenser's text does indeed refer to cosmos and to Queen, but to cosmos and Queen as signs and that, far from being reduced to a cosmological or political system of meanings, Spenser's text reconstrues those meanings and plays upon them. Yet, Spenser's text read allegorically does not necessarily break down verbal or textual differences. Instead it exhibits various sorts of tension and paradox, each producing a distinctive hindrance in the process of reading, a hindrance that in turn opens up further lines of interpretation. Paradoxes do not necessarily lead to the dissolvings of meanings.

In order to understand how a text can be read allegorically in relation to a second system of signs and meanings without being reduced to that system, I compare a deconstructionist reading with the reading of riddle. Riddle also helps us to understand why a formulation of the purely linguistic character of the fictional is inadequate to explaining a traditional allegorical reading of Spenser's text. Whereas Goldberg's deconstructionist and Lacanian approach reads a process such as the self's desire and search for a lover as involving a paradox in which "characters . . . in the text enact verbal relationships and structures," Renaissance cosmological allegory works in a reverse way.[8] There the reader moves from a paradoxical or suggestive verbal surface to an analogue, shifting levels of meaning from the verbal to the iconic or to signs that mean through tension and process. Where Goldberg finds differences fading, the allegorical reader discovers a relation.[9] He or she moves from the verbal surface as pattern to a secondary set of signs. The relation to the secondary signs (such as those of cosmology or philosophy) changes the way we read the text. Movement does not endlessly undo meaning, it changes it.

Let us now see how a reading that emphasizes textual differences and a (traditional) allegorical reading work by comparing two examples. In a reading of a portion of *The Faerie Queene,* Book IV, Jonathan Goldberg argues that paradox undermines the distinctions between characters. Drawing upon the work of Lacan, he reads love in Spenser's book IV as desire.[10] Desire becomes a trope in which characters like Scudamour are caught up; they lose themselves in the trope of desire. Selves can lose themselves in this way because the self can become defined by its desire for another whom it lacks.[11] This emergence of desire from a lack gives rise to the paradox that even if a lover possessed his love, his possession would not fulfill his self, since possession would involve a kind of falsification or substitution of another for the self. When characters love, they become caught up in a desire that has its own power.

For example, Scudamour loses himself in his desire for Amoret. Even if he succeeded in possessing Amoret, his doing so would involve a loss of self. As Scudamour becomes possessed by desire and then by jealously, he loses his status as character. Blandamour, also jealous, then replaces him, breaking down the distinction between himself and Scudamour. Eventually, characters become "examples, names, words — not selves — that can be devoured or that will devour."[12] Earlier allegorical readers might have understood this change as a process of abstraction through which a character becomes an idea. Goldberg's reading, on the other hand, reads what could be described as a process, the self's desire and search for a lover, as a "paradox" that "brings together having and losing. . . . It is generated in loss and sustained by loss."[13] As characters pursue other characters in the effort to fulfill a lack, differences between characters become blurred, and "episodes fade into one another."[14] The text "generates itself from itself":

> In book IV, . . . textual structures are the structures of relationships between selves and between incidents. The difficulty of the text is nothing other than the difficulty of sorting these structures out, establishing their differences, and thereby, their meanings. The text proclaims, explicitly, that these differences are blurred. It demands of us what it does not do itself and what cannot be done — to move outside of the patterning of the text in its replications in order to determine the significances.

Although the text may demand that readers move outside of the text, it "demands of us what it does not do itself and what cannot be done." In Goldberg's view, characters must be read textually rather than being referred to ideas or systems of meanings outside of the text.

Renaissance allegory in its more obscure forms works in a reverse way from Goldberg's reading; the allegorical interpreter moves from a puzzling verbal text to an analogue that exists in some sense "outside" of the text.[15] Peacham's definition of allegory will help us understand why. Peacham writes, "An Aligory is a sentence, which sheweth one thing in wordes, and another in sense."[16] Words that appear enigmatic on the surface become full of sense when read analogically. This process is easier to understand in the case of riddle than it is in allegory, so I will use the example of a riddle first.

As Michael Murrin has shown, riddles, like enigmatic allegories, work to stimulate thought by presenting an opaque surface.[17] The language presents an obstacle to reading:

'It is my mother well I wot,
And yet the daughter that I begot.'[18]

Taken literally the sentence is self-contradictory. How can someone be both a mother and a daughter to the same person? The analogical reading of the riddle involves looking for a process analogous to begetting but (in this case) reversible. The reader who seeks such an analogue may light upon physical processes which are reversible as birth is not, the processes of ice turning into water and water into ice. As deconstructionist readers sometimes do, we move from the literal to the figural, but because we establish a relation between the verbal surface and a different sort of sign, we find that meaning changes and grows.[19]

A second kind of riddle requires the rhetorical reader to think through a sentence that states a general but self-contradictory meaning:

Men do not understand how that which draws apart agrees with itself; harmony lies in the bending back.[20]

Paradoxically, the sentence suggests that opposites are the same. A drawing apart agrees with itself. One might read this puzzle as an instance of the way differences blur, but the allegorical interpreter uses the words as metaphors for a cosmos in tension with itself. We might think, as Heraclitus did, of the bow and the lyre as embodying relations of drawing apart and agreeing with itself, using these in turn as analogues for a cosmos where the tension of opposites holds together a unity. However, our interpretation does exactly what Paul de Man forbade; we resolve a verbal paradox by appealing to physical things that embody tension. The deconstructionist might argue that this move is naively referential, though the Renaissance reader would see it as inevitable.

Scholars of traditional allegory can resolve this difference by affirming a commitment to understanding allegory as read historically. Yet we may also admit the contribution of a modern semiologist who provides a powerful systematic explanation for how cosmic processes, psychological patterns and arguments mean as signs. Modern semiotics is helpful here as a bridge between ourselves and the past because, extending beyond the sphere of the verbal, it offers us a more comprehensive theory of signs than deconstruction. Charles Sanders Peirce argues that symbolic, verbal signs presuppose simpler, non-verbal sign functions such as the icon and index.[21] The icon and index are sign functions that mean through the kinds of physical patterns and tensions that one finds in Renaissance cosmology, psychology and moral thought. An icon relates through resemblance. Think of a diagram of an electrical circuit or a sketch of a painting. An index implies a binary relation like the push someone exerts in opening the door and the equal resistance someone else exerts in keeping it closed. Cause and effect presuppose this notion of push/being pushed. According to Peirce, the relation of cause and effect involves the category of struggle or tension such as we found in the bow and the lyre.[22] Things can function as icons and indices. So a weathervane is an icon in that its direction is like that of the wind and an index in that the direction in which it points is an effect of the wind's blowing. The weathervane as sign must be interpreted by someone but its meaning is not purely linguistic.

Once we extend our semiotics to include non-verbal signs, we are faced no longer with a chasm between language and the world. Peirce's concept of non-verbal binarity ("secondness") is especially helpful for understanding the cosmological type of allegorical interpretation involving as it does tension, process and cause. Consider that non-verbal binarity can be exemplified in the relation between pushing and resisting, action and reaction, cause and effect. If we express these tensions verbally as in "every action is reaction" or "action reacts" we create a verbal paradox. One might read this paradox as dissolving differences. The traditional reader penetrates through the paradox to another level of meaning, by shifting from verbal to physical sign, as from mother/daughter to ice and water, or from "that which draws apart agrees with itself" to the bow and the lyre. This effort to make a satisfactory shift alerts us to our own interpretive activity, making us self-aware in our interpretation of signs and freeing us from that naive referentiality into which a deconstructionist such as de Man may believe that earlier ages have fallen.

Peirce provides a modern semiotics that facilitates an understanding of the interpretive practices of the Renaissance. The Renaissance was permeated with Stoic and Presocratic cosmology, especially Pythagoreanism; the cosmos as sign was characterized by tension, organized mathematically. Peirce's concepts may give some readers access to earlier practices and theories whose sophistication they overlook. His recognition of non-verbal signs as important constituents of language also allows us to analyze areas of signification where the verbal, the kinesthetic, the aural and the visual play together. At one time, de Man avoided the reading of literature "by analogy with the plastic arts and with music," believing that "we now have to recognize the necessity of a non-perceptual, linguistic moment in painting."[23] Contrarily, Peirce understands the importance of a semiotic that generates signs for all of these. Movement back and forth between visual, aural, kinesthetic and verbal signs characterizes analogical interpretation of allegory.

Traditional allegorical readings informed by Peirce also recognize different kinds and levels of tension and aporia. Whereas Goldberg's deconstructionist reading plays upon textual difference, allegorical readings recognize various kinds of sign and, hence, various kinds of difference and contrast.[24] For example, the allegorical reader finds multiple kinds and degrees of tension and difference in The Temple of Venus, each presenting an aporia to the reader and each opening up a network of signs and meanings. Tension occurs on the level of action, where Scudamour's desire to penetrate to the island meets obstacles and hindrances that impede that desire. (X. 6–20) As Peirce suggests, action implies reaction, pressure against the self. This binary relation of secondness is not reducible to a purely verbal difference between words. Yet another sort of tension binds conflicting forces that distort the group of figues that Scudamour encounters after his visit to the garden.[25] (X. 31–3) The awkwardness of the Dame Concord's forcing Hatred and Love to join hands while Hatred turns his face away, biting his teeth and gnashing his iron tusks, spurs the reader toward the discovery of an analogue that makes significant the characteristics and gestures. Through analogy the allegorical reader may use the relations of the turning away of Hatred to the mastering power of Love and the tempering power of the Dame to reconstrue a cosmos based upon the proportion of contraries. The interrelation of Hatred whose impulse is to resist and turn away, with Love who has the mastery over the divisive power of Hatred analogizes the cosmological tension between a Love that unifies and a Hatred that separates and differentiates. This cosmic tension is an instance of secondness or struggle in Peirce's sense. Opposing forces moving toward unity and toward differentiation work like the string and bow of Heraclitus's riddle.

An approach that emphasizes difference as a feature of textuality might read such figures as exhibiting verbal antitheses or as dissolving such antitheses. On the other hand, non-verbal opposition or struggle as Peirce characterizes it involves a pushing and a pushing against that mutually implicate one another. Spenser's figure, Concord, expresses the necessary equivalence of these forces without dissolving them into one another. Yet, those who disallow analogies between non-verbal and verbal signs might resist readings that relate the text to icons and indices such as those implicated in the figures of the bow, the lyre and Spenser's cosmos.

De Man suggests that the rules by which we understand language and phenomena may be very different. Yet, if we read the cosmos not as phenomenon but as non-verbal sign, iconicity between language as sign and cosmos as sign becomes possible and potentially fruitful.

The oppositions between male and female united in the figure of the androgyne indicate another level and kind of tension and of mystery. Like Wind's account of Neoplatonism as paraphrased by Goldberg, the mystery may be a mystery of endless veils; "explicating goes on in an attempt to remove a veil that is never finally removed — indeed is constructed in this endless activity."[26] Yet such endlessness leads to skepticism only if one has an idea that there should be some external, central reality that could eventually be uncovered. For the Renaissance, the veils of language and non-verbal signs existed to *cover* a deeper mystery out of which came the infinite generativity of signs and meanings.[27] The paradoxical text protected the mystery from an easy and misleading construal by the uninitiated.

The notion of explicating a text in order to remove a veil implies that allegory invites its readers to use the text to find a center of meaning. In this view, the reader's attempt to explicate only proliferates words that take him or her ever further from the androgynous Venus. Elizabeth Bellamy develops such a reading of Spenser's images and namings of Queen Elizabeth, drawing on the work of Geoffrey Hartman and Jacques Derrida.[28] An analysis of her argument concerning Spenser's naming of Elizabeth shows that whereas her deconstructionist reading understands naming to seek a transcendental signified, an allegorical reading relates names and patterns of the Queen to a second sets of *signs* (not a transcendental signified) constructed by the Queen herself and by the courtiers and writers who surrounded her or who wished to gain her attention. The allegorical reader, by relating Spenser's text to a second set of socially constructed signs, also changes those signs. Peirce's concept of the metaphor enables us to understand how one sign may enable the reconstruing of an object (such as the Queen), which is also a sign. According to Peirce, a metaphor represents the sign character of a second sign through its own sign character.[29] Using this understanding of metaphor, we can regard the Queen as a socially constructed object, a set of signs with cultural and political meanings that can be metaphorically reconstituted by a text. Let us examine the relations between Bellamy's reading of Spenser's naming of Queen Elizabeth and an allegorical reading of Spenser's "goddess."

Elizabeth Bellamy's reading of Spenser's addresses to the Queen calls into question the power of the text to name the Queen at all. Bellamy argues that Spenser's text seeks to call forth Elizabeth from behind her veil but that it fails in its drive toward Elizabeth as "unmediated Pure Name."[30] In attempting to name his Queen, Spenser's text becomes caught up in a chain of figural substitutions. Because he cannot name her, he substitutes instead "faire patterns" of queenly courtesy, "which delay true knowledge of Elizabeth and can only serve to remind the poet that Elizabeth-as-Presence is missing."[31]

Like de Man, Bellamy challenges the power of the text to refer to something outside of itself, but her challenge is formulated in terms of Derrida's understanding of the name as attempting to reach a transcendental signified. She also draws on Hartman's reading of Derrida and Lacan according to which the name seeks to produce a "haunting, fixative, unifying effect of 'being named'."[32] If Spenser could name Elizabeth, he would fix her as the object and addressee of his poem. However, Bellamy argues that Spenser cannot do so; she understands the readability of his text to emerge from his unsuccessful attempt to name Elizabeth. Spenser's epic remains unfinished insofar as it fails to remove Elizabeth's veil and to name her "as a transcendental signified."[33] If Spenser could name Queen Elizabeth, if he could call her forth from her veil, he would sanction his own epic task.[34] Because she is unrepresentable, the poet finds himself in a futile search for a signifier, looking not for the Queen but for images of her virtue. Thus, the images and patterns serve not as occasions for allegorical readings in a traditional sense, but as replacements for or deferrals of reference.

Bellamy's reading of Spenser is informed by Derrida's response to the projects of Heidegger and Husserl as seeking words that uncover Presence. Derrida believes that self-presence "has never been given but only dreamed of and always already split."[35] Derrida understands language to inscribe within a difference, to classify. For Derrida, to name involves the "originary violence of language which consists in inscribing within a difference, in classifying, in suspending the vocative absolute." To name is to make a distinction, a difference (between the name and the named, between one name and another) and hence to invoke a whole system of differences. Bellamy's reading of Spenser enacts such differences as she follows through the chain of figures that substitute one for another as Spenser strives to name Elizabeth. So Elizabeth is dispersed into Belphoebe, "herself bifurcated as Phoebe and Cynthia."[36]

An allegorical reading of Spenser's text, on the other hand, understands the text not so much as seeking to reveal the Queen Elizabeth behind the veil as to interpret her as "*enfold*[ed] in couert vele" (II Proem 5). The allegory *wraps* the "fairest Princess" in shadows. Spenser's text emphasizes the distance between the text and the Queen as sign by reiterating its own status as veil, shadow, image, sign, and mirror (II Proem 4–5).

The "faire patterns" that Spenser constructs to mirror the Queen, are themselves "shadows" of a network of allegorical signs that she used to figure herself. Read as social, political, and (as we shall see) cosmological allegory, Spenser's text relates not to a transcendental signified but to a social construction which it both reflects and reworks. Spenser's text figures the goddess as veiled androgyne; Queen Elizabeth constructed herself in the figure of a goddess, a fecund virgin who could reproduce without the need of a "sire" and whose children were the subjects of her kingdom. The phoenix was her emblem, representing her ability to reproduce without a mate, and suggesting some of the same ideas of rebirth arising out of self-destruction that one finds in the snake that curls at the feet of Venus in The Temple of Venus.[37] Though we may wonder how the "promised virgin of imperial reform be also the goddess of love," Roy Strong responds that it is "less curious in the context of Renaissance monarchical mythology, which tries by the use of extreme forms of contrasting imagery somehow to reconcile the dual nature of royalty, divine and human, soul and body, mind and passions," and, we might add, male and female. Strong suggests that the cult is held together by such paradoxes. Moreover, "in [the] Venus-Virgo Renaissance Platonism [also] found the confirmation of its doctrine of the union of love and chastity."[38] Elizabeth used the available terms of the culture, turning her "vulnerability of gender . . . to her own advantage," "styling herself as the unattainable, hence endlessly pursued, Virgin Queen. . . . She ruled not so much by the 'arduous and constant wooing of the body politic,' as Wallace MacCaffrey once suggested, as by inducing it to woo her."[39]

Whereas Bellamy's reading understands Spenser's addresses to the Queen as striving to name Elizabeth and treats the text's rendering of patterns of her virtues as deferrals of meaning and reference, the allegorical reader uses the addresses and the patterns to relate the text to the Queen's own allegorization of herself through such signs as phoenix, snake, goddess of love and virgin. These allegorical signs, paradoxical as they are, image enigmatically greater mysteries—mysteries of change and regeneration. Each sign relates an icon or paradox to processes of

change in a manner similar to the way the riddles I discussed earlier relate
to signs that express process and tension. The phoenix finds new life by
being extinguished in the fire, then rising out of it as the new might
destroy but rise out of the old. The snake swallows its own tail, thus sus-
taining itself afresh by destroying its old self. These paradoxical emblems
of change and regeneration shadowed the mystery of a Queen who as
Pocock writes, "based [her] claim to a mysterious and quasi-divine
authority . . . on [her] expertise in . . . the *arcana imperii* or secrets of
power, in judging the fluctuations of times and seasons, events, circum-
stances and human wills."[40] The paradoxical emblems, like the riddling
words that suggested enigmatically process and tension in the Renaissance cosmos, become readable in relation to a political world characterized by events that were regarded as unique, contingent and fluctuating
and where the monarch's role was to make change and process fruitful
and generative. The snake with its tail in its mouth can also be read as an
icon of a Neoplatonic balance between a divine descent into particulars
and the particulars' reascent into the divine source of love and bounty.
Queen Elizabeth became an emblem and instance of this Neoplatonic
process insofar as she functioned as a source of office and wealth (love
descending to particular courtiers) at the same time they ascended to her
through their praise, their work on her behalf, and their pleas for grace.
To read her names and icons of herself as the virgin goddess of love, as
phoenix and snake is to interpret an emblematic paradox by relating it to
cosmological, political, and psychological processes which have a sign
character of their own rather than to seek a Presence that functions as a
transcendental signified, independent of social or historical construction.

Spenser's text understood as having an external allegorical reference
to the Queen invites readers to use a paradox as an occasion to shift to
another kind of sign, one that suggests process and change. Yet, Spenser
does not merely incorporate signs associated with Elizabeth. When
Spenser shadows the Queen as a system of signs, he also refigures her.
As in the case of the cosmological allegories discussed earlier, Spenser's
text reconstrues signs and meanings outside of the text, playing upon
them. Yet, such mirrorings do not endlessly defer a transcendental signified. To "mirror" is to rework and hence redefine the Queen. An episode like The Temple of Venus plays upon and changes the terms of the
Queen's discourse, shadowing them in ways that defeat or correct certain implications of those terms.

Louis adrian Montrose suggests that Elizabeth "had the capacity to
work the available terms to serve her culturally conditioned needs and

interests. By the same token, however, her subjects might rework those terms to serve their turns."[41] Spenser "reshapes the Queen by the very process of addressing and representing her allegorically."[42] Here language is regarded as having a pragmatic, rhetorical power for reshaping signs and meanings in a cultural system that exists outside the text as well as within it.

Spenser shadows the Queen differently in The Temple of Venus and in "Colin Clovts Come Home Againe," and a brief contrast of the two illustrates ways allegorical texts play upon both cosmology and Queen as signs.[43] The contrast between "Colin Clovts" and the Temple appears sharply in their different allegorizations of the "same" cosmology. Whereas in "Colin Clovts" opposites are drawn to each other in love and their union produces naturally an abundance of offspring, in the Temple, one finds many kinds and levels of opposition and hindrance, as we have seen. Conflict is never fully changed into amity. Love and Hate endure in perpetual opposition, held in balance and contained by Concord. This balance itself is imperfect as Hatred tries to brain Scudamour. Though the garden supplies a vision of perfect happiness in friendship and love, Scudamour mentions as he thinks of it that he himself "never tasted blis nor happie howre." The worshippers of Venus complain piteously of loss and delay, and Scudamour himself groans deeply within. The love of animals and human beings in the Temple never fully satisfies itself even in union. Desire produces offspring as in "Colin Clovts" but the individual remains unsatisfied, ready to quench his burning in another act of union. Spenser depicts a striving for good that continually encounters hindrances; the woes of suitors are increased by the reluctance of Venus to be gracious. The Temple of Venus can be read as allegorizing the relationship between the courtiers and the Queen that indirectly chastises her while also praising her powers.[44] It is an indirect plea for the queen's mercy, grace, and bounty, but is also questions a honey in which there is so much gall.[45] While praising the power of Venus and the joy she gives, while at times questioning and at times justifying suffering and hindrance, the episode persuades the Queen toward the concord, peace-making, and grace which her own discourse already claims as part of her meaning.

In "Colin Clovts Come Home Againe," Spenser employs the icon of androgyny to make a distinction between the Court with its supreme Cynthia and a pastoral ideal of love adumbrated through the figure of Venus and the God of love. The Temple, on the other hand, leads both Scudamour and the allegorical reader through a process of discovering the nature and value of eros as a source of hope, of productive action, and of fertility, while also bemoaning the bitterness and pain that the courtier experiences within the framework of the court. The episode acculturates the courtier, works through many of the challenges posed by strife, discord, and disappointment and, at the same time, clarifies some of the costs of a system in which few are rewarded. These specific criticisms and disagreements and Spenser's thoughtful refigurations of figures like the androgyne engage the power of a partial not a radical openness in language. Allegorical reading allows one to explore historically particular ambiguities, conflicts, and negotiations of meaning and to understand the edge and force of Spenser's particular rewritings of his culture.

The University of Chicago

NOTES

1.   I gave a briefer version of this article as a paper entitled "Love's Desire: Allegory and the Temple of Venus," at the Sixteenth Century Studies Conference in St. Louis, Missouri, October, 1988. I am grateful to William Olmsted for his comments on drafts of the paper and the article.

2.   Paul de Man, "The Rhetoric of Temporality," *Interpretation: Theory and Practice,* ed. by Charles S. Singleton (Baltimore: Johns Hopkins University Press, 1969), 173–209.

3.   Paul de Man, "The Resistance to Theory," *The Resistance to Theory* (Minneapolis, University of Minnesota Press, 1986), 11. Reprinted from *The Pedagogical Imperative,* ed. by Barbara Johnson, *Yale Fench Studies* 63 (1982).

4.   Michel Foucault, *The Order of Things* (New York: Random House, Vintage Books, 1970), 17–44.

5.   Michael Murrin's *The Veil of Allegory: Some Notes Twoard a Theory of Allegorical Rhetoric in the English Renaissance* (Chicago: University of Chicago Press, 1969) is helpful on this issue.

6.   Jonathan Goldberg, *Endlesse Worke: Spenser and the Structures of Discourse* (Baltimore: The Johns Hopkins University Press, 1981), 75.

7.   Spenser critics emphasize the dangers of trying to find point for point correspondences between the text and an analogue in allegorical reading. Attempts to attach particular meanings to terms and to make these meanings function at all times ruin the poem. Thomas P. Roche, Jr. argues that "when the structural patterns of the narrative coincide with the structural patterns of any other events of nature or supernature, we as readers are entitled to view the conformity or analogy as an allegorical meaning. This, I take it, is what Elizabethans meant when they called allegory a 'continued metaphor.' They do not mean a point-for-point correspondence between the narrative events and any meanings they may derive from the narrative." *The Kindly Flame: A Study of the Third and Fourth Books of Spenser's Faerie Queene* (Princeton: Princeton University Press, 1964), 10. See also 10 ff., 95, 122. Rosemond Tuve, *Allegorical Imagery; Some Medieval Books and Their Posterity* (Princeton: Princeton University Press, 1966). Tuve emphasizes the importance of not equating images with concepts (p. 21)

and of not confusing allegory with "a discussion of ideas carried on by having some concrete equivalent stand for each one," p. 28. See also 21 ff., 28 ff., 106. Murrin discusses this issue on pp. 56 ff. and 101 ff. Maureen Quilligan writes that "hunting for one to one correspondences between insignificant narrative particulars and hidden thematic generalizations, he [the reader] is frustrated when he cannot find them and generally bored when he can." *The Language of Allegory: Defining the Genre* (Ithaca: Cornell University Press, 1979), 32.

8. Goldberg, 112. See also 84–86.

9. See ibid., especially 116–117.

10. Ibid., esp. 75 ff.

11. On p. 79 Goldberg argues that the "self . . . exists only in relation to another" whom it lacks. On p. 85 he suggests that the self lacks "whether it achieves its desire or not."

12. Ibid., 112.

13. Ibid.

14. Ibid., 117.

15. Sometimes Spenser makes this move explicitly as when he writes of the dwelling of Ate:

> It is a darksome delue farre vnder ground,
> With thornes and barren brakes enuirond round,
> That none the same may easily out win;
> Yet many waies to enter may be found,
> But none to issue forth when one is in:
> For discord harder is to end then to begin.
>
> (IV. I. 20)

The story tells rather straightforwardly of the dark, underground den, surrounded by thorns and bracken so that none may find a way out. Stranger is the comment that "many waies to enter may be found, but none to issue forth when one is in." The reader needs to shift referents in order to make sense of a physical impossibility. Spenser shows us how by providing the moral commonplace, "for discord harder is to end then to begin." The historical progress of conflict and discord can be irreversible where paths usually are not.

16. Henry Peacham, *The Garden of Eloquence* (1597) (Menston, Eng.: The Scholar Press, 1971), paragraph on "Aligoria." See Murrin, especially Chapter III, pp. 54 ff. In its more limited sense, allegory is metaphorical; in a broader sense it includes all sentence tropes including enigma and irony. Among the works that describes allegory as continued or extended metaphor are Puttenham, "The Arte of English Poesie," *English Reprints*, ed. by Edward Arber (rpt. New York: AMS Press, 1966) and Richard Sherry, *A Treatise of Schemes and Tropes (1550)* (Gainesville, Florida: Scholars Facsimiles, 1971). See also William Nelson, *The Poetry of Edmund Spenser: A Study* (New York, Columbia University Press, 1963), 128.

Isabel MacCaffrey, *Spenser's Allegory: The Anatomy of Imagination* (Princeton: Princeton University Press, 1976), argues that "allegory belongs to Aristotle's fourth type of metaphor" and that "in a complex metaphor . . . only the third and fourth terms of the analogy will be visible, but their relationship can indicate, implicitly, the direction commentary should take. The *action* of the allegory is, therefore, a main avenue of accessibility to its possible meaning," 46–47.

17.   See Murrin on the relation of riddle and allegory, 59–61.

18.   Puttenham, 198.

19.   See Murrin's analysis of Peacham's riddle, "As long as I liue, I eate, but when I drinke, I die," 59.

20.   Heraclitus 51. Hermann Diels, *Die Fragmente der Vorsokratiker,* ed. W. Kranz (Berlin: Weidmann, 1951), vol. 1, 162. G. S. Kirk and J. E. Raven, *The Presocratic Philosophers: A Critical History with a Selection of Texts* (Cambridge: Cambridge University Press, 1964), 193.

21.   Charles Sanders Peirce, *Collected Papers,* ed. by Charles Hartshorne and Paul Weiss (Cambridge: Harvard University Press, 1974), 2. 247–49. 274–91.

22.   For Pierce's analysis of secondness or struggle, see 5. 45–58.

23.   De Man, "The Resistance to Theory," 10

24.   See, for example, Goldberg's emphasis on textual difference at p. 116. "Repetition and sameness absorb differences, and difference — as a textual matter and as a matter of characterization — is the most problematic area in *The Faerie Queene.* The problem is central to the nature of language itself, for it is composed of differences that are unremarked and unremarkable."

25.   See Berger, "The Spenserian Dynamics," *Studies in English Literature,* 8 (1968): 3 ff. See also "Two Spenserian Retrospects: The Antique Temple of Venus and the Primitive Marriage of Rivers," *Texas Studies in Literature and Language* 10 (Spring, 1968): 5–25 for analysis of discordia concors.

26.   Goldberg, 69.

27.   See Murrin, 46–47 on the obscurity of truth.

28.   Elizabeth J. Bellamy, "The Vocative and the Vocational: The Unreadability of Elizabeth in *The Faerie Queene, ELH* 54 (1987): 1–30. See Geoffrey H. Hartman, *Saving the Text: Literature/Derrida/Philosophy* (Baltimore: Johns Hopkins University Press, 1981), Jacques Derrida, *Glas,* trans. by John P. Leavey, Jr. (Lincoln: University of Nebraska Press, 1986), and Jacques Derrida, *Of Grammatology,* trans. by Gayatri Chakravorty Spivak (Baltimore: Johns Hopkins University Press, 1976). Spivak's introducton is very helpful with respect to the relationship between Derrida and Heidegger.

29.   In Peirce's terms metaphors "represent the representative character of a representamen [such as the Queen] by representating a parallelism in something else [such as a goddess]." 2.277.

30.   Bellamy, 5.

31.   Ibid., 10.

32.   Hartman, 101.

33.   Bellamy, 4.

34.   According to Bellamy, Spenser's quest is to interrelate his "*vocational* goal in *The Faerie Queene,* the fulfillment of his epic role as England's Virgil, and his *vocative* goal, his desire quite simply to name his queen, to call forth her image from behind her 'couert vele' (2 Proem 5.2) as the ultimate sanctioner of his epic task," 1.

35.   Derrida, *Of Grammatology,* 112.

36.   Bellamy, 4.

37.   Roy Strong, *The Cult of Elizabeth: Elizabethan Portraiture and Pageantry* (London, Thames and Hudson, 1977), 73. Robin Headlam Wells, *Spenser's Faerie Queene and the Cult of Elizabeth* (Totowa, New Jersey: Barnes & Noble, 1983), 101.

38.   Strong, ibid.

39.   Steven Mullaney, "Brothers and Others or the Art of Alienation," *Cannibals, Witches and Divorce: Estranging the Renaissance* (Baltimore: Johns Hopkins University Press, 1987), 74.

40.   J. G. A. Pocock, *The Machiavellian Moment: Florentine Political Thought and the Atlantic Republican Tradition* (Princeton: Princeton University Press, 1975), 28.

41.   Adrian Montrose, "The Elizabethan Subject and the Spenserian Text," *Literary Theory/Renaissance Texts,* ed. by Patricia Parker and David Quint (Baltimore: Johns Hopkins University Press, 1986), 310.

42.   Ibid., 303.

43.   Edmund Spenser, "Colin Clovts Come Home Againe," *The Poetical Works of Edmund Spenser,* ed. by E. de Selincourt (London, 1959), 536–45.

44.   For interesting analyses of the uses of rhetoric to praise and correct a prince, see Murrin and Daniel Javitch, *Poetry and Courtliness in Renaissance England* (Princeton: Princeton University Press, 1978).

45.   Goldberg's reading emphasizes gall even more strongly, 73 ff., esp. 84.

RICHARD MALLETTE

Book Five of *The Faerie Queene:* An Elizabethan Apocalypse

*I*N HIS TREATISE OF 1587, "A Fruitfull Dialogue concerning the End of the World," William Perkins fabricates an eschatological exchange between Worldling and Christian. Naturally they consider the arrival of the Final Day. Worldling offers the popular opinion of the moment: "They say euery where, that next yeare eighty eight, Doomes day will be."[1] Although Christian prudently denies the feasibility of exact calculation, he agrees that the Day of Judgment is inevitable and possibly at hand. Their debate typifies late Elizabethan preoccupations. Throughout the 1580s, as the great struggle with Spain reached a crisis and war became certain, voices both religious and political became growingly apocalyptic. After the Armada invasion of 1588, eschatological zeal increased and continued unabated for over a decade, often nationalistic and always anti-Catholic in emphasis. Among those voices is Book V of *The Faerie Queene,* whose final episodes partake of the apocalyptic fervor after the Armada invasion and contribute to the surge of religious and political zeal surrounding that pivotal event. The second half of Book V is constructed as an apocalyptic exegesis of contemporary history and is inseparable from a variety of post-Armada apocalyptic texts. The Protestant historiography of which these texts comprise a chapter has only recently been the subject of extensive scholarly investigation.[2] This inquiry has documented the degree to which the self-determination of Tudor England was shaped by apocalyptic discourse. Spenser's Legend of Justice needs to be squarely located among these apocalyptic texts, for the final "international" episodes of the Book are a product of this peculiar historical moment. They also reformulate the issues of late Elizabethan apocalypticism and thereby contribute to a striking confluence of religious polemic, the discourse of foreign policy, and prophetic historiography.

Book V has frequently alienated readers who object to its political views, particularly its presumptive support of the Elizabethan imperium. The Book is often pronounced a literary failure even by critics who have taken pains to interpret the topical allegory.[3] Attention over the last decade to the Book's negotiation of distinct, often contradictory voices about power and its justification has not fully dislodged these negative estimates.[4] While this historicist criticism has revitalized our understanding of the poem's political assumptions, it has not centered Book V within the contemporary religious upheavals inseparable from the nation's political life and hence has missed how the Book is embedded in the crucial public questions of the period. But with the efflorescence of Protestant studies and its recent impact upon our understanding of the literature of the English Renaissance, Book V has begun to attract scholars who have seen how Book V incorporates biblical apocalypse.[5] The most richly detailed of these studies is by Kenneth Borris, who supplies irrefutable evidence that the final three cantos employ Revelation as their main textual source.[6] The present essay will draw on Borris's work and that of recent historians of Tudor religion and politics to document how Book V not only is shaped by biblical apocalypse but also, just as pervasively, confronts and so becomes a part of apocalyptic commentary of the post-Armada period. To accomplish this task will mean examining exegetical texts insufficiently appreciated in previous criticism but central to a comprehensive reckoning of Reformation England's national self description.

This commentary is distinguished by its view of the English Reformation as a national struggle whose concerns are manifested in current political events, including foreign relations. Unlike an earlier generation of apocalyptic commentators (represented notably by John Bale and John Foxe), those of the late 1580s and 1590s are less interested in the remote future or the remote past and the history of the Church and its martyrs.[7] Instead much post-Armada exegesis encompasses political affairs of the present and the recent past and excludes the wider frame of historical reference evident, say, in Bale or Foxe. The Armada event looms largest among the contemporary occasions that occupy the exegetes' attention, because it is the most pressing example of the perils facing England from Antichrist and his adherents, embodied most alarmingly in Spain and its Roman Catholic allies. The commentators are also pointedly aware of other immediate political events, which they interpret in the light of apocalypse. This post-Armada commentary mediates between biblical apocalypse and Spenser's poem. To sort out the complex hermeneutical status of Book V, this essay will determine how the Legend of Justice partakes of biblical apocalypse throughout the final six cantos, how it forms part of late Elizabethan apocalyptic commentary, and how that commentary bridges biblical texts and the allegory that comments on current events. Finally, I will suggest that in the last canto the Book transcends some of the more nakedly polemical features of post-Armada hermeneutics.

Apocalypse exercised a lifelong fascination for Spenser, as it did for Reformation culture generally. For van der Noot's *A Theatre For Worldlings* the young poet translated four *Visions From Revelation,* a series of verse commonplaces capitalizing on the ecclesiological meaning the Reformation saw in John's text.[8] Apocalypse plays greater and lesser parts throughout the Spenserian canon, most preponderately of course in the Legend of Holiness.[9] Almost from its inception readers have recognized that Book I of *The Faerie Queene* is modelled on Revelation and draws its primary images from that enigmatic testament.[10] The Book exploits the rich visions of apocalypse not only to allegorize the Redcrosse Knight's individual struggle for redemptive faith but also to comment congruently on the fortunes of the English Reformation Church in a titanic struggle against its sinister and mighty opposite.

The Book's employment of biblical apocalypse to allegorize ecclesiastical history accords with how most English commentators between 1540 and 1590 generally understood the genre. Luther had identified Antichrist with the papacy and then in 1530 initiated a historicist exegesis of Revelation, interpreting it as a prophecy of Church history.[11] His goal was to "take from history the events and disasters" of Christianity and to find in them exegetical lessons about the monumental tasks he and his followers were caught up in.[12] For early Reformation England these lessons meant reading apocalypse primarily as a history of persecution and a theology of history. Its chief subjects were three: the doctrine of the two Churches, one true and oppressed, the other false, idolatrous, and powerful; the identification of the papacy as Antichrist; and the imminence of the Last Judgment.[13] These themes remained fairly consistent throughout the century, as apocalyptic commentary became the primary means of unfolding Church history and the chief instrument for Protestants to proclaim their historic destiny and to justify their rebellion from Rome.

Developing an idea first propounded in England by Tyndale, Bale's *Image of Both Churches* (1540–47) sets out in vivid detail the doctrine of the two Churches. Bale claims that historical research should be guided by apocalyptic exegesis; therefore, he says, in an apothegm that will direct exegetes for several generations, ". . . the texte [is] a lyght to the cronycles, and not the cronycles to the texte."[14] Apocalypse becomes a light by which history may be made fully visible. It reveals the wickedness of Rome and the truth of Protestantism. By closely correlating apocalypse and history, Foxe's *Actes and Monuments* and other works amplify Bale's dichotomies and historiographic outlines into a fully articulated Church history. Particularly in his late unfinished work *Eicasmi,* Foxe represents a signal historiographic advance on Bale.[15] In Foxe's hands Bale's doctrine of the two Churches becomes a guide to history and a means of judging truth and falsehood in the consuming crises of the Reformation. By establishing the historiographic principles of apocalyptic exegesis, Bale, Foxe, and their followers make possible many of the great commonplaces of Reformation discourse, such as the universal belief that the papacy was Antichrist[16] or as when William Fulke pronounces in his popular and quite unoriginal *Sermon Preached at Hampton Court* (1570): "I shal plainly shew and proue that Babilon is Rome."[17]

Apocalypse, especially Revelation, attracted early Reformation commentators because it offers readers burdened with a strong sense of persecution a theodicy and a hope for future redress. Its clashing dichotomies foster this hope: Christ and Antichrist, Mother and Whore, right and wrong, true and false. Daniel and Revelation were written in times of crisis: their purpose is to rally suffering readers with faith in the ultimate justice of history and God's vindication of the faithful. Their goal is to give a higher meaning to history by correlating the particularities of fallen experience to transcendent patterns accessible to the prophetic vision. Reformation apocalypticists see themselves in this line of vision, as latter day prophets as well as exegetes. Finding multiple links between history and apocalypse, they not only justify their own theological convictions but also find ample evidence of a teleology in the historical and political maelstroms swirling about them.

It comes as no surprise, then, to find apocalyptic exegesis and political polemic so closely intertwined in the period. As Bernard Capp has pointed out, this is a natural link, for princes were instrumental, indeed essential to the success of the Reformation.[18] Throughout the century, as apocalypse is scrutinized for evidence of papal corruption, the prince is increasingly hailed as the hope of Antichrist's destruction and the instrument of the elect. Foxe dedicates *Actes and Monuments* to Elizabeth I. The frontispiece to the 1563 edition depicts the Queen enthroned in triumph over a defeated papal Antichrist, declaring her the apocalyptic hope of the nation.[19] Just after her accession John Aylmer (later Bishop of London) writes that the Queen wields the "sworde of our defence" to "cutt the head of that Hidra, the Antichrist of Rome, in suche sorte, as it neuer growe againe in this realme of England."[20] Both Bale and Foxe are partly responsible for the nationalistic strain that runs through later apocalyptic commentary; Foxe, for example, claims apostolic roots for the English Church and promotes the crown as the source of God-given government.[21] But these voices are sporadic; the nationalism that becomes a chorus in apocalyptic commentary late in the century is, on the whole, relatively muted between 1540 and 1590.

Instead most English commentators follow Luther's lead and stress the "preaching of God's word in history" as the key to squelching the dark forces of Antichrist.[22] Although no commentator appears to have doubted his ultimate overthrow any more than his identification with Rome, many worried about his interim perfidies. Hence the chief question centered on how he was to be overpowered. Given the supremacy in Protestant thought of preaching the Word, it is natural that commentators promote this activity as the instrument of victory. The great apologist of the English Church, Archbishop Jewel, may be the most representative spokesman for this position. His undated sermon on 2 Thessalonians (he died in 1579) typifies Reformation apocalyptic exegesis before the Armada. He rejects the notion that Antichrist will be routed literally "by Michael." Instead, he says,

> The preaching of the Gospel . . . shal consume the kingdome of Antichrist. . . . Princes make their conquests by power and strength, by fyre and sworde, and engines of warre, but God shal beate downe his aduersarie with the rod of his mouthe. By true preaching of his worde. His worde is mighty, it is his sworde, it is his mace: it is the rod of his mouth.[23]

The opposition Jewel draws between preachers and princes (and his implicit admission that the power of the prince is available as an option) underscores that Protestant writers are often unsure about where to look for leadership in resisting Antichrist. Aylmer had endorsed the Queen's sword as the preferred weapon. The fact remains, though, that early in the reign, preaching was endorsed as the most suitable means of subduing Antichrist.

A quite different approach to the issue comes from Arthur Dent, writing *The Ruine of Rome* at the end of the Elizabethan reign (and published thereafter). He considers the question explicitly: is preaching the most effectual means of conquering Antichrist?

> Of all other meanes, the Gospell is strongest, but the thing is this. First, the Gospell being set abroach, shal detect and discouer the Whoore of Rome, and all her abhominable doctrine and filthinesse, which the Christian Princes espying, shal renounce her, make warre vpon her, and slay in the field thousande thousandes of her soldiers.[24]

The gospel alone is insufficient; to complete the great task the arms of the godly prince are needed. In his *Sermons Vpon the Whole Booke of Revelation* (1596) George Gifford makes a similar point. After acknowledging the role that preaching might play, he turns to the power of statecraft:

> . . . we . . . stand in neede of noble warriors and mighty men, who in so great and waighty causes are to be guided by the most high God, euen by the light of his sacred worde . . . Among other bookes of the holy Scripture, this Reuelation doth giue both special instruction and direction, and also incouragement vnto these warres.[25]

The Protestant princes, says Gifford, "are the ministers of the true Gospell upon earth, and all the right valiant men of warre which fight with the material sworde against Antichrist."[26] Jewel's spiritual reading has been literalized and materialized. The physical sword of the righteous prince has replaced the spiritual armor of Ephesians donned by the Redcrosse Knight. Laurence Deios, in *That the Pope is That Antichrist,* observes that while faith and prayer are appropriate as "spiritual armour, . . . as men, we must arme our selues if neede require otherwise."[27] Anthony Marten asks: "When had euer England so iust a cause to fight as now? . . . When had we euer a more louing Prince to her subiects then now?"[28]

As the nation edged toward war with Spain and a general mood of crisis deepened, particularly after the execution of Mary Queen of Scots made armed conflict inevitable, apocalyptic commentary, increasingly politicized, intensified the already vital role demanded of the prince by the events of the Reformation. In 1593 John Napier writes to James VI of Scotland in *A Plaine Discouery of the Whole Reuelation of Saint Iohn* that "it is the dutie of Gods seruants in this age, interpreters of Prophecies, as well as (according to examples of Prophets) to incourage and inanimate Princes, to be ready against that greate day of the Lords reuenge."[29] James himself has already virtually invited such a call-to-arms. His own apocalyptic pronouncement of 1588 warns that Antichrist has "sent out the Iesuites, his last and most pernicious vermin, to stirre vp the Princes of the earth his slaues . . . And are not the armies presently assembled, yea vpon the very point of their execution in France against the saints there? In Flanders for the like?"[30]

James's urgency characterizes the moment. The Armada and its attendant national furor heightened the expectation, already prevalent from Luther and Bale on, that the Reformation signalled the End.[31] After the Armada, exegetes assume a combative posture far different from Jewel's pacific confidence that preaching will bring victory. English Protestants see themselves not as preachers but as warriors, determined to trounce Antichrist with the force of dire arms.[32] Their exegesis takes on a bellicose tone commensurate with the current mood of political crisis. Napier claims that Revelation entreats "most speciallie of the destruction of the Antichristian seat, citie, and kingdome, doth directe the execution of that great work of Gods Iustice and iust iudgement to the kings of the earth."[33] Deios asserts that "popish legions . . . make warre vpon vs only for religion, & in those wars in *France* and *Germanie* & the low countries, & in all places where by inuasion or rebellion they can preuaile, haue made infinit slaughters."[34] Marten exhorts his countrymen to take up arms against "this very Antichrist" even as he asks God to "stretch out the Arme of Moses, that thy Christian Souldiers may valiantly fight for their Prince, their Countrey, and thy true Religion." He entreats God to "destroy their Armies, confound their forces, terrifie their Captaines. Scatter, breake, and sinke into the Sea, their huge and strong vessels."[35]

This militancy corresponds closely with shifts in foreign affairs and policy. From 1558 until the 1580s Elizabethan policy had been on the defensive, and relations with Philip II had been relatively amicable. But by the late 1580s foreign relations had deteriorated markedly. The

Netherlands, France, and Ireland were all areas of danger, and increasingly the English saw themselves sequestered by Roman Catholic adversaries, led of course by Spain. In the Netherlands the situation was especially perilous (especially after the fall of Antwerp in 1585), for the inviolability of England was, in the view of Elizabeth and her advisors, dependent upon the defense of the Low Countries. The danger from Spanish troops in those nearby lands was reinforced by hazards on other fronts: at home, fears persisted of papal plots against the Queen's life, carried out by the Jesuits, often in collaboration with the Spanish and (before 1586) Mary Queen of Scots; Irish resistance to English rule continued to prompt worries about European Roman Catholic intervention; the Roman Catholic Guise party in France became subsidized dependents of Philip II, leading to renewed anxieties about a Guise invasion of England led by Spanish troops.[36] The Armada invasion brought to a climax these mounting apprehensions, and the years following that heady event saw little diminution of the alarm over Roman Catholic encroachments. As Gifford puts it: "The enemies prepare themselues with mighty forces, threatening great terror vnto this land, euen as the waues of the sea, ready to ouerwhelme vs."[37] The passion of the apocalyptic commentators is that of the nation at large; the nationalistic zeal so marked in the commentary after 1588 is proportionate to unease about national self-preservation in the discourses of the moment.

Book V of *The Faerie Queene* responds to this historical urgency when in its second half it becomes both fully topical and apocalyptic. The national and historical drama now unfolds, and so the allegory shifts to the spacious arena sanctioned by the late Elizabethan apocalyptic habit of viewing political events of the present and recent past hermeneutically. It is appropriate, then, that the figures of the conflict assume the contrasting proportions of good and evil typical of apocalypse. Mercilla, figuring Elizabeth, a maiden queen of "soueraine grace" (V.8.17), is oppressed by that "mighty man" (8.18), the Souldan, figuring Philip II, who would slay her "sacred selfe" (8.19).[38] Upton in 1758 was the first to note the Souldan's associations with the Roman Catholic enemies of England, associations evident in the apocalyptic battle between Arthur and the Souldan.[39] The "pagan" is "[s]wearing, and banning most blasphemously" (8.28); he "bannes, and sweares, and rayles" (8.39). In view of the maritime threat the Armada epitomized, it is hermeneutically appropriate that the Souldan figure the Beast from the Sea that has upon its heads "the names of blasphemy" (Rev.13:1,5–7; cf. Dan.7:3,11:36).[40] The Souldan's activities illustrate how this Book employs simultaneously both apocalypse and its mediating post-Armada exegesis. Revelation and Daniel are the source of the Souldan's blaspheming; the commentary is the source of his "banning," one of the papacy's more notorious ecclesiastical practices, tirelessly denounced by the Reformers.

It is challenging to untangle the scriptural from the exegetical sources of the episode. The Roman Catholic Mass is condemned in Article 31 of the Thirty-Nine Articles as "blasphemous," an epithet with which the exegetes persistently malign the papacy.[41] In the same fashion, the Souldan, who "neither religion hath nor fay," is said to serve "Idols" (8.19), a term attached to Antichrist in apocalypse (e.g., Rev. 17:3 and gloss; 21:8; cf. Dan.11:31) as well as a common charge from the 1540s on in other anti-Catholic writings.[42] The Souldan is guilty of "cruell tyranny" (8.20) and is vilified as a "tyrant" (8.45), one of the favorite terms of execration heaped on the papacy throughout the period, especially by the apocalyptic commentators,[43] and an objurgation transferred to Philip as he became increasingly fearsome.[44] The battle between Arthur and the Souldan is based on both the triumphant accounts of the Armada "victory" as well as the victories in Revelation and Daniel. Acting the apocalyptic role of the conquering Christ, Arthur's arms "glister . . ." and shine "as bright, as doth the heauen sheene" (8.29), terrifying his enemy (as Alastair Fowler has noted) with a vision of Judgment (cf. Rev.1:16, 19:11–12, 22:16; cf. Dan.10:6). The aftermath is portrayed with eschatological joy: Arthur is declared "victour of that day" (8.51); Artegall's "warlike rout" is accomplished with "finall force" (8.50), when, Michael-like, he dispatches the pagan's followers "lyke wyld Goates" (8.50; cf. Rev.12:7; Matt 25:32–33). As Dent comments on the victory in Revelation 19: "Now all this is to be vnderstood of the battels betwixt the Papists and the Protestants in these last dayes."[45] The triumph over the Souldan, then, is modelled on a variety of apocalyptic battles as mediated by the commentary that saw Philip as the tyrant representative of Antichrist.

In this respect the Book is part of a wider cultural self-understanding, what we might label the discourse of foreign policy and also a newly developing discourse of nationalism. Post-Armada commentary contributes to this discourse by encouraging the nation to think of itself as oppressed, righteous, and engaged in a struggle under providential auspices. Critics earlier in this century make this point: Greenlaw maintains that the "whole Book treats of the danger to England from Spanish aggression"; Jones that "its main themes present different aspects of the Catholic danger in England, France, the Low Countries, and Ireland."[46] Recently Richard Helgerson has amplified our understanding of how the language of a developing nationalism shapes a variety of discourses in the period.[47] The rapid political shifts in the sixteenth century that lead English people by the 1590s to write about themselves as a "state," where they had not before, has startling manifestations; such changes can lead Aylmer (a post-Armada apocalypticist *avant la lettre*) to the conclusion that "God is English."[48]

Like other apocalyptic and patriotic polemic, the Souldan episode has little moral nuance, for the struggle is simply between right and wrong. Hence the poet claims that the Souldan "breakes all bonds of law and rules of right"; Adicia is "mortall foe to Iustice." The dichotomy is pellucid: the Souldan "[s]ought onely slaughter and auengement / But the braue Prince for honour and for right" (8.30). The apocalyptic outcome is suitably public and providential: "How worthily, by heauens high decree / Iustice that day of wrong herself had wroken" (8.44). As part of post-Armada apocalyptic commentary, the episode elicits a patriotic *frisson*, not to mention a quelling of fears about national self-preservation. It surely provided Spenser's original audience the same hopeful satisfaction that Dent does: "let us obserue for our comfort, that whensoeuer we shall see Kings and Captains, Nobles, and Potentates of the earth, being solicited by the Iesuites, priests, and False Prophet, to leuy great armies . . . they shal not preuaile, but bee vtterly ouerthrowne and destroyed. As in part we see fulfilled in the yeare our Lorde 1588 when the great and inuincible Armado of the Spaniards . . . came to Armegeddon. . . ."[49]

The long, vexed history of apocalyptic exegesis reflects the dichotomy of right and wrong it has found in its biblical originals. These dualities are also those of political polemic to which the genre has been tied throughout its history. Here, too, we see what has alienated so many readers of the Legend of Justice. The nation is at war, hemmed in by the enemies of truth, justice, and international Protestantism. Gough speaks for many later critics of the Book when he observes that "very recent history is seldom a fit matter for poetry, especially when the poet's country is engaged in a fierce national and religious struggle."[50] Doubtless, though, this is exactly why apocalypse attracted Spenser in this Book. Drawing upon the intense interest of apocalypse in justice, and with the example of both Bale and Foxe identifying the papacy as the source of injustice in Church history, post-Armada exegetes repeatedly appeal to supreme standards of justice, usually in political and military terms.[51] Addressing James VI, Napier

calls for "iustice to be done" against the "enemies of Gods Church, and
. . . most cruell oppressors." If James will "ministrate Iustice to them,
God the supreme Iudge shal ministrate Iustice to you against your
enemies."[52] Marten claims that the Spanish have "neither Iustice nor
religion, nor charity, nor conscience, nor yet good cause on their side. If
they had been iust, they would not have pretended peace, and yet swear
our destruction . . . neither have they God on their side."[53] Justice
derives from God in all apocalyptic commentary, most emphatically in
the post-Armada commentators, as it does in the Legend of Justice. The
power of the prince needs to uphold and defend that originating source
of her authority.[54] She engages her statecraft on behalf of both God and
justice: "Power is the right hand of iustice truely dight" (4.1). The proem
explicitly links this God-given virtue to the monarch:

> That powre [God] also doth to Princes lend,
> And makes them like himselfe in glorious sight,
> To sit in his owne seate, his cause to end,
> And rule his people right, as he doth recommend.
> (Proem 10)

Book V cannot be comprehended as apocalyptic commentary without appreciating, then, the role of Elizabeth in this text. Readers have
always seen the Queen in both Britomart and Mercilla, as warrior and
ruler. The imagery of apocalypse contributes significantly to Britomart's
vision in Isis Church; the New Jerusalem surely figures in the extended
description of Mercilla's throne and person. The two loci comprise the
iconographic centers of the Book, where the Queen's presence is felt
keenly. In Isis Church Britomart's vision before an "Idoll" (7.6,8) pro-
leptically summons up and transfigures apocalyptic imagery of later
cantos. Her "Moon-like Mitre" becomes a "Crowne of gold"; her "lin-
nen stole" a "robe of scarlet red"; she is "adorn'd with gems and iewels
manifold" (7.13). Imagery later associated with figures modelled on
the Whore and Antichrist (e.g., the scarlet robe and the mitre) in the
environment of Isis Church instead summons up the New Jerusalem
and also makes Britomart the Woman Clothed with the Sun. In her
subsequent dream vision she fights a flaming battle with a beast (a crocodile) that she overcomes with her rod (7.15).

With similar iconographic fluidity the description of Mercilla follows another great contest, the defeat of the Souldan. Her depiction,
too, taps a variety of scriptural and iconographic sources; unnoticed

perhaps are the echoes of the New Jerusalem (which itself follows a great victory in Revelation [cf. Rev.21:9–27]):

> Vpon a throne of gold full bright and sheene,
> Adorned all with gemmes of endlesse price . . .
> All ouer her a cloth of state was spred . . .
> Sunny beams . . . glistering like gold . . .
> Seemed those litle Angels did vphold
> The cloth of state, and on their purpled wings . . .
> Besides a thousand more of such, as sings
> Hymnes to high God, and carols heauenly things . . .
> Whilest kings and kesars at her feet did them prostrate.
>
> (9.27–30)

Both scenes have a nationalistic dimension. Britomart, the "Magnificke Virgin" (7.21) is promised union with Artegall, ultimate deliverance from the "raging flames, that many foes shall reare," and inheritance of her "countrey deare" (7.23). Mercilla's court recalls both Parliament and the grandeur of the Elizabethan court.[55]

But Elizabeth I in her own person, as it were, plays the leading apocalyptic role, right from the start in the Proem. Artegall is named as an "instrument" (Proem 11) of her justice, the only time any knight is joined so clearly to Elizabethan policy. The depiction of the Queen, one of the most fervent in Spenser's canon, is explicitly apocalyptic:

> Dread Souerayne Goddesse, that doest highest sit
> In seate of iudgement, in th'Almighties stead,
> And with magnificke might and wondrous wit
> Doest to thy people righteous doome aread
> That furthest Nations filles with awfull dread . . .
>
> (Proem 11; cf. Dan.7:13)

The "doome" (a word that has an apocalyptic career of its own in this Book: it is employed variously over twenty times) delivered to the Queen's subjects is a version of the divine doom, the ultimate justice of the Last Day when God shall sit in the "seate of iudgement" now occupied by the Queen. These lines reverberate throughout the final cantos, where, as the Proem has forecast, the "furthest Nations" are filled with "awfull dread" (cf. Rev.15.4). In the Proem the Queen exercises the authority attributed to her by some post-Armada exegetes, who praise her as the hope of Protestantism, the agent of divine retribution, and the instrument of justice.[56] They say, with Leonard Wright in his perfervid tract, *The Hunting of Antichrist* (1589), the Queen has "so hunted, tossed, and chased that Romish Antichrist, with all his superstitious trash and traditions, out of the forests of England: as (except by stealth in priuie corners) he dare not shew his head."[57] Gifford asserts that the Queen has "made the whore desolate and naked." Although "Antichrist and his adherents" will attempt the "subuersion of our religion, Queene, and countrie," the "wars and enterprises" of the "Romish beast" are "to smal purpose, vnlesse they could first supplant and destroy her Maiestie."[58]

Many critics have observed close affinities between the first and fifth Books. Like the Legend of Holiness, Book V turns to apcalypse as a generic model.[59] It is worth sketching the relation of the two Books to apocalypse, for the differences between each Book's handling of the genre suggest some of the distinctive features of the Legend of Justice. Florence Sandler has suggested that Book I be understood as apocalyptic insofar as Spenser read Revelation primarily as a moral and spiritual allegory where "historical" elements are subordinate.[60] Redcrosse's individual struggle to add "faith vnto [his] force" (I.1.19) compels the reader's attention as least as powerfully as the national saga that his story allegorizes. In Book V this situation is somewhat reversed, or at least considerably altered. The Legend of Justice, far from subordinating "historical elements," draws upon contemporary apocalyptic commentary that eagerly seeks historical and immediately topical application in Revelation. The struggles of the final cantos comprise not only or not even chiefly a spiritual warfare, but rather a literal, physical warfare, grounded in the material of history and politics. The difference partly resides in the general movement of the poem from the "private" virtues of the first half to the "public" virtues of the second half. In apocalyptic terms, Book I dramatizes the individual's thwarting of Antichrist by faith and the Word at least as much as (and arguably more than) it allegorizes the fortunes of the national Church. Book V, however, stresses that feature of Elizabethan apocalyptic commentary preoccupied with the nation's overthrow of Antichrist. Its contests have historical, national referents, impinging daily on the original readership. Furthermore, in the earlier Book contact with scripture is more direct and immediate than in the later Book, where apocalypse is mediated more thoroughly by contemporary commentary.

A consequence of these differences, then, is that Book V uses apocalypse more obliquely than Book I. In the earlier Book Redcrosse journeys toward the New Jerusalem encountering en route figures modelled on those from Revelation. The False Prophet and the Whore of Babylon, to take two outstanding examples, are incarnated in Archimago and Duessa. In Book V the relationship to apocalypse is less systematic and direct. The characters are not modelled as closely and uniformly on figures from Revelation. Instead we find refractions of apocalyptic figures in the characters of Book V. The chief villains of the Book—Radigund, Duessa, the Souldan, Geryoneo, Grantorto—form a composite portrait of Antichrist.[61] Furthermore, these characters are heavily bridged by contemporary exegesis, which itself refracts Antichrist. Some commentators locate Spain in the Beast, others in the Whore, still others in Antichrist.

Let us take Duessa as a case in point. Her manifestation in Book I is anything but simple; but there is no doubt, from her first appearance on, that we are encouraged to recall the Whore of Babylon. Those powerful affiliations remain through her exposure and defeat. In Book V Duessa has a rather more limited role, of course, as an avatar of Mary Queen of Scots, and, as such, she is indebted to the Elizabethan conception of Mary as the representative of a pernicious "papism." Among Protestants Mary was commonly regarded as one of the current embodiments of the Whore or, as she was called in the English Parliament, a "professed member of Antichrist."[62] Duessa is a political threat, and the allegory treats her accordingly. With typical Spenserian flexibility, the episode of her trial pays almost no attention to what had been a principal focus in Book I, her danger as a seductive woman.[63] The gloss of the 1560 Geneva Bible at Revelation 17:2,3 concurs: "Antichrist compared to a Harlot because he seduceth the worlde with vaine wordes." Nor does the post-Armada commentary treat the Whore as an erotically alluring woman, but rather as a political and even a military peril. Her role in Book V is almost exclusively public; she has virtually nothing of the personal menace she had in the earlier Book. The judgment delivered on Duessa in Book V is political, mediated by the apocalyptic commentary. Hence the eschatological diction: she is "brought to her sad doome" (9.42); her "doome" is heard "a-right," and she is "damned" (10.4). Furthermore, this judgment is rendered in the international context favored by the late Elizabethan exegetes: "And then the law of *Nations* gainst her rose/ . . . Next gan Religion gainst her to impute/ High Gods beheast . . . and lastly *Iustice*" (9.44; cf. Dan.7:26).[64]

The judgment against Duessa, political and transparently figuring the trial of Mary Queen of Scots, is the second defeat in the poem of the Scottish monarch, for she is recognizable in Radigund. Mary, then, is twice demonized in this Book (or more—since her mother was a Guise, she is also implicated in the Bourbon episode). Radigund is labelled a "harlot" and a "Tyrannesse" (6.11), terms from both apocalypse (Whore) and its exegesis (tyrant). The combat between Britomart and Radigund signifies not merely the triumph of Elizabeth over Mary but also a version of an apocalyptic battle urged on the Protestant prince against England's Roman Catholic adversaries. Indeed after the contest Britomart "there as Princess rained / . . . changing all that forme of common weale" (7.42). She rules as the idealized mighty sovereign, who, through power of arms, institutes a just peace: "There she continu'd for a certaine space" (7.45). Britomart brings about what in the Proem is attributed to the Queen: a political peace issuing from her might.

It is significant that intervening between the Souldan episode and the Duessa episode is the incident with Malengin. This protean figure, with his numerous literary forebears, has been persuasively identified as an allegorical representation of the Jesuits.[65] Known for their treasonous guile and their efforts to assassinate the Queen, the Jesuits are the targets of ceaseless excoriation in apocalyptic commentary and elsewhere. The 1560 Geneva gloss of the "croking frogs" of Revelation 16:3 singles out the Jesuits, "who speak nothing but lies all manner of craftie deceite." Dent glosses the same verse similarly and adds that the Jesuits show forth the Harlot and Antichrist, "liuing dayly in whoredom, Sodomitrie, and al kind of outragious beastlinesse."[66] Malengin epitomizes "forged guile" (7.7), one of the obstacles to justice. His deviousness also aligns him with Despaire, on whom he appears modelled in part. Both live in hollow caves (I.9.33,35; V.9.10) and have wild hair and hollow eyes. Malengin's "crafty" practices and "forged guyle" (9.25), his "guilefull words" that his "false intent to shade" (9.12), his "slights and iugling feates . . . of legierdemayne" (9.13): all recall Despaire's subtly deceptive rhetoric. Despaire himself is certainly modelled in part on the biblical False Prophet (e.g., Rev.19:20) an especially pernicious example of religious abuse.[67] In "quoting" himself, a typically Spenserian as well as an apocalyptic trait, the poet draws attention to the uses he makes of scriptural narrative technique. By recalling (among others) both Despaire and the biblical False Prophet, Malengin fits the bill as a cunning enemy of justice. As the representative of the

Jesuits, he is vilified as a religious and political enemy of the nation, one of the exegetes' chief straw men.

These three consecutive episodes — the Souldan, Malengin, Duessa — incorporate the apocalyptic triumvirate of Beast, False Prophet, and Whore. Together they sum up this Book's emphasis on "forged guile, / And open force" (7.7) as the principal antagonists of justice.[68] All three stand in for Antichrist, acknowledged throughout the Reformation for his ghastly strength as well as his deceit (Jewel: "He is suttle and cunning, hee that shal deceiue the learned and the wise."[69]). In post-Armada commentary, too, Antichrist is condemned for both his duplicity and his might,[70] but, as England's Roman Catholic enemies figure more ominously in the national life, force becomes the dominant theme. Especially in the wake of the invasion, commentators concentrate on the military power of "the Romish beast and his company," who "prepare themselues with mighty forces, threatening great terrour vnto this land, euen as the waues of the sea, ready to ouerwhelme vs."[71] Geryoneo and Grantorto impress their brutality on the final cantos, when the allegory downplays earlier emphasis on guile. Given the contemporary dread of invasion and other military depredations, it is not surprising that in the international episodes the preponderance of indictment falls on force.

The locus of these fears in Book V, as in other political discourse of the period, is Spain. Anticipation of Spanish hostility, not to mention actual examples of it, is of the greatest urgency in the last two decades of the Elizabethan reign. Hence Spain is repeatedly detracted in apocalyptic exegesis, which finds considerable evidence in scripture of Spanish perfidy as well as its ultimate vanquishing.[72] It bears examining how Philip II is depicted in the Legend of Justice. Besides his most obvious manifestation as the Souldan, he is reproduced in Geryoneo, Grantorto, perhaps even in Dolon and in the Samient episode.[73] His role in this Book reflects his multiple international crimes in late Elizabethan discourse. He was held responsible for plots to assassinate the Queen (Dolon), to monopolize the seas (Samient), for the oppression of the Low Countries (Geryoneo), the troubles in France (Burbon), and the subversion of Ireland (Grantorto). Philip is demonized repeatedly in the Book, even more strenuously than Mary. He is also crushed repeatedly. That he is variously condemned speaks to his minatory role, one commensurate with the historical facts of Philip's seemingly ubiquitous presence in Western Europe. The multiplicity of Spenser's portrayal of Philip is unmatched in The Faerie Queene by that of any historic personage, with the exception of Elizabeth I. Philip's daunting presence in the Book bears witness to his military, political, and religious importance and to the magnitude of the anxieties he instilled in his Protestant English contemporaries.

His continuous re-appearance also reflects his apocalyptic function. The narrative principles of incremental repetition and overlapping work powerfully throughout apocalypse, not only from Daniel to Revelation and other Christian loci, but also within the confines of a single text. Antichrist enjoys numerous modes and faces in scripture; Philip and Spain have multiple modes and faces in post-Armada commentary. Sometimes Philip is identified as the Beast, at other times Antichrist, even, in the "maiden face" of Geryoneo's monster, as the Whore.[74] The fluidity of Philip's representation in this Book exemplifies the apocalyptic view of the world, where a multiplicity of figures represent either good or evil. Throughout Reformation commentary apocalyptic figures are interchangeable. The numerous trouncings of Philip express the longing of apocalypse for the undoing of the wicked and the triumph of divine justice.

In the Belge episode Philip appears most complexly as a politico-religious malefactor. We need not examine these episodes in detail, because Kenneth Borris has recorded conclusively the multiple correspondences between the episode and Revelation, particularly the ways its monsters are modelled on apocalyptic beasts. Borris makes clear how Geryoneo refers to both the papacy and Spain, "the monstrosities of tyrannical government and religion," and he has pointed out how Spanish rule in the Low Countries had become a byword for tyranny.[75] Hence Geryoneo is "tyrannizing, and oppressing all" (10.14), forcing the people of Belge's land to "beare the yoke of inquisition" (10.27). His parent Geryone, "that whylome in Spaine so sore was dred / For his huge powre and great oppression" (10.9), expresses English fear of the Spanish menace. "Are not all places full of forraine powres?" (10.23) asks Belge. She herself, a Woman in the Wilderness who has been banished "mongst the croking frogs" (10.23; cf. Rev.16:3), is a Mercilla manquée, a monarch shorne of her rightful sovereignty by a predatory invader. She embodies the most sinister English dread for their own monarch and nation. English distress over the impingement of those "forraine powres" on the nation's autonomy, as well as panic over the loss of Antwerp, formed the basis of Elizabethan intervention in the Low Countries. This worry is reflected in the commentary as outrage against the Spanish Antichrist. One may then modify Borris's remark that "it would be wrong to identify the abuses of Gerioneo and his

Beast with Roman Catholicism exclusively. The episode allegorically attacks political as well as religious tyranny."[76] For the post-Armada apocalypticists these tyrannies are inseparable, and so it is in this Book.

The description of Geryoneo's Chapel is worth looking at from this perspective. It is described fully twice (10.28–29; 11.19–20), with detailed horror rare even in Spenser's most vivid depictions of idolatry. Geryoneo has erected a "cursed Idole," proclaims it God, and offers it in "sinfull sacrifice / The flesh of men" (10.28; cf. Dan.7:19). A "hideous monster" accepts these sacrifices, one whose "dreadful shape was neuer seene of none / That liues on earth" (10.29). In the next canto Belge repeats the description, adding that before being fed to the monster on the altar the victims are tortured and "burnt in flame" (11.19–20). A "huge great Beast it was" (11.23) and recognized since Gough's edition as an allegory of the Spanish inquisition and its idolatrous papism.[77] As conflated allusions to the Mass and the Spanish Inquisition, these re-iterated depictions comprise an unusually ferocious attack, even for this period, on Roman Catholic religion.

They are surpassed in their zeal, however, by the narratives of Arthur's battles, first against Geryoneo and even more in the subsequent combat against the monster beneath Geryone's altar. Critics often remark that the defeat of Geryoneo recalls Arthur's defeat of Orgoglio. But the two contests differ in this major detail: Orgoglio is a mythical giant; Geryoneo refers quite specifically to a historic personage (or nation, led by Philip). This battle is in turn outstripped in its violence by Arthur's encounter with the Beast in Geryoneo's Chapel. The event is portrayed as an apocalyptic battle, which we may legitimately see as the English wish-fulfillment in the conflict with Spain. Belge hopes Arthur's "victorious arme will not yet cease / Till ye haue rooted all the *relickes* out / Of that vilde race" (11.18; emphasis added). Arthur does just this. As Geryoneo goes down to defeat, he "curst and band, and blasphemies forth threw" and "gnasht his teeth" (11.12; cf. Matt.25:30; Rev.1-6: 10,11; Dan.7:11,12,26) — a conflation of terms exemplary of how the commentary bridges apocalypse and the poem. Having begun to rid Belge of that "yoke of inquisition" (10.27), Arthur then fells the beast, a creature of "fowle blasphemous speaches . . . and bitter curses" (11.28).

As religious invective, the episode is matchless. The narrator fiercely attacks Spain; the hatred of Roman Catholicism (the "hideous monster" [11.20] in its defeat becomes, as Borris points out, a "deformed Masse" [11.32])[78] is the equal of any contemporary anti-Catholic diatribe. Philip is demonized here even more bitterly than in the Souldan episode. The allegory is becoming more belligerent with each incarnation of the Spanish monarch. The intensity of the episode must lead one to conclude that, if it does not actually celebrate violence in the name of religion, it surely relishes the violence deemed necessary to defend religion and punish the sacreligious. After the slaying—a public gesture, as it were, that is this Book's eschatological counterpart to Redcrosse's slaying of the dragon as well as a repetition of the vanquishing of the Souldan—the public reaction echoes those found in Revelation: "Then all the people, which beheld that day, / Gan shout aloud, that vnto heauen it rong" (11.34; cf. Rev.19:1; Dan.7:9–10).

In the Burbon episode Philip is attacked yet again, albeit indirectly, for it was generally reported, quite accurately, that the rebellious subjects of Henry IV were supported by Spain. The two episodes—Belge and Burbon—need to be understood as a kind of apocalyptic diptych. They represent the two approaches we have seen taken by the exegetes to the question of how Antichrist is to be defeated, by preaching the Word or by wielding the Sword. Arthur's success against Geryoneo and his Beast answers the call of the post-Armada exegetes that the prince's arms smite Antichrist. On the other hand, Artegall's encounter with Burbon is presented as an example of what may be expected if Antichrist is confronted mainly by the more pacific, traditional Reformist strategy of preaching the Word to enhance faith.

The poet takes considerable trouble to link the episode expressly with Book I and its concern with faith as the agency of redemption. Burbon announces that he had been "dubbed knight / By a good knight, the knight of *Redcrosse*" from whom he received his shield with his "deare Redeemers badge vpon the bosse" (11.53)—a shield he has forsaken. He presents his problem as one of faith: he has been "forelore" (49) by Flourdelis, who has withdrawn "her faith" (50) from Burbon. Artegall upbraids Flourdelis, who is figured as a Harlot, "richly clad / In roiall robes, and many Iewels dight," (60) and impervious to "prayer [and] meed" (61). Furthermore, Burbon thanks Artegall for "sauing him from daungerous despaire" (48). But the episode is (in the words of one commentator) "remarkably unheroic."[79] Artegall barely rescues anybody; indeed he must deploy Talus to effectuate what limited heroic success the episode has. In apocalyptic terms the questions are clear: can Artegall "save" Burbon by means of the Word? Is preaching the Word of faith enough to defeat Antichrist, as earlier Elizabethan apocalypticists had averred? Can France be rescued from the forces of the Beast by non-violent measures?

Here, I believe, we may detect a reason why Spenser chose to place this episode in the same canto as the defeat of Geryoneo. The Argument to the final canto indicates that the Burbon episode may have originally been included in canto 12, along with the Grantorto episode. Mrs. Bennett's conjecture that a last minute change took place as the poem went to press is supported by other bibliographic evidence.[80] But the final disposition of the episodes is imaginatively just: Arthur's conquest of Geryoneo and Artegall's meeting with Burbon belong together in the same canto as twinned examples of how the faithful may confront Antichrist. Arthur's purely military exploit is unequivocally triumphant: the power of his arms gets the better of the Beast. Artegall's rescue of Burbon is patently less heroic, for he employs almost no physical might of his own but relies rather on almost exclusively verbal resources to end the episode. His homily about a "breach of faith" (62) seems feeble when compared to Arthur's victorious purging of Belge's lands.

The episode asks us to compare Burbon's situation with that of Redcrosse for this very purpose. For Redcrosse, too, the issue is one of faith. Una's salvific words about "heauenly mercies" and "grace" (I.9.53) snatch him from the brink of suicide in the Cave of Despaire and direct him to the House of Holiness, where he learns to deepen his faith so as to destroy the dragon. The Burbon episode, with its explicit links to Redcrosse's situation, calls into question the reliance placed in the earlier Book on the Word of faith as the most efficacious means of foiling Antichrist. Arthur's sword rids Belge's land of bestial "forraine powres"; Artegall's non-belligerent homily fails to rid Burbon's land of its molesters. Burbon, of course, is freed from his assailants, at least temporarily, but the episode lacks the aura of a final victory or the conclusive emergence of the good. Flourdelis has been held "by force" (11.54), and the two episodes taken as companions suggest that force may be needed to free her for the long term. As the poet says, "No faith so firme . . . that may enduren long" (12.1), a truth to which "[w]itnesse may Burbon be" (12.2). Certainly the historical events motivating the allegory would bear out such a disheartened conclusion. Elizabeth bowed to the dictates of Realpolitik in not opposing the right of Henry IV, a newly converted Catholic, to sit on the French throne in 1595, a practical political compromise that could not but offend those who advocated an aggressive opposition to the advances in Europe of Antichrist. In the international political arena, where he rages, the Word alone is insufficient: "loue of Lordship and lands / Made [Burbon] become most faithlesse and vnsound" (12.2). Although Henry IV enjoyed English support, his recent apostasy could hardly be seen as affirming the value of non-aggressive tactics against Rome. The post-Armada apocalypticists assert instead that the Book of Revelation encourages war and "setteth forth how the Lord himselfe doth as it were sound the trumpet vnto this battaile against *Babel*, saying Reward her euen as she hath rewarded you, and giue her double according to her works, and in the cup that she hath filled vnto you fil her the double."[81]

In canto 12 this is exactly what happens. The previous paired episodes of Geryoneo and Burbon dramatize the superiority of Arthur's weaponry in overpowering the Beast. Why, then, is the Belge episode not placed at the Book's conclusion? If that episode were the Book's ultimate, we could say confidently that the Legend of Justice replicates the recommendations of other post-Armada apocalyptic exegesis: use the sword to subdue Antichrist. Instead, this Book concludes with not only the most vexing and ambiguous test case in English foreign policy but also the unleashing of yet one more Beast, the Blattant Beast. Why is the Irena episode last, where it is certain to generate doubt and protest and controversy? Why does this Book move from chivalric rescue of beleaguered Belge to the ironies and perplexities of the contest on Irena's behalf?

Book V has always been faulted for its presentation of violence. Critics have noted that its presiding genius appears to be Talus, his merciless iron flail mowing down all resistance. If we examine the second half of the Book under its apocalyptic aegis, we find that violence is legitimated in biblical terms. When Gifford cries out for vengeance against the foreign Antichrist, when Dent forecasts the beneficent slaughter of thousands of the enemy, when exegetes call out for the shedding of blood as demanded by prophecy, the violence of Book V seems less extreme, more the pronouncement of a nation at war, hedged in by bloodthirsty enemies. Post-Armada commentaries are often calls-to-arms, based on fears of persecution, responses to the crises of the moment. Richard McCabe has noted that the Book's villains are more easily defeated once transformed into monsters.[82] However that may be, Book V is but one of a number of texts of the day to treat the enemies of England like beasts from Daniel and Revelation. Biblical apocalypse dehumanizes God's enemies, and much of its exegesis treats the enemies of the faithful similarly. (Dent: "The popish armies [will] go downe by heapes in all countries and kingdomes, and be made meate for the foules of the aire.")[83] Hermeneutics is used to validate bloodshed, particularly when the exegete advocates the "material sword" as the divinely sanctioned weapon to destroy Antichrist.

Little sanction is needed in the case of the Souldan, who is, after all, an invader, and a universally loathed one. There can be no question why Spenser violates chronology and places this first among the international episodes. From a contemporary English perspective the moral issue is plain and needs little justifying. But as the righteous triumphs of self defense give way to the quandaries of foreign intervention and colonialism, the allegory becomes more ambiguous. Grantorto is both man and monster, "[t]yrant" (12.25) and "[g]iant," less monstrous than Geryoneo's beast but more so than the Souldan: "whether man or monster one could scarse discerne" (12.15).

The episode is presented in similar apocalyptic terms to its predecessors. The battle is heralded by trumpets to take place on a "dismall [i.e., *dies mal*] day" (12.11) — an Eschaton of sorts but also morally overcast. As she awaits the "doome of her decaye," Irena "no redemption nigh . . . did nor heare nor see" (12.11). The Burbon episode has demonstrated the insufficiency of defeating Antichrist by peaceful, homiletic means. Artegall now follows the example set by Arthur in performing apocalyptic violence so prosperously in the Belge episode. And indeed at first Artegall proves the equal of Arthur and fully overcomes Grantorto. He acts out the Arthurian role of both Michael and Christ, who are themselves interchangeable in apocalyptic commentary. Having quashed this "tyrant" (12.3) in the fashion advocated by the exegetes, Artegall faces a problem that has plagued English rulers in Ireland since: "[h]ow to reforme that ragged common-weale" (12.26). Here is an issue not addressed by the exegetes, who confidently champion Arthur's policy and who (to my knowledge) make no mention of Ireland.

But, better informed by bitter experience, Spenser does, both in Book V and in *A View of the Present State of Ireland*. Considerable notice has been taken of this document in recent years, particularly its links to the Irena episode.[84] We may best approach the *View* from its estimates of the religion of Ireland. When the interlocutors turn specifically to the issue, Irenius laments that the Irish are "all Papistes by theire profession but in the same so blindelye and brutishly." His phrase implies a kind of patronizing exoneration, for indeed "what other Could they learne then suche trashe as was taughte them[?]" The Irish had been instructed with all other Christians ("[c]orrupted with . . . Popishe trumperie") to "drinke that Cupp of fornicacion with which the purple

Harlott had then made all nacions drunken." Therefore "purgacions" are needed to remove these pernicious practices, but they will have to await quieter times: "it is ill time to preache amongest swordes." Instead of endorsing the violent coercion he sees imperative to reform most other aspects of Irish society, Irenius implies that non-violent preaching will best serve the purpose of bringing religious truth to Ireland. He sets up an opposition between preaching and violence that we have seen elsewhere and develops it in this section of the *View,* as he segues from matters of religion to matters of civil order. He does not, in fact, keep the terms in opposition but rather as complements. Reformation must come first in matters of government, only thereafter in religion. He posits that religious reform will be the effect of governmental reform. When Eudoxus asks how such "reformacion" is to be achieved, Irenius responds that "the sworde" must help bring into effect "[l]awes and ordinaunces." By this he means the "Royall power of the Prince." Though he disavows widespread slaughter and endorses only limited bloodshed as a short-term policy, Irenius' proposed solution to Irish disorder is that of the exegetes and Book V: "must needs this violente meanes be used." [85]

The proximities, associations, and connections among colonial policy, religion and violence in the *View* are distanced in Book V by its multivalent and syncretic allegorical methods. The sharp pragmatism of the *View* is blunted in the allegory—although perhaps not thoroughly enough, for *Realpolitik* emerges despite the amelioration and has alienated modern readers. As an apocalypse the Book makes no attempt in the final victories to downplay the bloodshed or its celebration. To impose on the allegory a distaste for violence is both sentimental and anachronistic—especially against a foreign enemy, especially in a religious war—as any cursory reading of the chronicles demonstrates. Throughout *The Faerie Queene* we find ample evidence of violence; it appears to embarrass and outrage twentieth century (idealist) critics, however, chiefly when the allegory becomes "historical" or "topical." Religious discourse has always been deployed to justify war ("neither is God on their side"), and this Book is no exception. Scripture and its commentary serve the purpose, as they have in countless cultures and crises, of legitimating aggression.

Book V is distinctive not in advocating warfare to enhance the aims of foreign policy nor in its harnessing of scripture and hermeneutics to justify the goals and methods of the prince. What finally makes Book V unusual as a commentary on contemporary history is its conclusion.

One presumes that Spenser could have chosen to place the Belge episode last or to give the Irena episode a Belge-like triumph and end the Book at that. Had Spenser elected some such course he would have been following one set down by his exegetical contemporaries in locating the ideal patterns of apocalypse behind the chaotic particulars of history. In fact, the Belge episode reflects just such a plan of action, for its unqualified triumphs do not conform closely to the often ignoble events of Elizabethan intervention in the Low Countries. Instead, though, the Book ends on the distressing notes of the inconclusive Irena episode, followed by the unleashing of the Blattant Beast.

It seems certain that the final stanzas are intended to provide an unsettling conclusion — or inconclusiveness — to the issues raised in the international episodes. The hags Envy and Detraction represent two more Harlot figures, more deformed than any others in the Book, and the Blattant Beast is obviously designed in part on the beasts of apocalypse. These "griesly creatures" (12.28) resurrect the Book's emphasis on deceit (the hags "weaue false tales" [12.36], "make much worse by telling / And take great ioy to publish it to many," [12.35]) rather more than force, although they are nothing if not aggressive. They reflect the emphasis throughout the Book (indeed throughout the Spenserian canon) on fraudulent speech. Like blasphemy, with which it is consonant, this speech cannot easily be contained.[86] (Bonfont's tongue is nailed to a post for having "blaspheme[d]" Mercilla "for forged guyle," 9.25.) On the other hand, the coloration of the final vignette is decidedly domestic. The malice of these creatures seems contained at least by the borders of England: gone is the interest in foreign affairs motivating the allegory for several cantos. Nonetheless, when the final stanzas are examined from the apocalyptic perspective encouraged by the second half of the Book, we may discern how hesitant the Book has been to advance a complete eschatology. The widespread Reformation belief in an imminent End is not part of this Book's apocalypticism. The final dour notes suggest that evil will continue to rule the world indefinitely. Most readers have felt that the ending suggests a deep skepticism about the operations of justice. In fact, such a doubtful vision accords with the apocalyptic view of temporal justice. History cries out for a providential judge to dispel its corruptions and impose a higher form of justice. But as Merlin says to Britomart in his prophecy in Book III: "yet the end is not" (III.3.50). This Book is an Apocalypse Postponed.[87]

The ending of the Book conforms closely with the image of the present advanced in the proem: the world "growes daily wourse and wourse"

(Proem 1), as it moves "toward . . . dissolution" (Proem 4) and its "last ruinous decay" (Proem 6). However fervently the prince may be looked to for relief from injustice, her might is limited and evil is widespread. The apocalyptic view of the world comprehends human failure as deeply as tragedy does. The Eschaton may be imminent, but it is also delayed. Artegall is no exception to the rule that Spenser's heroes, like the policy of the Queen whom Artegall represents, are radically limited. No more than Redcrosse does he establish a New Jerusalem. We are not even vouchsafed a vision of it. Nor, for that matter, can he so much as "reforme that ragged common-weale" (12.26). Apocalypse and its exegesis dwell on the degradations of the present. Few see much hope of human redress of that deterioration. What future the world has will be marked by chaos and suffering.

Lake Forest College

NOTES

An earlier version of this essay was presented at Spenser at Kalamazoo, 1991, where I benefited from the responsive comments of William Sessions. I am also indebted to the expert advice of Anne Lake Prescott and Clark Hulse at later stages of this essay. My thanks, as usual, go to the Newberry Library for making available to me not only its vast resources but also a carrel from which to inspect them.

1. William Perkins, *Works* (London, 1618), vol. III, p. 467. Katherine R. Firth, *The Apocalyptic Tradition in Reformation Britain 1530–1645,* (Oxford: Oxford University Press, 1979), 151–53, discusses the apocalyptic significance of the year 1588.

2. I have learned the most from the following historians: Richard Bauckham, *Tudor Apocalypse* (Abingdon: Sutton-Courtenay Press, 1978); Paul Christianson, *Reformers and Babylon: English Apocalyptic Visions from the Reformation to the Eve of the Civil War* (Toronto: University of Toronto Press, 1978); Bryan W. Ball, *A Great Expectation: Eschatological Thought in English Protestantism to 1660* (Leiden: Brill, 1975); Katherine R. Firth, *The Apocalyptic Tradition;* Bernard Capp, "The Political Dimension of Apocalyptic Thought," in *The Apocalypse in English Renaissance Thought and Literature: Patterns, Antecedents, and Repercussions,* ed. C. A. Patrides and Joseph A. Wittreich, Jr. (Ithaca: Cornell University Press, 1984), 93–124. Although (or perhaps because) it is a literary study, Joseph Anthony Wittreich, Jr., *Visionary Poetics: Milton's Tradition and His Legacy* (San Marino: Huntington Library, 1979) illuminates the whole tradition of apocalyptic and its exegesis.

3. For example, Michael O'Connell, *Mirror and Veil: The Historical Dimension of Spenser's "Faerie Queene"* (Chapel Hill: University of North Carolina Press, 1977), 147–60: "The Legend of Justice fails finally to be prophetic poetry" (p. 156).

4. Two recent historicist treatments are especially provocative: Jonathan Goldberg, *James I and the Politics of Literature: Jonson, Shakespeare, Donne, and Their Contemporaries* (Baltimore: Johns Hopkins University Press, 1983), 2–11; Clark Hulse,

"Spenser, Bacon, and the Myth of Power," in *The Historical Renaissance: New Essays on Tudor and Stuart Culture,* ed. Heather Dubrow and Richard Strier (Chicago: University of Chicago Press, 1988), 316–46.

5.   David Norbrook, *Poetry and Politics in the English Renaissance* (London: Routledge and Kegan Paul, 1984), 133–36; John N. King, *Spenser's Poetry and the Reformation Tradition* (Princeton: Princeton University Press, 1990), 106–9, 227–29. King's insights into the relation of *The Faerie Queene* to English Protestantism are indispensable.

6.   Kenneth Borris, *Spenser's Poetics of Prophecy in "The Faerie Queene" V* (Victoria: English Literary Studies, 1990). Borris's monograph is a model of careful scholarship. He performs the rare feat of re-orienting critical understanding of a major work. I have benefited throughout from his study, although I disagree at various points. Borris makes no reference to the exegesis of the post-Armada apocalypticists and does not place the poem among other exegetical texts of the late Elizabethan era. Nor does he account for the apocalyptic features of the Book before the tenth canto. In notes to the following pages I will merely touch upon my chief debts to his work as well as our divergences.

7.   Angus Fletcher, *The Prophetic Moment: An Essay on Spenser* (Chicago: University of Chicago Press, 1971), 4, notes that Spenser "looks not to the future as a prophet but to the past, and even more, to the present." Fletcher's essay illuminates many features of Spenser's archetypes and their relation to prophecy, though he is not concerned with apocalypticism in detail.

8.   Jan van der Noot, *A Theatre for Voluptuous Worldlings* (London, 1569), sigs. D3ᵛ-D6ʳ. For useful commentary on the place of *A Theatre* in the Reformation see J. A. Van Dorsten, *The Radical Arts: First Decade of an Elizabethan Renaissance* (Leiden and London: Oxford University Press, 1970), 75–85; and Carl Rasmussen, "'Quietnesse of Minde': *A Theatre For Worldlings* as a Protestant Poetics," in *Spenser Studies* I (1980), ed. Patrick Cullen and Thomas P. Roche, Jr. (Pittsburgh: University of Pittsburgh Press, 1980), 3–27.

9.   For a comprehensive survey of Spenser's references to Antichrist see Joseph A. Wittreich, Jr., "Apocalypse," in *The Spenser Encyclopedia,* ed. A. C. Hamilton et al. (Toronto: University of Toronto Press, 1990), 46–48. Wittreich's article distills his copious knowledge of the subject, and I have found it rewarding at several points in research for this essay.

10.   There are three indispensable studies of the relation of Book I to Revelation: Josephine Waters Bennett, *The Evolution of "The Faerie Queene"* (Chicago: University of Chicago Press, 1942), 110–22; John E. Hankins, *Source and Meaning in Spenser's Allegory: A Study of "The Faerie Queene"* (Oxford: Clarendon Press, 1971), 99–127; Joseph Anthony Wittreich, Jr., *Visionary Poetics,* 59–78.

11.   Katherine Firth, *The Apocalyptic Tradition,* 23–26.

12.   Bernard McGinn, "Revelation," in *The Literary Guide to the Bible,* ed. Robert Alter and Frank Kermode (Cambridge: Harvard University Press, 1987), 529.

13.   Richard Bauckham, *Tudor Apocalypse,* 13. I am indebted to Bauckham's definitive exposition; he is especially lucid on the early sixteenth century exegetes, 68–90, 113–44.

14.   John Bale, *The Ymage of Both Churches* (London, 1550), sig A3ᵛ. See also Leslie P. Fairfield, *John Bale: Mythmaker for the English Reformation* (West Lafayette: Purdue University Press, 1976), 50–85.

15.   Richard Bauckham, *Tudor Apocalypse,* pp. 13, 125. See also V. Norskov Olsen, *John Foxe and the Elizabethan Church* (Berkeley and Los Angeles: University of California Press, 1973); Katherine Firth, *The Apocalyptic Tradition,* 69–110.

16.   Peter Lake, "The Significance of the Elizabethan Identification of the Pope as Antichrist," *Journal of Ecclesiastical History* 31 (1980): 161–78; Bauckham, *Tudor Apocalypse,* 91–112.

17.   William Fulke, *A Sermon Preached at Hampton Court* (London, 1574), sig. Aiv^r.

18.   "The Political Dimension," p. 94.

19.   John N. King, *Tudor Royal Iconography: Literature and Art in an Age of Religious Crisis* (Princeton: Princeton University Press, 1989), pp. 154–57; Kenneth Borris, *Spenser's Poetics of Prophecy,* 29–30.

20.   John Aylmer, *An Harborwe For Faithfull and Truwe Subiectes* (London, 1559), sig. R3^r.

21.   John Foxe, *Acts and Monuments,* ed. Josiah Pratt, 8 vols. (London: Religious Tract Society, 1931), vol. 8, pp. 673–79. These pages reward the student of apocalyptic, not least for the intimate connections Foxe avers among the accession of the Queen, the downfall of papal tyranny, and the triumph of justice.

22.   Bernard McGinn, "Revelation," p. 535; Richard Bauckham, *Tudor Apocalypse,* 129–30.

23.   John Jewel, *Upon the Second Epistle to the Thessalonians* (London, 1583), 362–63.

24.   Arthur Dent, *The Ruine of Rome* (London, 1603), 254.

25.   George Gifford, *Sermons Vpon the Whole Booke of the Revelation* (London, 1596), sig. A3^v.

26.   George Gifford, *Sermons,* 380. Compare I. L., *The Birth, Purpose, and Mortall Wound of the Romish Holie League* (London, 1589), sig. A3^v, who identifies the pope as "that purple Whore"; and yet "the most part of Christian Princes with their people haue imbraced the free libertie of the Gospel, and freed themselues from her Antichristian yoake."

27.   Laurence Deios, *That the Pope is That Antichrist* (London, 1590), 181. Deios begins his treatise by claiming that Revelation sets forth the "persecutions and rewardes of those that with true faith cleaue onely to Christ; secondly, the assaults and wicked attempts of the enemies of the truth against the Church, together with their punishments and ouerthrowe" (p. 1).

28.   Anthony Marten, *An Exhortation, to stirre vp the mindes of all her Maiesties Faithfull Subiects* (London, 1588), sig. E5^v. Marten's riproaring tract is not a proper apocalyptic commentary, but it gives a vivid sense of how the Armada event kindles apocalyptic passion. "For though the Spanish King lately approached to the kingdome with wonderfull force and preparation to haue conquered the same, yet he was but a deputie therein to the Pope, and should haue taken possession but of that which he gaue vnto him" (sig. B1^v). He exhorts the Queen's subjects to strengthen themselves against "that horrible beast [Spain], who hath receiued power from the Dragon [the papacy]" (sig. A2^v).

29.   John Napier, *A Plaine Discouery of the Whole Reuelation of Saint John* (London, 1593), sig. A3^r.

30.   *The Works of James I* (London, 1616), 78.

31.   Richard Bauckham, *Tudor Apocalypse,* 173–77.

32.   Bernard Capp, "The Political Dimension," 100.

33. John Napier, *A Plaine Discovery,* sig. A3ʳ. In *Visionary Poetics,* 243–44, Wittreich maintains that for Napier "such wars represent the way of Rome and Antichrist," but Napier's tone and diction at times are expressly militant. For example: "God hath shewed mervellous indices, that the Empire of Rome & Papistical Kingdom, shal shortly fal: the Antichristian and Spanish flote is destroyed: the late King of France, Duke of Guize, & his brother Papists, and committers of the Parisian massacre, al murthered by other: a Protestant nowe made King of France [Napier is writing on the eve of Henry IVs conversion to Roman Catholicism]: So that before the ende of this Iubelie (God willing) Rome and the whole Papistical kingdome thereof, shal be ruined" (p. 179). Wittreich goes on to say that "Spenser and Milton would clearly place themselves among those who extract from the Apocalypse the message that man must learn 'to War no more.'" This essay will make clear that in the case of Spenser in Book V I disagree.

34. Laurence Deios, *That the Pope,* 27.

35. Anthony Marten, *An Exhortation,* signs. E4ᵛ, F3ᵛ.

36. I have learned the most about Elizabethan foreign policy from the following political historians: Charles Wilson, *Queen Elizabeth and the Revolt of the Netherlands* (London: MacMillan, 1970); P. S. Crowson, *Tudor Foreign Policy* (London: Adam & Charles Black, 1973), 158–236; John Guy, *Tudor England* (Oxford: Oxford University Press, 1988), 309–51.

37. George Gifford, *Sermons* sig. A4ʳ.

38. All quotations from *The Faerie Queene,* cited hereafter parenthetically in the text, are from *The Faerie Queene,* ed. A. C. Hamilton (London and New York: Longman, 1977). A typical opposition, such as that between Mercilla and the Souldan, is drawn by I. L., *The Birth, Purpose, and Mortall Wound,* sig. A3ᵛ: *England* happie through her *Elizabeth,* fate crowned with a wreath of peace (making Christ her hope) . . . . *Philip* king of *Spaine* made drunke and deceiued with the superstitious cup of Romish abhomination."

39. *The Works of Edmund Spenser: A Variorum Edition,* ed. Edwin Greenlaw *et al.,* 11 vols. (Baltimore: Johns Hopkins University Press, 1932–57), vol. V, pp. 299–302. I refer to this edition hereafter as *Variorum.*

40. All scriptural references are from *The Geneva Bible: A Facsimile of the 1560 Edition,* introd. Lloyd E. Berry (Madison: University of Wisconsin Press, 1969), and are noted hereafter in the text.

41. *The Creeds of Christendom,* ed. Philip Schaff (New York: Harper and Brothers, 1877), pp. 494–95. Dent in *Ruine,* 172, for example, speaks of the "surpassing blasphemies of the Popes against God, and all goodnesse" (172). Laurence Deios in *That the Pope,* 33, claims that the Roman Catholic Mass and other practices are "vile and horrible blasphemies."

42. An officially sanctioned example comes from "An Homelie against perill of Idolatrie and superfluous decking of Churches," in *Certaine Sermons: The Second Tome of Homilies* (London, 1595 [first published in 1563]), sig. B6ᵛ: ". . . the corruption of these latter dayes [i.e., under the papacy] . . . hath brought into the Church infinite multitude of images . . . occasioning [Christians] to commit most horible idolatrie." Compare George Gifford, *Sermons,* 380: "If we follow the decrees of Popes and Emperours, setting vp Idolatrie and superstition, then as we worship diuels, so we worship the beast"; Laurence Deios, in *That the Pope,* 32, refers to the "whorish and idolatrous Religion" of Rome.

43.   Arthur Dent, *Ruine*, 170, speaks of the "tyrannie" of the papacy. It is, however, an almost official term of abuse, as evinced in "An Homelie against Rebellion," (1570): the "Byshop of Rome" is "spoyler and destroyer both of the church . . . and all Christian kindomes, as an universall tyraunt over all." (*Certain Sermons or Homilies [1547] and A Homily against Disobedience and Wilful Rebellion [1570]: A Critical Edition*, ed. Ronald B. Bond [Toronto, Buffalo, London: University of Toronto Press, 1987], pp. 238–39).

44.   For example, Anthony Marten, *Exhortation*, sig. A3^v. The term "tyrant," rarely used in other Books of *The Faerie Queene*, is employed, with its cognates, nearly thirty times in the second half of this Book.

45.   Arthur Dent, *Ruine*, 238.

46.   *Variorum*, Vol. V, 306, 316.

47.   Richard Helgerson, *The Forms of Nationhood: The Elizabethan Writing of England* (Chicago: University of Chicago Press, 1992). Helgerson's discussion of Foxe, 249–68, is especially pertinent in this connecion. He notes, for example, Foxe's assertion that Elizabeth I was sent to triumph over Antichrist by means of the Word.

48.   John Aylmer, *An Harborwe*, sig. P4^v.

49.   Arthur Dent, *Ruine*, p. 217. Compare I. L., *The Birth, Purpose, and Mortall Wound*, sig. B2^v: "To them [i.e., the Spanish] a certaine signe of Heauens heauie rod, / To vs a shewe of loue; let vs be thankfull then, / And praise that Lord, which is the Lord of hoast, / That doth defend and shield our English Coast."

50.   *Variorum*, vol. V, p. 312.

51.   Kenneth Borris, *Spenser's Poetics of Prophecy*, p. 32, notes that "Protestant historiography was ready-made for Spenser's endeavour to transform historical particulars into an epically appropriate paradigm of Justice in human history."

52.   John Napier, *A Plaine Discovery*, sig. A3^v.

53.   Anthony Marten, *An Exhortation*, sig. E4^v.

54.   For an illuminating amplification of this point, see Clark Hulse, "Spenser, Bacon, and the Myth of Power," 318–20.

55.   Douglas A. Northrop, "Spenser's Defence of Elizabeth," *University of Toronto Quarterly* 38 (1969): 277–94, identifies Mercilla's court as the English Parliament (280). Northrop provides a wealth of detail to interpret the historical referents in Book V.

56.   The point is confirmed by Richard Bauckham, *Tudor Apocalypse*, pp. 128–130, 173–180; and by Bernard Capp, "The Political Dimension," 95–100. See also Richard McCabe, *The Pillars of Eternity: Time and Providence in "The Faerie Queene"* (Dublin: Irish Academic Press, 1989), 123–25; Joseph A. Wittreich, Jr., *Visionary Poetics*, p. 59. See Edward Hellwis, *A Maruell Deciphered* (London, 1589), sig. B2^{v-r}, who identifies the Queen as the Woman Clothed with the Sun.

57.   Leonard Wright, *The Hunting of Antichrist* (London, 1589).

58.   George Gifford, *Sermons*, p. 339, sig. A3^r.

59.   Frank Kermode, *Shakespeare, Spenser, Donne: Renaissance Essays* (New York: Viking Press, 1971), 33–59, was the first to treat the two Books extensively in tandem. He argues that Spenser advances a "Protestant imperialist ecclesiastical history in Book I and . . . [a] Protestant imperialist equity in Book V." (p. 58). John King, *Spenser's Poetry*, 227, observes that Book V builds upon Book I as a "model for religious iconography." Josephine Waters Bennett, *Evolution of "The Faerie Queene,"* 189, comments that Book V "is, in a sense, a coda to the Book of Red Cross, bringing the

English phase of the religious struggle up to date." I hope that this essay illustrates the truth of her remark.

60.   Florence Sandler, "*The Faerie Queene*: an Elizabethan Apocalypse," in *The Apocalypse*, ed. Patrides and Wittreich, 148.

61.   John N. King, *Spenser's Poetry,* 229, makes a similar point.

62.   Richard McCabe, "The Masks of Duessa: Spenser, Mary Queen of Scots, and James VI," *English Literary Renaissance* 17 (87), 224–42; James E. Phillips, *Images of a Queen: Mary Stuart in Sixteenth Century Literature* (Berkeley: University of California Press, 1964) 200–203.

63.   Jonathan Goldberg, *James I,* 4, focuses on Duessa's alleged crime of "lewd *Impietie*" (9.48) as evidence that she is still perceived in this Book as sexually duplicitous. It strikes me that the phrase points rather to her religious criminality, which was certainly a political crime as well.

64.   Edwin Greenlaw in *Variorum,* vol. V, 303, notes that the execution of the Queen of Scots was a necessary step in repelling Spanish aggression.

65.   Josephine Waters Bennett, *Evolution,* 188–89; Douglas Northrop, "Spenser's Defence of Elizabeth," 281. Harold Skulsky, "Malengin," in *The Spenser Encyclopedia,* 450, provides Malengin's literary genealogy.

66.   Arthur Dent, *Ruine,* 217.

67.   Richard Mallette, "The Protestant Art of Preaching in Book One of "*The Faerie Queene*," in *Spenser Studies* VII (1986): 14–17.

68.   The first to outline how the Book develops force and fraud as enemies of justice is Jane Aptekar, *Icons of Justice: Iconography and Thematic Imagery in Book V of "The Faerie Queene"* (New York: Columbia University Press, 1969), 116–119 et passim.

69.   John Jewel, *Upon the Second Epistle,* 305.

70.   For example, Arthur Dent, *Ruine,* sig. B1^v: ". . . notwithstanding al forces and armies cunningly contriued and raised up against the Church by Seminary Priests, Iesuites, Pope, Cardinall, and King of Spaine . . . [Rome] shall fall as Dagon before the presence of the Arke."

71.   George Gifford, *Sermond,* sigs. A3^r, A4^r.

72.   Laurence Deios, *That the Pope,* 75, asserts that the "*Spaniard,* not in any regard of his Religion, but in hope of a Monarchie vnder [Antichrist's] title, hath stepped forth as his champion in this age, to fight his warres for him. By him the armies are renewed and supplied in the Lowe countries: by him the warres are holden vp in *France*: through his meanes, *Geneva* hath bin besieged: and he hath set his inuincible nauie to subdue vs: but God bee thanked, that hath drowned it in the seas."

73.   H. S. V. Jones in *Variorum,* vol. V, 211, identifies Dolon with Philip II; James Nohrnberg, *The Analogy of "The Faerie Queene,"* (Princeton: Princeton University Press, 1976), 406, interprets the Samient incident as a reference to England's contest with Spain for the privilege of the seas.

74.   Kenneth Borris, *Spenser's Poetics,* 12, identifies the analogy between Geryoneo's monster and the beast of the Whore of Babylon (Rev. 17:3–8).

75.   Kenneth Borris, *Spenser's Poetics,* 12, 40, 25–26.

76.   Kenneth Borris, *Spenser's Poetics,* 54.

77.   Edmund Spenser, *The Faerie Queene, Book V: The Legend of Artegall or of Justice,* ed. Alfred B. Gough (Oxford: Clarendon Press, 1918), p. 108; John N. King, *Spenser's Poetry,* p. 107.

78.   Kenneth Borris, *Spenser's Poetics,* p. 53.

79.   Anne Lake Prescott, "Burbon," in *The Spenser Encyclopedia,* 121; Prescott's article, "Belge," also in the *Encyclopedia,* 82–83, is equally incisive. In the latter she points out, for example, that Spenser would have read glowing reports of the campaigns in the Netherlands in Holinshed. Here is a fact put to good apocalyptic use in the Belge episode and an application of Bale's maxim that the text give light to the chronicles.

80.   Josephine Waters Bennett, *Evolution,* 188; A. C. Hamilton's edition of the poem, p. 603, cites support.

81.   George Gifford, *Sermons,* sig. A3^v.

82.   Richard A. McCabe, "The Fate of Irena: Spenser and Political Violence," in *Spenser and Ireland: An Interdisciplinary Perspective,* ed. Patricia Coughlan (Cork: Cork University Press, 1989), 109–25. McCabe's Machiavellian reading of the Book and its relation to *A View of the Present State of Ireland* is one of the most expert recent examinations of the two texts in tandem; like all McCabe's work on Book V it is grounded on a deep knowledge of history.

83.   Arthur Dent, *Ruine,* p. 240.

84.   The following are useful: Ciaran Brady, "Spenser's Irish Crisis: Humanism and Experience in the 1590's," *Past and Present* 111 (1986), 17–49; Sheila T. Cavanagh, "'Such Was Irena's Countenance': Ireland in Spenser's Prose and Poetry," *Texas Studies in Literature and Language* 28 (1986), 24–50; Richard McCabe, "The Fate of Irena."

85.   *Variorum,* vol. IX, 136–49.

86.   Angus Fletcher, *The Prophetic Moment,* 288 observes that "the Beast's cruelty seems to have something essentially verbal about it; his 'blatting' is a deformed kind of speech, the blasphemous perversion of eloquence."

87.   Joseph A. Wittreich, Jr., "Apocalypse," in *The Spenser Encyclopedia,* 48, observes that "it is a definition of an apocalyptic poem that until history is complete the poem cannot be complete . . . In the very act of postponing apocalypse, Spenser implies that the beast still rules history because it is still enthroned in man and so continues to manifest itself both there and in the world."

ELIZABETH J. BELLAMY

The Aesthetics of Decline:
Locating the *Post*-Epic in Literary History

I WOULD LIKE to begin with a series of questions. To what extent is epic narrative *consciously* seeking its own subversion when it undertakes the representation of civil war? Or, to phrase the implications of this question somewhat differently, to what extent can we properly view Spenser's account of civil war between England and Ireland in Book V of *The Faerie Queene* as a continuation of a larger tradition of representing civil war within the literary history of epic? Is it time to cease viewing Book V as a "dark" aberration from the overall epic design of *The Faerie Queene* and to place it more squarely within the bounds of the epic tradition as a whole? In short, can cynicism be an epic topos?

Spenser's Book V (and its precipitous plunge into history) has long been viewed as exerting a regressive, anti-prophetic pull on the epic teleology of *The Faerie Queene* — as, indeed, a portion of Spenser's narrative in which something has somehow *gone wrong*.[1] But, to my knowledge, never has its pervasive sense of fatigue and cynicism and its presentation of a world in decay (a world that "growes daily wourse and wourse" [Proem.5]) been viewed as an explicitly (and conventionally) *epic* gambit (almost, as I will argue, as the formulaic deployment of an epic topos) in the representation of civil war.[2] Every reader of Spenser knows that Arthegall, signifying the much-maligned figure of Lord Grey and his unsuccessful campaign in Ireland, and the hero's abuse by the Blatant Beast demonstrate what happens when the ideals of an allegorical justice must submit to the unpredictable contingencies of civil war—around the difficulties of making, as Gough phrased it long ago, "the petty military operations of Gray, with their accompaniment of ceaseless hangings, massacres, burnings, and harryings the crowning achievement of the heroic Knight of Justice" (317). And to be sure, Spenser's account of England's morally ambiguous and frustratingly prolonged civil war with Ireland (an ambiguity scarcely disguised by Arthegall's rescue of Irena from the tyrant Grantorto) presents a radical departure from his earlier, and seemingly more self-assured, accounts of epic heroism. But what, we must ask, are the precise reasons for this abrupt shift in tone of Book V? Some critics have interpreted the darkness of its narrative as a waning of poetic inspiration.[3] And virtually every reader of *The Faerie Queene* has rightly emphasized the book's anti-prophetic tendencies as resulting from Spenser's deeply personal disillusionments about the nature of his own involvement in England's use of force against Ireland. But my paper argues that the darkness of tone and even the seeming dissipation of epic purposiveness of Book V may (ironically) owe as much to Spenser's *calculated* imitations within the literary history of epic as they do to a sudden resurgence of personal doubt or to a mysterious waning of aesthetic inspiration.

My paper, which, I admit from the outset, will raise more questions than it will answer, will be argued in two parts. In the first part, I will offer some extended comparisons between Ariosto's *Cinque Canti* and Spenser's Book V in an effort to trace the lineaments of what I would call the "*post*-epic" as the genre of empire in decline. Some key questions I will be considering in my discussion are: What does it *mean* when an epic comes too close to (real) history?; how does the representation of civil war become its own critique of epic prophecy?; how much of the literary history of epic are we overlooking when we label an isolated epic event as "merely" topical?; what can a focus on the representation of civil war as a topos tell us about when an epic is "complete"? In the second part of my paper, I intend to use Spenser's Book V as the occasion for a broader theoretical discussion of the new historicism and its weaknesses in providing a conceptual framework for interpreting this, ironically, most "historical" of Spenser's books. My overarching purpose will be to offer some further considerations on how historical meaning is revealed through literature—and what is at stake for literary studies when literature and history confront one another as directly (and uncomfortably) as they do in Book V.

I. TRACING THE GENRE OF POST-EPIC

The representation of civil war within the bounds of epic is scarcely new with Spenser, but rather has its origins in Lucan's first-century *De Bello Civili*, the epic of Rome's civil wars between Pompey and Julius Caesar. As a kind of "anti-Virgil," the poet of Nero as opposed to Augustus, Lucan, with a misanthropy that borders on the macabre, portrays Roman history as a dead end with the onset of Caesarean tyranny. In his edition, A. E. Housman describes the poem as written in "repulsive detail," as if Lucan had designed it "less to charm his readers than to startle them and make their flesh creep" (xiii). Among other themes, Lucan proclaims as his central subject matter, "populumque potentem / In sua victrici conversum viscera dextra" ("how an imperial people turned their victorious right hands against their own vitals" [I.2–3]).[4]

But despite the popularity of Lucan's epic in Elizabethan England, I would suggest that Spenser's representation of civil war in Book V has as its more immediate (anti)epic prototype the *Cinque Canti,* Ariosto's depiction of the origins of the Roland saga.[5] Though Spenser's debt to Ariosto has long been acknowledged in Spenser criticism, the focus has remained on the *Orlando furioso* and the characteristic influence of its labyrinthine narrative structure on what is commonly referred to as the "romance middle" of *The Faerie Queene.* But there may be more at stake in the issue of Spenser's borrowings from Ariosto than the deferrals and "dilations" of romance narrative. There are a number of uncanny similarities between the *Cinque Canti,* Ariosto's oddly fragmentary account of the civil wars that led to the dissolution of Charlemagne's empire, and Spenser's Book V, a book not normally associated with Italian epic or with the "matter" of Charlemagne. Though Book V and its "poetics of violence" represent a break from the dream-like wanderings of Ariostan romance, it may not necessarily represent a break from Ariosto; for its disturbing portrayals of a frequently brutal justice and its explicit political allegory recapitulate the dark cynicism of the *Cinque Canti* and, like Ariosto's problematic fragment,[6] constitute a distinctly (post)epic struggle to represent real historical events that elude the larger vision of the narrative of epic imperialism.

The dissonant *Cinque Canti* seems designed as the apocalyptic end of epic itself. The work opens in a distinctly eschatological setting with a high consistory of fairies airing their grievances against past epic heroes in Demogorgon's temple by the Ganges.[7] The *Cinque Canti* is highly self-conscious of its roots in the literary history of epic, with its opening serving as a virtual review and denunciation of Boiardo's *Orlando innamorato* and Ariosto's continuation, the *Orlando furioso*. We observe Fallerina, for example, lamenting Orlando's destruction of her garden in the *Innamorato*, II (I.24). The Fata Morgana makes her first appearance since the *Innamorato*, "squalida e negletta, / nel medesmo vestir ch'ella avea quando / le diè la caccia, e poi la prese, Orlando" ("mournful, dirty and neglected, . . . in the same dress she had been wearing on the day when Orlando chased and later captured her" [I.10])[8] — a tousled reminder of the diminishing of her prior glory as the principal enchantress of the *Innamorato*. Morgana's sister Alcina is depicted as still smoldering in resentment at Ruggiero and his escape from her enchanted isle in the *Furioso*, VII. In the midst of these bitter reminiscences, the presiding Demogorgon, approving Alcina's plans of revenge against Carlomagno, urges,

> che sia Orlando, sia Carlo, sia il lignaggio
> di Francia, sia tutto l'Imperio spento;
> e non rimanga segno né vestigi,
> né put si sappia dir: "Qui fu Parigi." — [9] (I.30)

> (let Orlando, let Charles, let the lineage
> of France, let the entire Empire be extinguished;
> and let no sign or vestige remain, let no one even
> know enough to say: "Here once was Paris.")

Thus, in effect, Demogorgon calls for the end of epic and, for that matter, the annihilation of any "segno" or "vestigi" of the *translatio imperii* itself.

In the *Cinque Canti,* the machinations of Demogorgon's demonic council easily contaminate the real world of Carlomagno's court, which is depicted as having completely lost the heroic luster it enjoyed in the *Furioso*. Ippolito as benign imperial patron of the *Furioso* has disappeared. And Alcina's subsequent recruiting of the figure of "Invidia" (or "Envy") for her treacherous plots against Carlomagno demonstrates her conviction that his empire may already be in decline, already vulnerable to collapse from within through sedition and betrayal. She proclaims:

Alle mortal grandezze un certo fine
ha Dio prescritto, a cui si può salire;
che, passandol, serian come divine,
il che natura o il ciel non può patire;
ma vuol che giunto a quel, poi si decline.
A quello è giunto Carlo, se tu mire.

(I.48)

(God has ordained a certain limit for mortal achievement, up to which it is allowed
to rise, but passing beyond which it would
be almost divine, something which nature
and heaven cannot endure; He wished instead that, having reached that limit, it
may then decline. Charles has reached that
point, if you observe him well.)

Thus, Alcina isolates *un certo fine* as a late stage in the history of empire—
a characteristic state of decay that marks the inevitable collapse of empire not so much by epic "force" as by "fraud" (or "Invidia"). And we
might note here that Alcina's (Italianate) *certo fine* seems calculated as an
ironic echo of Jupiter's (Latinate) promise to Aeneas that he will found
an *imperium sine fine* (*Aeneid,* I). When viewed in light of Alcina's
warning, the *Cinque Canti* may be interpreted as Ariosto's narrative
documentation of empire's ineffable, but predictable *certo fine*—the
point at which empire must reckon with the possibility of its own end.

Under Alcina's direction, Invidia appears to the Maganzan Gano
(or Ganelon) in a dream, torturing him with visions of Carlomagno's
faithful followers insulting and mocking him. Goaded by l'Invidia
(much like Virgil's Amata, driven into a hysterical rage by the twisted,
slithering snake that Allecto unleashes deep into her breast in the
Aeneid, VII), Gano becomes "d'insidie e tradimenti il padre" ("the
father of treacheries and betrayals" [II.32]). To the unpredictable
Rinaldo, always on the verge of abandoning Carlomagno's cause in the
Furioso, Gano "sciolse la crudel lingua" ("loosed his cruel tongue"
[3.53]) with stories of Carlomagno's slander against the knight. His
treacherous campaign is so successful that Marfisa and Ruggiero, two
of the principal heroes of the *Furioso,* join forces with Rinaldo against
Carlomagno, who, by Canto V, puts a price on the brother and sister as
traitors. In Canto I.102, Alcina gives Gano a magical ring inhabited by

the shape-shifting demon Vertunno, who later, transforming himself
into Terigi, Orlando's squire, goes to Rinaldo with a forged letter from
Carlomagno slandering Rinaldo and announcing the Emperor's intention to take Rinaldo's command from him. Later Vertunno, disguised
as Ruggiero, is able to capture Ruggiero's spouse Bradamante, while
Baldovin works his treachery against his half-brother Orlando, once the
heroic embodiment of the consolidation of Carlomagno's empire. When
we consider that Gano and Orlando, too, are half-brothers, then we can
begin to see the extent to which the dissolution of empire in the *Cinque
Canti* is directly linked to, as in Lucan's *De Bello Civili,* the particular
outrage of "how an imperial people turned their victorious right hands
against their own vitals."

But the empire begins to crumble not just because of the betrayals of
key heroes from literary epic. In the *Cinque Canti,* "real" history intrudes upon "fictive" narrative when Gano, as part of his strategy to
unite much of Europe against Carlomagno, recruits Desiderio of Lom-
bardy, Tassillo of Bohemia, and Marsilio of Spain. Alcina kidnaps the
figure of Sospetto to Italy and orders the once-suspicious tyrant, now
transformed into the allegorical figure of Suspicion itself ("piggior di
tutti i mali," or "the worst of evils"), to enter Desiderio (II.24), who
then successfully unites the Bohemians and the Hungarians against
Carlomagno. And although Desiderio is later defeated (one of several
anti-climactic sub-plots in the *Cinque Canti*),[10] Carlomagno is unsuccessful in his attempts to capture Prague, as Gano widens his treasonous
alliance, uniting not only the Eastern European forces of Bavaria, Sax-
ony, Silesia, Hungary, Rumania, and Serbia (in short, all the countries
that were thought to be not *really* Christian), but also the kings of
Arabia, Syria, and Egypt (II.127). The "conclusion" of the *Cinque Canti*
breaks off abruptly with Carlomagno barely escaping an enemy attack
outside Prague (but suffering confusion in the midst of his own battle
strategy), with violent confrontation between Rinaldo's and Orlando's
troops, and with Ruggiero and Astolfo trapped inside the belly of
Alcina's whale[11] — with no end in sight to the deceit, envy, treachery,
sedition, and Machiavellian manipulation that have so completely
replaced the (by this point archaic) heroism of the *Furioso*.

The point to emphasize here is that Ariosto's oddly fragmentary account of the civil wars that led to the dissolution of Carlomagno's empire (not to mention his depiction of a real, geographically explicit
Europe) constitutes a distinctly *post*-epic struggle to represent real historical events that elude the larger vision of the narrative of epic imperi-

alism. Among other things, the *Cinque Canti* seems to be an extended meditation on the decline of chivalric ideals. In a world where Gano's "false ghigno" ("counterfeit smile" [I.36]) is a more effective weapon than Orlando's mythic sword Durindana, ambition is no longer defined as the *virtù* that defeats the enemies of Empire, but rather as the instigator of "calunnie, insidie e morte" ("calumnies, betrayals and death" [III.2]) that destroy empire from within. Even as the poet broods about the weak judgment of declining leaders, like Carlomagno, who "lascia il buono et il piggior sublima" ("neglect good men and exalt the worse" [II.134]), the *Cinque Canti* begins to form a depressing appendix to the wit, energy, and playful irony of the *Furioso* — an unexpectedly pessimistic twist to the chivalric heroism that had carried the day against the Saracens in Ariosto's earlier epic. Shaken by peripheral rebellion and internal sedition, Carlomagno's empire has indeed, as predicted by Alcina, reached its *certo fine* of decay. And thus the narrative of imperial ideology and of the purposeful formation of empire is made to cede place to the *Cinque Canti*'s cynical representation of history as "running out," an (anti)narrative where both the teleology of epic and the delicate and nimble *entrelacement* of romance are undermined by a detailed and deliberately inconclusive account of the *real* dissolution of empire (of, in other words, cynicism as a calculated narrative, and epic, effect).

Before we move to *The Faerie Queene,* it is tempting to speculate as to whether or not Tasso, Ariosto's epic successor in Ferrara, had a self-unravelling work like the *Cinque Canti* in mind when he warned against the use of contemporary history in epic. At the heart of Tasso's epic aesthetics, as meticulously outlined in his *Discorsi Dell'arte Poetica* (1587), is history — or, more accurately, the *representation* of a history that cannot be *remembered.* For Tasso, the subject matter of epic must be historical — not, however, the contemporary history *de' nostri tempi* (the immediacy of whose current events resist poetic representation), but rather the history of *tempi remotissimi.* The history of more distant eras naturally lends itself to representation (affords the most poetic freedom) because, quite simply, memory cannot recall it: "però che, essendo quelle cose in guisa sepolte nel seno dell'antichità ch'a pena alcuna debole ed oscura memoria ce ne rimane, può il poeta a sua voglia mutarle e rimutarle . . ." ("Because these things are so buried in the depths of antiquity that scarcely any feeble and dim memory of them remains, the poet can choose to change and rechange them . . .").[12] It is a "debole ed oscura memoria" of past history that effectively opens up the aesthetic space for the conscious poetic exercise of what Tasso refers to throughout his

Discorsi as a "gran commodità di fingere." Tasso warns, "però che di troppo sfacciata audacia parrebbe quel poeta che l'imprese di Carlo Quinto volesse descrivere altrimente di quello che molti, ch'oggi vivono, l'hanno viste e maneggiate" ("therefore, it would seem a very impudent boldness in a poet to wish to relate the undertakings of Charles V otherwise than many living today have seen and handled them").

Though its story occurred long before Ariosto's time, the *Cinque Canti* nevertheless refuses the luxury of a "debole ed oscura memoria," allowing contemporary events to intrude on its own narrative so completely that Ariosto in essence denies himself the opportunity to *represent* history. No longer "sepolte nel seno dell'antichità," the raw, unmediated events of a "recent history" undermine not only the integrity of Carlomagno's empire, but also the structure of Ariosto's epic narrative itself. Tasso's warning notwithstanding, however, we can assume that the dissolution of his own narrative was precisely what Ariosto had planned from the outset of the *Cinque Canti*. Even as empire crumbles from within, so also does Ariosto's narrative enact its own death wish as the conscious undermining of an archaic epic heroism. The *Cinque Canti*, in short, offers dissonance and cynicism as the distinctive topoi of *post*-epic—what Tasso might choose to call the genre of *le istorie moderne*.

As a document of political turmoil, civil war, and deceit, the *Cinque Canti*, then, affords a valuable backdrop for a larger understanding of Spenser's presumed aesthetic and narrative "disappointments" in Book V of *The Faerie Queene*—a work that, *pace* Tasso, quite *literally* confronts the immediacy of current events.[13] And when read in conjunction with the *Cinque Canti*, Book V can also be seen as tracing nothing less than the lineaments of the "decline of empire" as epic *topos*. The second canto of the *Cinque Canti* opens with nostalgic praise for the great justiciars of myth:

> Tal fu in terra Saturno, Ercole e Giove,
> Bacco, Poluci, Osiri e poi Quirino,
> che con giustizia e virtüose prove,
> e con soave e a tutti ugual domino,
> fur degni in Grecia, in India, in Roma, e dove
> corse lor fama, aver onor divino;
> che riputar no si potrian defunti,
> ma a più degno governo in cielo assunti. (II.3)

> (Such on Earth were Saturn, Hercules, Jove, Bacchus,
> Pollux, Osiris, and after them, Quirinus who with

justice and valiant deeds, and with a rule gentle and equal
for all, were worthy of heavenly honors in Greece, in In-
dia, in Rome, and everywhere their fame has traveled; so
that one cannot consider them dead, but only taken up to
a more worthy government in the heavens.)

In the opening of the first canto of Book V, Spenser gives vent to a
similar nostalgic yearning for the law-givers of "old times" (1.1):

> Such first was Bacchus, that with furious might
>   All th'East before vntam'd did ouerrone,
>   And wrong repressed, and establisht right,
>   Which lawlesse men had formerly fordonne.
>   There Iustice first her princely rule begonne.
>   Next Hercules his like ensample shewed,
>   Who all the West with equal conquest wonne,
>   And monstrous tyrants with his club subdewed;
> The club of Iustice dread, with kingly powre endewed.
>
> (1.2)

As in the *Cinque Canti,* the ideal of heroism is conspicuously absent
from Book V, which may be best interpreted as the aesthetic representation of the *end* of epic; and, like the *Cinque Canti,* Book V assumes from
its outset a distinctly apocalyptic tone with Astraea's fleeing to the
heavens (or, as Ariosto might have phrased it, "a più degno governo in
cielo"). Taking place, as it does, in "present dayes which are corrupted
sore" (Proem.2), the book laments a world that "is runne quite out of
square" (Proem.1) and lays bare an eschatological sense of the state of
mankind as "degendered" (Proem.2). And we should consider the
strong possibility that Spenser's tone of disillusionment is less a symp-
tom of an aesthetic crisis than it is his own *post*-epic depiction of Tudor
empire's *certo fine,* a narrative that, as its references become more and
more contemporary, presents the political pieces of a world that cannot
be put back together again.

Book V seems written almost in defiance of Tasso's warning that *le
istorie moderne* deny the poet "la licenzà di fingere" so vital to the project
of poetry itself. Within the "reception history" of Book V, it has
become a critical commonplace to dwell on what has been perceived to
be its distinctly *unaesthetic* failures. Every reader can perhaps agree that
Book V is, in some properly "epic" fashion, attempting to convert

brute violence to the foundation of *civitas;* but in the cynical, post-lapsarian world of this troubled book, history intrudes on the narrative so directly that it reaches (as Tasso might have predicted) neither imperial nor aesthetic resolution, with Arthegall prematurely recalled from Ireland before he can insure that his liberation of Irena will culminate in an imperial prophecy of peace. So seemingly depleted are the aesthetics of Book V that critics have without difficulty long made any number of "old historical," one-to-one correspondences between "literary" character and "historical" figure: Arthegall as, of course, Lord Grey, Elizabeth's beleaguered Lord Lieutenant in Ireland; Arthur as the Earl of Leicester in the Protestant Netherlands; Duessa as Mary Stuart; the Soldan as Philip of Spain; Sir Burbon as Henry IV of France; Malengine as the Irish kern.[14] And, like the encroaching, hostile periphery of Charlemagne's empire in the *Cinque Canti,* the Europe of Book V is very much a *real,* geographical Europe, no longer the dreamy *selva oscura* of epic romance.

Though epic prophecy is traditionally structured by millenarian visions and chiliastic anticipations, Book V's "desolate piratical violence," as Fletcher has described it (136), fails to achieve political stability or imperial resolution. Even as the "courses of the rowling spheares" have "wandred much" (Proem.5), so also is Arthegall, by the conclusion of Book V, his "course of Iustice . . . forst to stay" (5.12.27). All of which is to suggest the narrative problems inherent when the authority of Arthegall's peculiarly Iron Age heroism as the "Champion of true Iustice" (Proem.3) must be established within history when "history" is the "state of present time" (Proem.1) — the very history *de' nostri tempi* that Tasso warns the epic poet to avoid as hostile to the "gran commodità di fingere."

In short, prophetic vision in Book V deteriorates into heroic decline — a decline with its own "history" to consider. Of the decline of the hero in general, James Nohrnberg has argued that the loss of heroism is "in part the loss of his daemonological nature" (767). And Fletcher has argued that Book V seems to be positing, among other things, a "human, as opposed to divine culture" (138). Ancient history (of Tasso's *tempi remotissimi* as the more benign haven of the epic poet) was distinctly euhemeristic, a hybrid of history and mythology in which earthly heroes were portrayed as having divine origins. Spenser himself acknowledges the glory of the euhemeristic hero when he speaks nostalgically of "those great Heroes [who] got thereby / Their greatest glory, for their rightfull deedes, / And place deserued with the Gods on hy" (5.2.1). Thus, Spenser's central problem of Book V may have been the ongoing problem

within the literary history of epic of keeping its heroes properly "euhemeristic"—properly "Hesiodic," or "mythohistorical."

But as Nohrnberg has also observed, "It is a paradox that, as a literary
symbol, heroes in part exist to be superseded; they are supplanted by a
lesser, postheroic race whose unheroic stature thereby defines its predecessor as heroic" (768). Arthegall is both the daemonological, euhemeristic hero of conventional epic (having been tutored as a youth by
Astraea herself), and the "supplanting," *post*-heroic figure *de' nostri tempi*
whose failures in establishing a definitive justice may, in the end, be
serving merely to authorize the heroism of his epic predecessors *retroactively*. In this context one thinks, for example, of Arthegall's mythographic sword Chrysaor, "that all other swords excelled, / Well prou'd
in that same day, when Ioue those Giants quelled" (5.1.9). Throughout
Book V, Chrysaor fails to achieve mythic status in its brutal exercising
of a violent justice and, despite its role in the beheading of Grantorto,
seems to exist only as a nostalgic reminder of prior magical swords in
epic, such as Orlando's Durindana. Arthegall is both eminently heroic
(embodying the divine heroism of such figures as Bacchus, Hercules,
Osiris, Samson, Aeneas—figures whom Fletcher has called types of the
culture-bringing "social bandit"); but, as every reader of Book V has
perceived, Arthegall also seems repressively *post*-heroic in his inconclusive effort to impose "justice" in Ireland. One question posed by the
nature of Arthegall's declining heroism is: who gets to claim the cultural "prestige" of being Book V's definitive "social bandit"? Is it Arthegall—or is it rather the cattle-rustling Irish kern *de' nostri tempi*? Are
the Irish kern "merely" rebellious ("gainst lawfull gouernment"
[5.12.26])—or are they a new type of "social bandit," superseding the
outmoded epic heroism of Arthegall?[15]

As the hero of "justice," Arthegall is forced to become the "hero" not
of culture bringing, but of a repressive violence. And, like the *Cinque
Canti*, we can begin to view Book V as perhaps the genre of the euhemeristic hero in decline. Arthegall's "fall" from euhemeristic glory may
properly be viewed as Tudor empire's *certo fine*, its predictable point of
decay from within. Although Tudor imperialism enjoys a "prophetic
moment" of triumph in Arthur's expedition to liberate the Lady Belge
from Geryoneo, Arthegall's campaign in Ireland succeeds only in unleashing "fell contention," "bitter wordes," and "false sclaunders"
(12.41–42). And we can now immediately recognize the parallels between the *Cinque Canti* and Book V as narratives that begin to undo

themselves as the real world of present events threatens the ideals of empire. As in the *Cinque Canti,* the principal protagonist of Book V is not so much its titular hero Arthegall as it is Envy, Slander, and the Blatant Beast in all their manifestations as "piggior di tutti mali" ("the worst of evils") — the heirs of Grantorto as the "great wrong" of rebellion and sedition. In the anti-chivalric world of Book V, betrayal, not individual heroism, motivates (or undoes) much of the narrative; and the *Cinque Canti*'s many figures of deceit, when viewed as *post*-epic prototypes, suggest a more cohesive purpose for Spenser's seemingly endless recurrences of treachery: Pollente, the master of "many trap fals pight"' Dolon, who terrorizes his guests with "full many treasons vile," and his eldest son Guizor, characterized by "guilty wile"; Dolon's surviving sons who later revile Britomart for Guizor's murder; the "smooth of tongue" Malengin (or "Guyle"), the Protean shape-shifter (like Ariosto's Vertunno) representing the guerrilla tactics of the Irish rebels; Duessa, purveyor of "practise," "traynes," and "treasons"; Sedition ("breeding stryfe"), Murder, "lewd Impietie," and Ate, Duessa's accusers at her trial at Mercilla's palace; Malfont, the poet of "euill words, and wicked sclaunders"; Grantorto, who captured Irena "By guileful treason and by subtill slight"; Enuie and Detraction, the "griesly creatures" that slander Arthegall; and, finally, the Gano-esque Blatant Beast that looses backbiting and slander throughout the entire empire.

II. Post-epic / History / Literary history

In both the *Cinque Canti* and in Book V, the decline of the hero is precipitated by *le istorie moderne* and their panoply of slander, sedition, and betrayal — the "aesthetically lean" consequences of a "grantorto" that is inevitably complicit with the swiftness with which the imperial quest can deteriorate into the divisiveness of civil war (not to mention the unraveling of narrative itself). At this juncture in my paper, I would like to ponder a larger question that naturally arises from a consideration of Book V's "deep structure" of deceit and sedition: what is at stake in defining the genre of the *post*-epic? For one thing, such a generic classification, as we shall see later, provides us with a new way of interpreting Book V. Years ago, in her admirable study of the complex iconography of Book V, Jane Aptekar chose to read Spenser's work as an elaborate and extended interplay "between icon and signification" (2). But what happens, we may ask, when "real" power is being enforced by "literary" icons? More recently, Jonathan Goldberg, in a paradigmatic new historicist reading, has interpreted Book V as an extended meditation on how (real) imperial power seeks to justify its own oppressions. And thus, between Aptekar and Goldberg, we are presented with two sharply divergent options for interpreting Book V, options that reflect a perhaps over-dichotomized choice between "literary" and "historical" interpretation. On the one hand, we are presented with an iconographical reading that privileges the interpretive richness of the book's mythographic emblems, icons, and symbols of monarchy, of justice, and of Herculean myth, but at the expense of confronting the question of the book's very *real* violence and turbulence;[16] and on the other hand, we are offered an unabashedly historical reading that confronts only the operations of imperial power, at the expense of considering the book's inherently epic (i.e., *post*-epic) properties.

What I would suggest is that we need a new conceptual framework to fully understand the *post*-epic genre of *le istorie moderne*. How exactly are we to interpret, for example, Book V's peculiar tonal mix of nostalgia, cynicism, and insistence on envy, slander, and treachery as the replacement of heroic valor? How "literary" or how "historical" is the decline of the euhemeristic, daemonological hero? How "internal" is this process of decline to the literary text itself? What does it mean when "Sedition" itself becomes a literary character? And finally, what precisely is at stake when literature and history meet with as much tension as they do in Book V?

Before attempting to answer these questions, I would like to turn to a theoretical consideration of some of the weaknesses of the new historicism in interpreting the "historicism" of Book V. Such a digression is necessary for a full understanding of why we must re-think Spenser's use of "history" in this his most troubled book. From its inception, the new historicism has been reluctant to specify and debate its interpretive methodology—a reluctance that has not prevented others from proceeding to identify its theoretical weaknesses for it. For a full understanding of these weaknesses, we should first consider the broader intellectual currents that have shaped the new historicist project. As historian Lynn Hunt usefully summarizes, cultural history, the larger disciplinary frame for the more particularized new historicism, is concerned with fields of cultural production "which cannot be explained deductively by reference to an extracultural dimension of experience" (7). Among other things, cultural history has itself been influenced largely by anthropologist Clifford Geertz's concept of "local knowledge," specifically his rejection of positivist, explanatory, and causal (extracultural) "laws" of cultural phenomena in favor of a semiotic, hermeneutic approach that views culture as a concentrated "web of significance" to be deciphered. But we should turn at this point to Geertz's own frank acknowledgment of the weaknesses of his method of "thick description": "Cultural analysis," he admits, "is intrinsically incomplete. And, worse than that, the more deeply it goes the less complete it is" (29).[17] The subtly textured quality of the interpretations yielded by "thick description" may be, in the final analysis, merely self-generative of other interpretations in ways that are theoretically infinite. In his consideration of the problematics of the new historicism in particular, Vincent Pecora portrays the new historicist as, like the Geertzian anthropologist, "trapp[ed] . . . inside the semiotic systems he or she would wish to explain" (272). In other words, the more the interpretive power of the new historicism is exercised, the more it begins to recapitulate the operations of formalism, the very operations that the new historicism has accused of excluding "history" itself.[18]

A key question that the new historicism's obfuscation of its own critical methodology has failed to answer adequately is: how is historical meaning revealed? To confront this question more directly would be one way the new historicism could attain greater theoretical development—a possible way to break out of the unrelenting synchrony of its "thick descriptions." Is historical meaning revealed, as the new historicism would have it, *only* synchronically—only within textured "webs of significance"? At what point is historical meaning revealed through a more diachronic dimension? In its purusit of one of its more specific goals to unsettle the opposition between literature and history, the new historicism has failed to identify (an admittedly difficult task) what it is that precisely *links* history and literature—and, in the process, "literature" itself is in danger of disappearing from the critical scene.[19] How do we forge a link between literature and history (or "poetics" and politics) that is not merely contingent or arbitrary? What precisely *is* the dimension of history within poetry? The new historicism, as we all know, has conventionally insisted on the embeddedness of the text in history. But, in the case of Book V of *The Faerie Queene* as our particular prooftext, we have seen that history may be more accurately described as embedded in the *text*.[20] To explore the implications of this reversed embeddedness further, I propose that we take a fresh look at an old concept (an "old" concept that my paper has essentially been discussing throughout) long dismissed by the new historicism.

I would like to argue that the "thick description" of the new historicism could be considerably enriched by a reconsideration of literary history—that antiquated holdover from Frye's self-enclosed "literary universe," long since rendered *passé* by new historicist privilegings of a "cultural poetics." Such a reconsideration would itself depend, however, on a reconsideration of how historical meaning is revealed *temporally*. Expressing a typically new historicist position, Louis Montrose, for one, has explicitly called for a "substituting for the diachronic text of an autonomous literary history the synchronic text of a cultural system" (17); and in so doing, he has, among other things, pitched the debate between new historicists and literary historians as a debate between the relative merits of "diachrony" and "synchrony" as the preferred temporal dimension in which historical meaning is revealed. I have no quarrel with the new historicist axiom that a synchronically operative ideology always traverses the literary text. But should not the new historicism also be equally attentive to the literary text's own, self-conscious treatment of the ideological? The point I wish to make here is that the (diachronic) motivation of, specifically, the literary history of epic constitutes a special link between history and literature that, among other things, represents epic's (or *post*-epic's) particular way of treating the ideological—a representation that eludes a merely synchronic scrutiny of the epic text and its "webs of significance."

The concept of literary history has, of course, been rendered obsolete by the new historicism, almost completely effaced in a sweeping paradigm shift in textual studies that no longer sees the text as "autonomous," but rather as a non-transcendent, discursive "field." In its highly detailed and richly synchronic webs of "thick description," the new historicism has dismissed literary history as irrelevant to its goal of subsuming literature under larger historical or cultural processes. But my question is this: what if we were to view literary history as *itself* a discursive practice—the discursive practice *par excellence*, in fact, of any epic (or *post*-epic) which, as Nohrnberg has argued, always speaks by and through other epics? I want to emphasize first that to pose this question is certainly *not* to argue for a privileging of literary history over an attention to networks of cultural representation or fields of historical and political force being exerted on the text—nor is it to withhold appreciation from the new historicism's bold move of interpreting history itself as a text. What I *am* suggesting here is that the new historicism should also be attentive to how processes of signification, or structures of symbolic meaning, operate when they are deeply embedded in an at least *"semi*-autonomous" literary history (especially a literary history as authoritatively and powerfully defined as the literary history of epic).[21] I would argue that literary history, especially the literary history of epic, can itself be seen as a form of "cultural semiosis." If, in its broadest sense, "History" comprises everything that ever happened in the past, then a specifically *literary* history of epic, i.e., how epic texts choose to represent themselves *for* one another, can be a useful key to understanding how historical meaning is revealed *through* literature, as well as how literature becomes its own characteristic way of treating the ideological. To emphasize the *semi*-autonomy of literary history is an effort at forging a more precise link between history and literature, a link that can pose an at least brief alternative to the new historicism's theoretical fallacy of increasingly "thick (i.e., synchronic) description." To ask a simple question, *pace* Montrose: what's so bad about diachrony as one measure of historical meaning?

In his perceptive essay, "New Historicism: A Comment," Hayden White describes the conflict between diachrony and synchrony as a conflict in viewing what constitutes a genuinely "historical sequentiality" (300). And, in the process, he has gotten to the heart of what is so ironic about the new historicism's appropriation of the synchronic as its privileged temporal focus for the revealing of "history." As White argues, "The formulation [i.e., the new historicism's favoring of the synchronic] appears strange, because conventionally 'diachronic' is taken to be synonymous with a specifically 'historical,' and 'synchronic' with a generally 'ahistorical' treatment of phenomena" (300). In other words, the new historicism has, in its past successes, rather deftly managed to reverse the earlier structuralist understanding of "diachrony" and "synchrony," coding the operations of synchrony as "good" (i.e., rightly cognizant of historical and ideological pressures at work within cultural systems), while coding diachrony (and diachronic concepts such as literary history) as "bad" (i.e., escapist, too narrowly concerned with the literary text, insufficiently engaged with issues of ideology and power).

How can the prior (structuralist) meaning of diachrony as a more properly historical movement through time be recuperated for textual studies? Further defining his concept of "historical sequentiality," White explains how literary history is constituted diachronically: "Although each instance or exemplification [i.e., designating a period as the "Renaissance," identifying a work as an "epic," etc.] might be treated as a unique moment in the sequence, it is its status as a 'function, or articulation' of the fundamental structure (or code) of . . . literary history that reveals its meaning" (300). In other words, in a literary historical approach, the full meaning of a text is always revealed *retroactively*. But a new historicist approach holds that in the study of any given literary work, the "code" of literary history, in White's summary, "cannot be appealed to in order to account for the unique features of specific moments in the series that comprises the sequence" (301). The resulting problem for textual interpretation can be summarized as follows: the new historicism chooses to focus synchronically on what it perceives to be "unique features" in a given text, the same features that a literary historian might describe not as "unique," but rather as products of a broader "historical sequentiality."

Let us now consider how this impasse can have important consequences for how one chooses to interpret Book V of *The Faerie Queene*. The new historicism has built its interpretive agenda on what Dominick LaCapra might call "symptomatic" texts (i.e., texts that specifically reinforce certain perceptions of power codes and ideologies). In Book V, with its explicit "poetics of violence" and its brutal and competing regimes of power, the new historicist has found just such a privileged, "symptomatic" text in which the reader witnesses the weakening (or the repressive strengthening) of the dominant codes of imperial power and ideology.[22] Book V, in all its stripped down, "aesthetic leanness," is precisely the kind of literary work that the new historicism chooses to interpret as a "symbolic fiction"—a realm of Realpolitik endowed with signification, a virtual primer of how power constitutes itself as a "social trope."[23] With its extended "theater" of conflict, tension, rupture, and abjected marginalization, Book V is read by the new historicism as a record of the subversion, undermining, and dismantling of Elizabethan cultural codes. In effect, the new historicism proceeds under the assumption that, in Book V, it has located a "weak link" (i.e., a highly "symptomatic" link) in the diachronic "strength" of the literary history of epic; in the cynicism of Book V, the new historicism insists on having located one of its privileged "specific moments" (to echo White) in which epic, in ways that I discussed earlier in my paper, has somehow *gone wrong*—a "specific moment" in which epic implodes under the pressure of fields of historical and political force being exerted on it.

But the question that I propose as cutting to the heart of the interpretive matter would be: how textually disruptive *is* the explicit intrusion of history into literature in Book V? The answer depends on the emphasis the critic chooses to place on literary history. As we have seen, Tasso rejected *le istorie moderne* in epic, thereby suggesting, to phrase the problem "new historically," an avoidance of the complexities inherent in trying to absorb history into a text. But Spenser chose to confront the complexities of a contemporary history directly. And if we place Book V squarely within the literary history of epic, particularly the representation of civil war in epic (as evidenced by the *De Bello Civili* and the *Cinque Canti*), then we see that the peculiarities of Book V are less a "unique feature" of the sort new historicism is looking for than the characteristically generic features of *post*-epic; in other words, Book V can be seen as not a "symptomatic" text at all, but rather a *conscious* attempt to confront the discontinuous seams between literary representation and current history. To be sure, like the new historicism, a literary historical approach also "reads" Book V as a troubled investigation of the operations of power and ideology — but of power and ideology as *mediated* first through a generic representation of political reality, i.e., through a distinctly *post*-epic topos of depicting a world that "growes daily wourse and wourse." The poetics of violence that persistently disturbs the narrative of Book V is precisely the representational space of *post*-epic's depiction of empire's *certo fine* — an interpretation that occurs *retroactively* from a (diachronic) look back at the literary history of epic representations of civil war.

In its interpretation of Book V, the new historicism (not perhaps intentionally) tends to favor a view of literature as merely a *mimesis* of historical disruptions. But it is the very nature of *post*-epic to critique its own official discourse — its own implosive representations of the turbulent "state of present time" (or Tasso's *de' nostri tempi*). Book V may be more aware of its "technologies" of power than the new historicism is willing to admit.[24] Literature is not always *merely* mimetic, and, accordingly, Book V's poetics of violence is not always *only* "historical" (all of which may be to argue that, in the final analysis, we will have to devise more complex interpretive maneuvers if we are seeking to locate a "political unconscious" to Book V).

To identify the *Cinque Canti* and Book V as *post*-epic is to open up a rich series of questions that can only be posed (if not fully answered) by a literary historical approach: what is at stake in the textual *representation* of political reality? What happens when a "subversive" history is consciously *absorbed* into (or refracted by) the text? What can the new historicism tell us about an epic aesthetics that is always already self-conscious about a state of decline? What theoretical conceptualization is necessary when "real" history intrudes upon fictive narrative? And indeed, the difficulty of formulating such a theoretical conceptualization might very well have been uppermost in Tasso's mind when he counseled epic poets to avoid plunging into events *de' nostri tempi* altogether — to avoid, in effect, taking risky aesthetic chances with "real" history.

To extend the representational domain of the literary (to argue for the influence of a larger diachronic scope of literary history) is not itself an "interpretive" gesture, and, as such, it cannot answer to some of the larger criticisms of the new historicism.[25] And to be sure, we must continue to acknowledge Book V as a text "socially embedded" in history — to recognize its discursive field as produced and appropriated within history. But we should keep in mind, too, that much of that "discursive field" is produced within the literary, i.e., the "discursive field" of literary history. We should keep in mind that literary history is itself a "textualized trace" that participates in the process by which history can come to be viewed as a construct.

In the final analysis, Book V's "crisis of diachronicity" may be the crisis of trying to theorize "change" itself. The narrative paradigm of epic is, in effect, a comprehensive theory that attempts to make sense of history. Throughout *The Faerie Queene,* the concept of "history" itself (and how historical meaning is revealed through literature) is a privileged Spenserian preoccupation. And Book V in particular, where the synchrony of current history collides with the diachrony of literary history, would seem to be an extended meditation on the slippages that establish the difference between the past and the present. What Book V illustrates is that the crisis of diachronicity may be *first* a literary, not a historical problem; and thus a question to ask at this point is: can Book V (or any historical narrative) conceive of the temporality by which it processes its own historical material? The "endlesse exercise" of Eumnestes (2.10) and his chaotic *Briton moniments* are two notable Spenserian examples of the difficulties of such temporal processing — examples of the failure of historical meaning to integrate the immediacy of each changing moment.[26] As history changes from moment to moment, so also does the notion of what is "historical." When an epic chooses as its subject matter the *certo fine* of the decline of empire, then it becomes, among other things, an attempt to master diachrony itself, i.e., the relationship between the historical past and the "lived experience" of the present. But in Book V the "mastery" of diachrony merely ends up taking the form of a formulaic self-consciousness about the gap between a nostalgic "then" (or "the antique vse, which was of yore" [Proem.3]) and a turbulent "now" (a "world runne quite out of square").[27]

The euhemerism that structures Book V is a complex negotiation between myth and history (or in Spenser's case almost literally between Kronos, or Saturn, and Chronos as time itself) such that, for example, Astraea's presence (and subsequent fleeing to the heavens) embodies both the timelessness of political myth *and* the onset of the Iron Age. And thus Book V is an effort to imagine how a declining heroism can be accommodated into a diachronic, changing history. In Spenser's "Two Cantos of Mutabilitie," where no faerie knight comes to intervene heroically,[28] diachrony modulates into an ambiguous "mutabilitie" as the medium of change, the principle under which everything is always already in the making (even as the poet paradoxically insists that her "lineage ancient" can be found "registred of old,/In Faery Land mongst records permanent" [7.6.2]). Richard Terdiman has written that, in matters of cultural memory, "What is at stake is nothing less than the way a culture imagines the representation of the past to be possible" (19). If we focus on this "representation of the past" as the central (aesthetic) crisis of Book V, then the synchronic focus of a new historicist reading alone is inadequate for conceptualizing the crisis of change. To be sure, Book V is a highly unstable text — primarily because of its difficulties in comprehending its own temporal transformations. But that, in the final analysis, may be a *literary* (a *post*-epic) feature as much as a historical problem.

Notes

I owe a debt of gratitude to Albert Ascoli and David Quint, co-directors of the 1990 NEH Summer Seminar, "From Ariosto to Tasso: Genre and History in the Sixteenth Century," held at Northwestern University, where I was first introduced to the *Cinque Canti.* I also wish to thank Donald Cheney, Jonathan Crewe, Lawrence F. Rhu, and Joseph Wittreich for their reading of and helpful comments on my essay.

1. Joanne Craig, for example, remarks that "in the closing cantos of Book V archetype and history are so irreconcilable, so antithetical, as to drive one another out" ("The Image of Mortality," 540).

2. All references to *The Faerie Queene* are taken from A. C. Hamilton, ed., *Edmund Spenser: The Faerie Queene* (London and New York: Longman, 1977).

3. As T. K. Dunseath has argued, "The solving of historical equations in general tends to limit the suggestibility of Spenser's poem and in particular has led to the low critical fame of Book Five" (6). Even one of the book's great explicators, Angus Fletcher, has described it as "aesthetically lean" (137). And in his introduction to Book V in his edition of *The Faerie Queene,* A. C. Hamilton laments, "The application of certain episodes in Book V to events in Elizabethan history remains painfully obvious" (526) — as if it is somehow an inherently *unaesthetic* endeavor within epic to incorporate current events into its narrative.

4.   Readers of Book V of *The Faerie Queene* would benefit from noting that Lucan's epic is perhaps purposely incomplete and refuses to make sense out of a history that is increasingly perceived as aimless. (See Richard McCoy for a discussion of the influence of Lucan's "agonistic view of history" [117] on Samuel Daniel's *The Civil Wars* [1595].)

In his essay "Epic and Empire," David Quint has suggested that the Battle of Actium between Augustus and Antony, as depicted on Aeneas's shield in Book VIII of the *Aeneid*, is also simply "the climax of a civil war, Roman against Roman," where a propagandistic, imperial *telos* has intervened on "the winning side of Augustus bring[ing] into play a whole ideology that transforms the recent history of civil strife into a war of foreign conquest" (3). Civil war, in other words, may be nothing less than the constitutive form of any history of empire. (For more on the political cynicism of the *De Bello Civili*, see Quint's chapter on Lucan in his recent book *Epic and Empire: Politics and Generic Form from Virgil to Milton*.)

5.   The dating of the *Cinque Canti* presents a huge problem. It was probably begun no earlier than 1518–20, and Ariosto probably stopped working on it no later than 1525. It first appeared as an appendix in the 1545 edition of the *Furioso*. The controversies about its dating are matched by the controversies surrounding its status as a poetic fragment. The first stanza of the *Cinque Canti* is identical to stanza 68 in canto 46 of the *Furioso*, and the *Cinque Canti* was probably originally written as part of the *Furioso*, only to be omitted finally. In his *I romanzi* (1554), Giovanni Battista Pigna argued that it formed a new poem. More recently, James Nohrnberg, one of the few Spenserians even to make reference to the *Cinque Canti*, describes it as "an undigested block of narrative that seems to belong to the subject of the larger poem, and yet to go beyond it" (737). A number of critics, such as Eduardo Saccone, who has written extensively on the poem, now generally regard the *Cinque Canti* as a complete poetic work deliberately left as a fragment.

6.   Saccone, for example, describes the style of the *Cinque Canti* as "un poetare difficile . . . e rischioso" (132). Giorgio Petrocchio refers to "il clima di dubbio" that pervades the tone of the poem (282). And Albert Ascoli alludes to the *Cinque Canti*'s "bleak and desperate spirit" (9).

7.   Ariosto's airing of grievances at a fairy council could be viewed as a precursor of the opening of Spenser's "Two Cantos of Mutabilitie" (as starkly and fragmentarily entitled as the *Cinque Canti*), where the titaness Mutabilitie demands of Jove the restoration of her powers. Nohrnberg points out that Spenser links Demogorgon with Night, "to which Mutabilitie, given her head, would willingly return the cosmos" (739).

8.   All references to the *Cinque Canti* are taken from Lanfranco Caretti, ed., *Cinque Canti* (Turin: Einaudi, 1977). The English translation is from the unpublished manuscript of Alexander Sheers.

9.   Demogorgon's call for the annihilation of Paris seemingly echoes Virgil's Panthus who, urging Aeneas to flee his burning homeland, reminds the hero simply that "Fuimus Troes" ("Troy has been" [*Aeneid*, II.325]). Later in the *Cinque Canti*, Alcina slanders Charlemagne's ancestors as "una vil gente che fuggi da Troia / sin all'alte paludi de la Tana" ("a vile race that fled from Troy all the way to the deep marshes of the Don" [I.45–6]).

10.   Surely Ganelon's capture by Bradamante (III.91) is the most anti-climactic of Ariosto's narrative dead-ends.

11.   With this development, the *Cinque Canti* doubles back on the seventh canto of the *Furioso,* where Ruggiero is carried off by a whale to Alcina's enchanted isle. This "conclusion" also fulfills the prophecy in the *Furioso* 34.68 that Astolfo would suffer a second loss of his wits. Astolfo's imprisonment in the whale's belly is punishment for his amorous pursuit, as he narrates to Ruggiero in the *Cinque Canti,* of Cinzia, wife of Gaultier, an English baron.

12.   All references to the *Discorsi* are taken from *Torquato Tasso: Prose,* ed. Ettore Mazzali (Milan and Naples: Riccardo Ricciardi Editore, 1959). The translation is mine. (An excellent annotated translation of the *Discorsi* is forthcoming from Wayne State UP by Lawrence F. Rhu.)

13.   In his prefatory "Letter to Raleigh," Spenser explicitly announces his intention to avoid *le istorie moderne* through his choice of Arthur as the central protagonist of *The Faerie Queene:* "I chose the historye of king Arthure, as most fitte for the excellence of his person, being made famous by many mens former workes, and also furthest from the daunger of enuy, and suspition of present time." However, what is left unaddressed in the Letter to Raleigh is Spenser's decision to shift, in his middle books, to Arthegall as the central hero, who, as Lord Grey in Book V, is continually embroiled in "the daunger of enuy, and suspition" as the very heralds of empire's *certo fine.*

14.   These one-to-one correspondences are, as noted in an earlier footnote, disparaged by Hamilton as "painfully obvious," i.e., inherently unaesthetic.

15.   Fletcher notes that in Book V, "[w]e find a disturbing similarity between the psychology of rebellion and that of culture bringing" (249). As Jane Aptekar has observed, a recurring motif throughout the book is the rebellion of giants, such as the "strong tyrants" Geryoneo and Grantorto, the usurping, egalitarian "Gyant" of canto 2, the rebellious Irish kern, and, as mentioned earlier, even the giants that Jove once "quelled" with Chrysaor. In this sense, Book V anticipates the "Mutabilitie Cantos" and its anxiety about maintaining right rule and authority in the face of rebellion. The figure of Jove, the original owner of Chrysaor and the arbiter in Mutabilitie's dispute, is himself ambiguous — part right ruler of the universe and part "social bandit," having once usurped the just Titan Saturn.

16.   The "ontology" of the Blatant Beast serves as a useful example of the tensions inherent in interpreting the key symbols of Book V. Aptekar rightly interprets the Blatant Beast as "remarkably iconographically orthodox" (201); and Nohrnberg, too, has traced the origins of the Blatant Beast through literary history back to such sources as Virgil's Fama and Ovid's "biting Envy" in his *Ars Amatoria* (688). But in a new historicist reading, the emphasis would be placed not on the Blatant Beast's iconographical past, but rather on its very real power in the present to destroy empire from within.

17.   In his essay, "The Thick and the Thin: On the Interpretive Theoretical Program of Clifford Geertz," Paul Shankman has characterized "thick description" as "turning inward on itself. There are more and more 'exotic' descriptions — denser, more detailed ethnographies — but they do not seem to yield greater theoretical development" (269). Vincent Pecora refers to Geertz's interpretive method as "a rather empty gesture, because by the end of 'Deep Play,' it is almost impossible to decide what sort of experience would *not* constitute cultural semiosis" (262). And the intellectual historian Dominick LaCapra has argued that "an appeal to *the* context is deceptive. . . . The assumption that one does [have *the* context] relies on a hypostatization of 'context,' often in the service of misleading organic or other overly reductive analogies" (35).

18.   Alan Liu argues that "it is simply not the case that the new historicism is essentially different from formalism. It is more true to say that it is an ultimate formalism so 'powerful' that it colonizes the very world as its 'text'" (755).

19.   As Liu writes of this failure, "To argue . . . repeatedly that texts are historical, and history textual, I suggest, is to draw yet another version of the hermeneutic circle" (755). (For an astutely perceived account of how the new historicist ideal of demonstrating how "text" can actually influence "context" is "rarely achieved in current practice," see A. Leigh DeNeef, "Of Dialogues and Historicisms," esp. p. 502.)

20.   Here I consciously echo Jean Howard's rhetorical question posed in her excellent overview of the new historicism: "Does the text absorb history into itself?" (25). I would suggest that we can turn to Fletcher for as critically sophisticated an answer as any to Howard's question as it might relate to Book V:

> Very simply, before we try to account for political ideas in the poem, we have another problem to face: that insofar as any great and complex poem is a unity, it is also something of a political metaphor—it is a nation or state, in some sense—and thus Spenser is finally writing a poem which, expressing ideas and aspirations and happenings occurring outside itself, also is a cosmogonic allegory whose main intent is to watch its own coming into being. . . . By the time the critic grasps the full range of its allegory, he finds himself lapped in vision, as if its world were more real than any world outside it.
>   (204)

21.   We might consider, in this context, Spenser's own "idea of a literary career." As Richard Helgerson has argued in his *Self-Crowned Laureates,* Spenser (at a "synchronic" moment in time) sought to shape a poetic career as "England's Virgil." But it was a pragmatic decision very much determined by a (diachronic) consideration of the prestige of the career of the epic poet throughout literary history.

22.   Book V is generally considered to be Spenser's most violent book, a virtual study of how imperial justice uses pain and repressive violence to impose its restrictions—of how valuations of the body are written into the political discourse of Elizabeth's imperial state. As grisly punishment for beheading his own lady, Sanglier is forced to wear her severed, bloody head around his neck (1.28); Munera's hands of gold and feet of silver are "Chopt off, and nayled on high, that all might then behold" (2.26) by Talus, even as Pollente's "blasphemous head" is "pitcht vpon a pole on high ordaynd . . . / To be a mirrour to all mighty men" (2.19) by Arthegall; the "Gyant" is tumbled off a cliff, "His timbered bones all broken" (2.50); the Soldan is "Torne all to rags" (8.42) by his runaway horses, "rapt and all to rent, / That of his shape appear'd no little moniment" (43). With his tongue "Nayled to a post," the poet Malfont is stripped of a semiotic capacity to signify anything other than the legal and penal discourse of the Queen—with his tongue becoming, in effect, a synecdoche for the power of the Queen.

23.   To suggest only the briefest of overviews here, Stephen Orgel argues that "in the latter books of the *Faerie Queene* Spenser repeatedly confronts the realities of his society with his poetic mythology, and keeps making the same point: it doesn't work" (43). In his extended analysis of Duessa's trial, Goldberg reads Book V as a "discourse of sovereign power," claiming that "what it enacts is outside itself and transcendent" (6). In this context, it should be mentioned that Clark Hulse has criticized Goldberg for his

"over-dichotomi[zation] between the authoritarian and the subversive and between non-poetic and poetic language" (328).

24. As Hulse has suggested, "[T]he reality of power in Tudor England does not seem to have been shocking news for it did not lurk very far beneath the surface of things" (329).

25. One such criticism would be Nigel Smith's simple, but resonant question, "But what happens after representation?" (quoted in Liu, 734).

26. In her attempt to isolate what she refers to as "the cardinal moment of historicist inquiry," Marjorie Levinson has defined it as "the transformation of the past from an object into a subject" (30) — surely as apt a summary as any of the confusion that reigns in Eumnestes' chamber of memory and historiography.

27. For more on Spenser's self-conscious use of the concept of "antiquity" and a consequent "shifting but developing sense of the past" (199), see Judith H. Anderson, "The Antiquities of Fairyland and Ireland," *JEGP* (1987): 199–214.

28. As Nohrnberg argues, "If the loss of the hero's heroism is in part the loss of his daemonological nature, then it is crucial to an understanding of the Mutabilitie Cantos to observe that no champion of faerie makes his presence felt there" (767).

Works Cited

Anderson, Judith H. "The Antiquities of Fairyland and Ireland." *JEGP* 86: 2 (1987): 199–214.

Aptekar, Jane. *Icons of Justice: Iconography and Thematic Imagery in Book V of "The Faerie Queene."* New York and London: Columbia University Press, 1969.

Ascoli, Albert. *Ariosto's Bitter Harmony: Crisis and Evasion in the Italian Renaissance.* Princeton: Princeton University Press, 1987.

Craig, Joanne. "The Image of Mortality: Myth and History in the *Faerie Queene.*" *ELH* 39 (1972): 520–44.

DeNeef, A. Leigh. "Of Dialogues and Historicisms." *SAQ* 86:4 (1987): 497–517.

Dunseath, T. K. *Spenser's Allegory of Justice in Book Five of "The Faerie Queene."* Princeton: Princeton University Press, 1968.

Fletcher, Angus. *The Prophetic Moment: An Essay on Spenser.* Chicago and London: University of Chicago Press, 1971.

Geertz, Clifford. *The Interpretation of Cultures.* New York: Basic Books, 1973.

Goldberg, Jonathan. *James I and the Politics of Literature: Jonson, Shakespeare, Donne, and Their Contemporaries.* Baltimore and London: Johns Hopkins University Press, 1983.

Gough, A. B., ed. *The "Faerie Queene" V.* Oxford: Clarendon, 1918.

Hamilton, A. C., ed. *Edmund Spenser: The Faerie Queene.* London and New York: Longman, 1977.

Helgerson, Richard. *Self-Crowned Laureates: Spenser, Jonson, Milton and the Literary System*. Berkeley: University of California Press, 1983.

Housman, A. E., ed. *M. Annaei Lvcani: Belli Civilis*. Oxford: Basil Blackwell, 1926.

Howard, Jean E. "The New Historicism in Renaissance Studies." *ELR* 16:1 (1986): 13–43.

Hulse, Clark. "Spenser, Bacon, and the Myth of Power." In *The Historical Renaissance: New Essays on Tudor and Stuart Literature and Culture*. Ed. Heather Dubrow and Richard Strier. Chicago and London: University of Chicago Press, 1988.

Hunt, Lynn. "Introduction." In *The New Cultural History*, ed. Lynn Hunt, 1989.

LaCapra, Dominick. *Rethinking Intellectual History: Texts, Contexts, Language*. Ithaca: Cornell University Press, 1983.

Levinson, Marjorie. "The New Historicism: Back to the Future." In *Rethinking Historicism: Critical Readings in Romantic History*. Ed. Marjorie Levinson, Marilyn Butler, Jerome McGann, Paul Hamilton. Oxford: Basil Blackwell, 1989.

Liu, Alan. "The Power of Formalism: The New Historicism." *ELH* 65:4 (1989): 721–71.

McCoy, Richard C. *The Rites of Knighthood: The Literature and Politics of Elizabethan Chivalry*. Berkeley, Los Angeles, and London: University of California Press, 1989.

Montrose, Louis A. "The Poetics and Politics of Culture." In *The New Historicism*. Ed. H. Aram Veeser. New York and London: Routledge, 1989.

Nohrnberg, James. *The Analogy of "The Faerie Queene."* Princeton: Princeton University Press, 1976.

Orgel, Stephen. "Making Greatness Familiar." In *The Forms of Power and the Power of Forms in the Renaissance*. Ed. Stephen Greenblatt, special issue of *Genre* 15 (1982): 41–47.

Pecora, Vincent P. "The Limits of Local Knowledge." In *The New Historicism*. Ed. H. Aram Veeser. New York and London: Routledge, 1989.

Quint, David. "Epic and Empire." *Comparative Literature* 41:1 (1989): 1–32.

Quint, David. *Epic and Empire: Politics and Generic Form from Virgil to Milton*. Princeton: Princeton University Press, 1993.

Saccone, Eduardo. *Il sogetto del "Furioso."* Naples: Liguori Editore, 1974.

Shankman, Paul. "The Thick and the Thin: On the Interpretive Theoretical Program of Clifford Geertz." *Current Anthropology* 25:3 (1984): 261–70.

Terdiman, Richard. "Deconstructing Memory: On Representing the Past and Theorizing Culture in France since the Revolution." *Diacritics* 15:4 (1985): 13–36.

White, Hayden. "New Historicism: A Comment." In *The New Historicism*. Ed. H. Aram Veeser. New York and London: Routledge, 1989.

THEODORE L. STEINBERG

Spenser, Sidney, and
The Myth of Astrophel

*M*OST COMMENTARY ON Spenser's pastoral elegy *Astrophel* has called attention to the poem's alleged lack of passion. As S. E. Winbolt wrote, Spenser's "heart was, apparently, not in the work".[1] C. S. Lewis's comment was that "*Astrophel* has none of the elaborate ugliness of *Daphnaida*. It is merely insipid. The eighth stanza has some merit,"[2] and more recently Michael O'Connell has commented on the poem's "cool tone."[3] Such opinions indicate not only that there is something odd about the poem, but also that the critics, like so many of Spenser's contemporaries and like so many readers since the sixteenth century, have been seduced by the Sidney myth. Their expectations for a Spenserian elegy on the dead knight have led them to see the poem as a disappointment, even a failure. What I shall argue is that the poem is not a failure and is far from cold or insipid, but that it is passionate in an unusual and unexpected way, a way that reflects Spenser's state of mind and his understanding of Sidney's life in the early 1590s, including his rejection of parts of the Sidney myth. Unlike other pastoral elegies, which invariably glorify their subject in the process of focusing ultimately on the speaker, *Astrophel* simultaneously glorifies and criticizes its subject, and the speaker remains distinctly secondary in importance, as I will try to demonstrate.

187

We have become so accustomed to the picture of Sidney as the glorious courtier, as England's Renaissance man, that it may be difficult for us to conceive of anyone being critical of him; but we must realize that this attitude, whatever Sidney's real virtues may have been, is the result of highly effective Elizabethan propaganda. We know, for example, that for Elizabeth Sidney was often an annoyance. Sir Robert Naunton offers a revealing glimpse of Elizabeth's attitude when he quotes her upbraiding a courtier who, like Sidney, had tried to sneak away on a military expedition: "'Serve me so,' quoth she, 'once more and I will lay you fast enough for running. You will never leave till you are knocked on the head as that inconsiderate fellow Sidney was.'"[4] Even if Naunton has only captured her sentiment rather than her exact words, it hardly sounds like she was deeply upset at Sidney's memory; and we should keep in mind the possibility that Sidney's elaborate funeral was an entertainment designed to distract attention from the execution of Mary Stuart.[5]

Furthermore, Sidney's early reputation, as shown in the Oxford and Cambridge memorial volumes, was not that of a poet but that of a soldier and courtier and a martyr to the Protestant cause.[6] Alan Hager has written of the two "propagandistic motives" that lay behind the Sidney memorial literature: the promotion of Protestant militarism and Elizabeth's desire to have her court regarded "as the late flowering of chivalry in fealty to the virgin queen."[7] The image of Sidney that resulted from these propagandistic motives has been incredibly attractive, and from what we can tell, Sidney truly seems to have been an admirable character. We love his writing, we admire his wit, and we wish that he had trounced the Earl of Oxford in tennis. Consequently, we are not prepared to encounter criticism of the hero who died young while fighting for God and country, and we are especially unprepared for it in a pastoral elegy, which, according to tradition, should focus on its subject's virtues, and especially in a pastoral elegy by Spenser, who surely admired Sidney. Spenser, however, having waited nine years to publish an elegy for his fallen colleague, not only manipulated the elegiac tradition, he almost completely inverted it. When the poem is viewed through that inversion, it proves to be quite moving.

Spenser's praise for Sidney is both obvious and genuine: Astrophel is an extraordinary shepherd, excelling in all the activities that traditionally occupy literary shepherds, especially, and not coincidentally, the literary activities. As the opening stanzas of the poem's introduction indicate, the poem is addressed specifically to "Shepheards that wont on pipes of oaten reed, / Oft times to plaine your loves concealed smart" — that is, it is addressed to poets, and it is the literary Astrophel that the narrator mourns so deeply, the Astrophel who "could pipe and daunce, and caroll sweet" (31),[8] who could compose lays of love and charm the shepherd girls but who was faithful to his Stella.

But there are other aspects of Astrophel that are more problematic. Almost from the poem's beginning we can sense trouble, for despite his favorable genealogy, his Arcadian background, and the love and praise of the Arcadian shepherds and lasses, he was, we read, "not so happie as the rest" (12). William Oram, in his interesting introduction to the poem, interprets this line as pointing to Astrophel's lack of luck, not joy,[9] but both external and internal evidence indicate that while Astrophel may be unlucky, he clearly does lack joy. The external evidence can be found in comments by Sidney's contemporaries. On January 15, 1574, for example, Languet wrote to him, "I am very much troubled by the letter in which you write that you are not in very good health and are even more melancholy than usual";[10] and a week later Languet, apparently having contemplated Sidney's melancholia, wrote, "Since you are not at all cheerful by nature you should seek out companions in whose honourable society you can find good cheer."[11]

The internal evidence can be found throughout the poem, in the picture of Astrophel as an overachiever, as a shepherd who is not content with the important work of being a shepherd but who must seek to prove himself in other ways. Thus, the narrator tells us, he wooed Stella not with "ydle words . . . / And verses vaine (yet verses are not vaine) / But with brave deeds to her sole service vowed" (67–69). Astrophel feels that words are "idle" and verses are "vaine," a sentiment that the narrator, a poet himself, counters with his parenthetical "yet verses are not vaine," but Astrophel insists on coupling his literary deeds with physical ones. He vanquishes everyone in "all the sports that shepheards are emong" (76), but in his pursuit of happiness he also partakes in such unshepherdish activities as hunting, which is the occasion of two very interesting lines:

> Besides, in hunting such felicitie
> Or rather infelicitie he found . . .
>   (79–80)

Read one way, these lines mean that he found felicity, or rather infelicity, in hunting — that is, he seemed lucky and happy while hunting but ultimately was unfortunate. Read another way, however, with "felicitie as the object of "hunting," these lines say that in hunting for such felicity, he actually found infelicity. Whichever way we read these lines, or if we read them both ways, Astrophel loses: his pursuit of happiness, and his extension of that pursuit beyond the shepherd's life, must and did result in tragedy. He was, as the narrator says, a "Full happie man (misweening much)" (101). His happiness was a false happiness, based on his misunderstanding of his own situation and on his misunderstanding of what constitutes happiness.

What we have, then, is a fairly strong criticism of Astrophel, who excels as a shepherd but who, unlike the Colin Clout of *Colin Clout's Come Home Again,* is not content with the pastoral world and insists on leaving that world for another one. William Oram says that "Astrophel is indeed not an ordinary shepherd: he belongs to a less peaceful and more heroic world" (566). There is that myth again, but as we can see in both *Colin Clout's Come Home Again* and *Astrophel,* that other world is clearly not more heroic. It may pretend to be heroic both to itself and to others, but it is actually a world of sterility and death, and Astrophel is quite mistaken when he abandons the pastoral world of poetry in order to join it.[12] We can see how Spenser makes this point in two ways: in his depiction of Astrophel as a version of the Redcross Knight and in his use of the Venus and Adonis story.

Again, there can be no doubt about the narrator's love and admiration for Astrophel or about his grief at Astrophel's death, but he fills his descriptions of Astrophel with verbal echoes of the young, deeply flawed Redcross Knight, the major distinction between the two characters being that Astrophel is less successful and learns less, dying before he can grow into knowledge. Astrophel is like a Redcross Knight who dies in his clash with Orgoglio. Thus, to return to the question of Astrophel's lack of happiness, we can say that he is quite literally sansjoy, and we can recall that Redcross, too, "did seeme too solemne sad." So when we read that Astrophel was "Both wise and hardie (too hardie alas)" (72) or

> Such skill matcht with such courage as he had,
> Did prick him foorth with proud desire of praise:
> To seek abroad, of daunger nought ydrad,
> His mistresse name, and his owne fame to raise
>
> (85–88)

we might well think of Redcross at the cave of Errour, where he is too "hardie" and where he fights through pride to raise, or at least to preserve, his fame. It is worth emphasizing here that Astrophel's motivation is a combination of his Arcadian unhappiness and his pride. He is not described as fighting for God or for the Protestant cause or for any other worthy cause. There is, in short, no good reason for him to abandon his proper station as shepherd-poet and seek the death he finds. As the narrator says, "Ill mynd so much to mynd another's ill, / As to become unmyndfull of his owne" (111–12), and if he then seems to blame the "cruell skies" for Astrophel's lack of self-concern, he quickly focuses attention back to Astrophel's fatal error, the kind of error that Redcross escapes. Heaven may help the one and not the other, but the fault is in them, not in their stars.

This picture is reinforced by Spenser's skillful use of the Venus and Adonis myth, which, of course, he had used earlier in Book III of the *Faerie Queene,* where, in keeping with the dual nature of Venus as both the goddess of evil sensuality and the goddess of blessed procreation, we have two versions of the story, one *in malo* and one *in bono.* In both of these versions — and in Shakespeare's *Venus and Adonis* — this fertility myth is used to explore various aspects of sexuality, but in "Astrophel" the myth is used to explore a different kind of fertility.

We might recall here that the poem is addressed to those poetic shepherds who "have learned to breed / Compassion in a country lasses hart"; if they are successful, the likelihood is that they are breeding more than compassion. In fact the early part of the poem is full of images of fertility, from the reference to Astrophel's distinguished genealogy through his charming of the nymphs who bring him gifts of flowers and fruit. The Arcadian world, the world of shepherd-poets, is fruitful, even if it is, as the narrator points out, not free of dangers: "What needeth perill to be sought abroad," he asks, "Since round about us it doth make abroad?" (89–90). In contrast, that "forreine soyle" where Astrophel goes to hunt is a land of "waste" and the poetry that describes it relies heavily on images of death and sterility, from the "subtil traines" that Astrophel uses through the spoil he hopes to claim and ultimately to the deaths of himself and his beloved Stella. In fact, according to the mythographers, for whom Adonis represents the sun, the boar is winter, the season that banishes the sun and that produces sterility and death on earth.[13]

Astrophel, then, more closely resembles the Adonis of Book III canto i than the Adonis of Book III canto vi, as he turns his back on the fruitful world of Arcadia and chooses the sterility of the hunt. His life, as the narrator says, is "wasted," that is, both laid waste and put to waste, and the only way he and his Stella can be revivified is through poetic transformation into a fictional species of flower and into the subject of this poem.

What does this reading of the poem tell us about Sidney and Spenser? The Arcadian world that Astrophel abandons is the poetic world that Colin Clout refuses to abandon in *Colin Clout's Come Home Again.* We can see this point both in the opening address to an audience of poets, whose society Astrophel has left, first by choice and then permanently through death, and in Spenser's choice of *Astrophel,* Sidney's poetic persona, as the name of his poem and his hero. In this context, Donald Cheney's suggestion about Spenser's apparent misidentification of Stella seems perfectly on target: "She is . . . quite simply the Stella of Sidney's sonnets; after the death of the maker of those sonnets, she continues to live only as he does, a part of the flowering of Sidney's poetic genius."[14] Just as Astrophel now lives only as part of Spenser's poetic universe, so Stella now lives only as part of Sidney's. The world of the hunt is not precisely the world of the court — that is the province of *Colin Clout's Come Home Again* — but it is the related world of the campaign in the Low Countries, which Spenser glorified in a limited way in Book V of the *Faerie Queene* but of which he is here obviously critical, a point to which I will return.

This poem, then, published nine years after Sidney's death, mourns not only Sidney himself but also the wastefulness of his death, the loss of a great poet in an unnecessary adventure. Anthony Esler says that Sidney's "generation was shocked by the tragedy of his death — but not by the folly of such honorable recklessness as that which killed him."[15] Perhaps many — perhaps most — of Sidney's contemporaries, having accepted the current mythology, felt this way, and this sentiment may explain the orgy of grief that followed his death; but we should remember that Sidney's death was immediately co-opted by the propagandists and the apologists for the war, and Spenser in the 1590s would have no part of that. Sidney was a great poet, and as a poet he was engaged in divine labor. That was his talent and therein lay his duty. Oram may say that Sidney's "motive for fighting Elizabeth's wars was not only love of glory as the narrator implies (85–90) but love of God,"[16] but Spenser most emphatically does not say that. Despite his love and admiration for Sidney, Spenser is highly critical of him and of the whole ethos that idolized the fallen soldier without understanding not only the uselessness but also the wastefulness of his death. Consequently *Astrophel,* unlike so many other pastoral elegies, does not even pretend to offer consolation. Instead it both mourns and blames the deceased, as does the "Doleful Lay of Clorinda," which celebrates Astrophel's "happie, happie spirit" but which ultimately, as we shall see, draws little consolation from it. As Annabel Patterson says about *The Shepheardes Calender,* "It is a tribute to Spenser's intelligence and his courage that he conceived a way to say, as it were, both things at once, to publish the unspeakable criticism alongside the celebration. . . ."[17]

There is, however, one more question I would like to discuss before examining the "Doleful Lay." If Spenser is so critical of Sidney's decision to go to war, how can we explain his apparent support for the war in Book V? Was Spenser the kind of "patriot" we may remember from the Vietnam War who maintained that the war was a very good thing as long as no one he cared about had to fight it? I do not think so. A better explanation is that in Book V Spenser was contrasting, sometimes implicitly, sometimes explicitly, the ideal of justice with the reality of justice. Thus in the Belge episode we have an ideal: if there were justice, this is how it would work; but there isn't so it doesn't. It would be good to help the Low Countries if it could be done well, although Belge has been seduced, not conquered.[18] By the early 1590s, however, if not earlier, it was clear that Leicester's expedition had been an utter failure, that its greatest accomplishment, indeed its only accomplishment worth noting, had been the death of Sidney. Spenser makes this failure clear when he notes in *Astrophel* that after the shepherd is wounded, "the captiue heard his nets did rend, / And hauing none to let, to wood did wend" (125–26). Astrophel's efforts, and Astrophel's death, have actually accomplished nothing. Perhaps Spenser recognized that one of Elizabeth's greatest strengths had been her ability to maintain England's status with a minimal involvement in war. We may recall that at Mercilla's feet

> her sword was likewise layde,
> Whose long rest rusted the bright steely brand;
> Yet when as foes enforst, or friends sought ayde,
> She could it sternely draw, that all the world dismayde.
>   (V.ix.30)

Her sword is there and it can be used, but it is rusty from lack of use, because Mercilla finds other ways to accomplish what she wants. She must be convinced to execute Duessa, just as Elizabeth had to be convinced to send Leicester and Sidney to war. And clearly Elizabeth's initial reluctance was more prudent than their fervor. Sidney, in urging battle, and in urging that he be in the battle, had abandoned his proper realm as poet, had denied his identity as Astrophel, and had entered the sterile forest, where, in an important sense, both he and Astrophel met their deaths. Sidney was responsible for the Astrophel in him, for the divine poetic gift with which he had been entrusted and which he sacrificed in the quest for glory.[19] Spenser mourned those deaths, of course, but he was also angry about them, and it is those conflicting emotions that account for the peculiar tone of the poem. Spenser was of course not a pacifist, and he illustrated the concept of the "just" war more than once in his poetry; but he recognized that Sidney's military venture was not a just war and that Sidney was the wrong person to be in it. Is this my rationalization, because I love Spenser's poetry and I want him not to be hypocritical, not to have been seduced by the war party? Perhaps, but I think that this reading of *Astrophel* is supported by such Spenserian evidence of disillusion as Book VI of the *Faerie Queene* with its contrast between the courtly world and the pastoral poetic world of Colin Clout.

"Astrophel," in fact, calls to mind Benjamin Britten's *War Requiem,* that extraordinary work in which Britten combines the Requiem Mass with the poetry of Wilfred Owen, a work that is both saddening and infuriating. It is saddening in recalling the wasteful deaths of so many young men, including such poets as Owen and Isaac Rosenberg, and it is infuriating in reminding one of the ethos that proclaimed that such deaths had value and glory. Perhaps Spenser, too, arouses these feelings, grief at Sidney's useless death and anger at Sidney's complicity in that death. *Astrophel* is not, then, a cold pastoral, but it expresses a grief that is far different from the grief expressed in other elegies. Spenser's honesty, his refusal to accept the Sidney myth, reflects his state of mind in the 1590s, his disillusionment with the court and with the Elizabethan world. Because the poet could try to improve that world, Spenser had remained true to his calling; but Sidney, he regretted, had not.

Still, *Astrophel* is not Spenser's last word on Sidney, for we must now consider "The Dolefull Lay of Clorinda." Approaching the "Dolefull Lay" is, at this time, a risky proposition, largely because of the question of its authorship. Margaret Hannay, for example, presents a strong case for Mary Sidney as the author, but she also makes it clear that in her opinion arguments against Mary Sidney's authorship are at base sexist, stemming from conceptions of "the improbability of such an achievement by a woman."[20] Despite Hannay's strictures, however, critics are not unanimous on the question of authorship: Beth Wynne Fisken, for example, assumes that Mary Sidney wrote the "Lay" while Peter Sacks just as clearly attributes authorship to Spenser.[21] There is no way to prove conclusively that either position is historically correct; but from the evidence at hand, it does not seem possible that that Mary Sidney actually wrote the "Lay," although she certainly would have voiced the sentiments it contains. Furthermore, the two poems, unlike any of the other poems in the *Astrophel* volume, are closely related not just in their sorrow over Astrophel's death but in their thematic and imagistic patterns. In addition, the "Lay" shares *Astrophel*'s straightforward, uncomplicated style:

> Ay me, to whom shall I my case complaine,
> That may compassion my impatient griefe?
> Or where shall I unfold my inward paine,
> That my enriven heart may find reliefe?
> (1–4)

Compare these lines to the far more ornate and mannered opening of Mary Sidney's "To the Angell spirit . . .":

> To thee pure sprite, to thee alone's addres't
>   this coupled worke, by double int'rest thine:
> First rais'de by thy blest hand, and what is mine
> inspird by thee, thy secrett power imprest.
> (1–4)[22]

It is no insult to Mary Sidney to doubt that the same author wrote both of these poems. In those poems that we know are by Mary Sidney, she shows herself to be a skilled poet, but her skill as a poet does not require that we accept her as the author of the "Lay."

If Spenser wrote the "Lay," however, we must ask why the poet would write two elegies for Sidney in the same volume. Of course, two of the other poems in the *Astrophel* volume are by Lodowick Bryskett, but those poems are related only in being elegies for Sidney, whereas *Astrophel* and the "Lay" form an obvious unit.

As we have seen, *Astrophel* is clearly insufficient in the traditional terms of the pastoral elegy. Written from the point of view of a fellow shepherd-poet, it mourns its subject somewhat less than it condemns him. It lacks even the conventional sense of "I weep for Astrophel—he is dead!" The "Lay," written not from the public stance of *Astrophel* but from the private stance of a mourning sister, contains more grief, though even here Spenser manipulates the conventions. The "Lay" begins with

Clorinda asking to whom she can complain, whether to the "heavenly powres" or "unto earthly men," and the first answer is to neither but only to herself. The heavenly powers knew what was about to happen and did not intervene, and men are incapable of altering their mortality.

This opening to the poem would be blasphemous if the poem stopped there, just as we might wonder what Jesus meant when he said, "My God, my God, why hast thou forsaken me?" if we did not understand that Jesus recited the whole of Psalm 22, which moves from the doubt expressed in its first line to the certainty of divine salvation in its closing verses. Just so Clorinda's opening doubts find resolution by the poem's end, resolution for what has happened to her brother. When she asks about his "immortall spirit," "Ay me, can so divine a thing be dead?" (66), the obvious answer is no, and what follows is a description of her brother's soul in heaven, freed from the travails of the world. Thus, despite the condemnation of *Astrophel,* we have a confirmation of Astrophel's essential goodness and of his eternal repose in heaven. Here is the consolation that was missing from *Astrophel.*

Even this consolation is tempered, however, for in the last verse of the elegy itself, she says

> But live thou there still happie, happie spirit,
> And give us leave thee here thus to lament:
> Not thee that doest thy heavens joy inherit,
> But our owne selves that here in dole are drent.
>> Thus do we weep and waile, and wear our eies,
>> Mourning in others, our owne miseries.
>
> (91–96)

Since Astrophel is peacefully in heaven, since he is now a "happie, happie spirit," as *Astrophel* showed us he was not in life, we cannot be lamenting for him. Rather it is for ourselves, having to live not only with his absence but with the human condition in general, that we lament, according to Clorinda. Compare this sentiment with that which closes Ralegh's contribution to the *Astrophel* volume:

> That day their Hanniball died, our Scipio fell,
> Scipio, Cicero, and petrarch of our time,
> Whose vertues, wounded by my worthlesse rime,
> Let angels speake, and heaven thy praises tell.[23]

The subject of Ralegh's poem, like those of Bryskett and Roydon, is the dead Astrophel, but that is not the subject of either *Astrophel* or the "Lay." In these poems Spenser focuses on Astrophel's unhappy life and the part that life played in the unhappiness of his friends and family, concentrating in the earlier poem on Sidney's public life and in the later on his private life.

Like the theme, the imagery of the poems also overlaps. Michael O'Connell has pointed out the continuity between the flower imagery of *Astrophel* and the "Lay," concluding that "The flower . . . becomes a very delicate symbol for Sidney's poetry." [24] It is interesting to note how carefully Spenser uses the word "flowre" in the "Lay," recalling the Penthia of *Astrophel*. In its first appearance in the "Lay," the flower is explicitly a metaphor for Astrophel himself:

> And all the fields do waile their widow state,
> Sith death their fairest flowre did late deface.
> The fairest flowre in field that ever grew,
> Was *Astrophel*; that was, we all may rew.
> (27–30)

In the next stanza, however, Clorinda asks

> What cruell hand of cursed foe vnknowne,
> Hath cropt the stalke which bore so faire a flowre?
> (31–32)

Astrophel was in one sense the flower, but in another sense he, the physical Astrophel, was the stalk that bore the flower, indicating that the flower itself was something else. This pattern is repeated again when Clorinda tells the shepherd lasses to break their garlands, "Sith the faire flowre, which them adornd, is gon" (38) and then asks

> What is become of him whose flowre here left
> Is but the shadow of his likenesse gone.
> (57–58)

This alternation between Astrophel as flower and Astrophel as producer of flowers is entirely appropriate in view of the previous imagery of sterility and death and of Astrophel's transformation into a flower in *Astrophel*. In the earlier poem, the dead poet is transformed through poetic art into a flower. He continues to exist as a flower, in combination with Stella, his own poetic creation, but he no longer exists as a producer of flowers. In the "Lay," as the lines just quoted indicate, he continues to exist as the producer of flowers, although flowers are only shadows of himself and he can produce no more. But he no longer exists as an earthly flower. There is, in the "Lay," no flower called Astrophel.[25] But—and this is an important "but"—that immortal spirit now exists in Paradise, the original garden, lying in a bed of lillies, surrounded by roses and violets (70–72). And he is also surrounded by other flowers, the verses that constitute the *Astrophel* volume, as the "Lay's" last lines indicate:

> The which I here in order will rehearse,
> As fittest flowres to deal his mournfull hearse.
> (107–108)

In this poem, then, Spenser conflates the fruitfulness of poetry, the fruitfulness of nature, and the fruitfulness of Christian belief, while at the same time acknowledging the grief and sorrow to which human beings are prey. He offers some consolation, especially after the criticism in *Astrophel,* but this is not an untempered Christian consolation.[26] It is, perhaps a consolation that bids us abide with a world in which even Astrophel can make such dreadful mistakes, a world in which poetry can do so much and so little, a world in which we can proclaim the consolation of religious belief and yet be unable to restrain our grief over worldly mutability, at least until such time as we gain "that Sabaoths sight."

Astrophel, then, along with its companion piece, is hardly "cool" or "insipid." These are poems that probe the heart of matters that were central to Spenser and that challenge conventional attitudes. Our response to them requires that we also not rely on convention, that we attend closely to what Spenser had to say, for Spenser's reflections on the concerns of his time continue to resonate in ours.

NOTES

1.   S. E. Winbolt, *Spenser and his Poetry* (London: G. G. Harrap, 1911), 64.

2.   C. S. Lewis, *English literature in the Sixteenth Century Excluding Drama* (Oxford: Clarendon Press, 1954), 372.

3.   Michael O'Connell, "*Astrophel:* Spenser's Double Elegy," *Studies in English Literature* 11 (1971): 27.

4.   Sir Robert Naunton, *Fragmenta Regalia, or Observations on Queen Elizabeth, Her Times & Favorites,* ed. John S. Cerovski (Washington, D.C.: Folger Books, 1985), 56.

5.   See Alan Hager, "The Exemplary Mirage: Fabrication of Sir Philip Sidney's Biographical Image and the Sidney Reader," in *Essential Articles for the Study of Sir Philip Sidney*, ed. Arthur F. Kinney (Hamden: Archon Books, 1986), 22. Originally published in *ELH* 48 (1981), 1–16.

6.   W. A. Ringler, Jr., "Sir Philip Sidney: The Myth and the Man," in *Sir Philip Sidney: 1586 and the Creation of a Legend*, ed. Jan Van Dorsten, Dominic Baker-Smith, Arthur F. Kinney (Leiden: E. J. Brill, 1986), 11. See also the account in Raphael Falco, "Instant Artifacts: Vernacular Elegies for Philip Sidney," *Studies in Philology* 89 (1992): 1–19.

7.   Hager, "Exemplary Mirage," 17–18.

8.   All references to Spenser's poem are to *The Yale Edition of the Shorter Poems of Edmund Spenser*, ed. William A. Oram, et al. (New Haven: Yale University Press, 1989).

9.   *Shorter Poems*, 565.

10.   James Osborn *Young Philip Sidney, 1572–1577* (New Haven: Yale University Press, 1972), 131.

11.   Osborn, *Young Philip Sidney*, 138.

12.   Peter Sacks in *The English Elegy: Studies in the Genre from Spenser to Yeats* (Baltimore: Johns Hopkins University Press, 1985) makes a similar point when he mentions "Spenser's hostility or at least ambivalence toward Astrophel's lethal pursuit. At an obvious level, Spenser finds it difficult to approve the very choice that led to Sidney's death" (53). Sacks, however, subordinates this point, which I find central to the poem, to his interest in how the poem functions in the elegiac tradition. What Sacks interprets as Astrophel's "rejection of language" in favor of "the unmediated and here almost [!] suicidal pursuit of violent action" (54) I see as Astrophel's rejection of his fruitful poetic calling in favor of the sterile and clearly suicidal military option. Sacks is interested in the way "the poem achieves its work of mourning . . . by resolving [the] question of the adequacy of language and its figures of consolation" (54). He sees this resolution being achieved "by the thorough way in which the second part of the poem, 'The Lay of Clorinda,' questions and moves beyond the consolation figured in the earlier part" (54). I shall argue that *Astrophel* and the "Doleful Lay" present Astrophel in two completely different ways, and that while the private grief of the lay does present the possibility of consolation, there is no consolation in *Astrophel*, which laments Sidney's abandonment not of language but specifically of poetry. In short, Sacks is examining the mechanics of mourning, often with great insight (and often with a bit too much Freud), while I am trying to examine Spenser's attitude toward Sidney's life and death as he expressed it in 1595.

Raphael Falco says that in Spenser's poem "the dead knight is seen by Spenser to have been misguided in his foreign exploits, more like a hubristic Adonis than an exemplary Alexander" ("Instant Artifacts," 14), which is closer to the point that I am trying to make.

13.   See, for example, Natalis Comes, *Mythologiae sive explicationum fabularum libri decem* (Venice, 1567), 287 and Vincenzo Cartari, *Le imagini con la spositione de i dei de gli antichi* (Venice, 1556), 118.

14.   Donald Cheney, "Spenser's Fortieth Birthday and Related Fictions," *Spenser Studies* 4 (1983), 14.

15.   Anthony Esler, *The Aspiring Mind of the Elizabethan Younger Generation* (Durham: Duke University Press, 1966), 91.

16.   *Shorter Poems,* 567.

17.   Annabel Patterson, *Pastoral and Ideology: Virgil to Valery* (Berkeley: University of California Press, 1987), 131.

18.   As Michael O'Connell explains in *Mirror and Veil: The Historical Dimension of Spenser's Faerie Queene* (Chapel Hill: University of North Carolina Press, 1977), "Spenser's Legend of Justice, published as it was in 1596, is caught uneasily between . . . national moods. In its explicit argument it is a patriotic defense of Elizabeth and her policies. But we catch sight of Spenser's discomfort from time to time, and the gloom at the end of the book seems indeed suggestive of the mood to come. There appears no open expression of political skepticism, but the tone of the conclusion implies dissatisfaction and a basic doubt of the processes of political reward. Spenser, in fact, writes himself into a decidedly awkward position: while praising Elizabeth's justice, he portrays a final lack of justice for the human instruments of her policy" (157–58).

19.   According to Ralph Sargent in *The Life and Lyrics of Sir Edward Dyer* (Oxford: Clarendon Press, 1968), "Throughout the negotiations between the Dutch and the English, Edward Dyer preserved a steadier head than either Sidney or Leicester. His concern was more honestly directed toward the welfare of England itself, less deflected by love of personal glory or political idealism" (48–49). Anthony Esler reinforces this point when he says, "The Spanish War, beginning with the English intervention in the Netherlands in 1585, was the first watershed in the careers of the aspiring generation of 1560. In responding to the opportunities for quick gain and rapid advancement opened up by the war, the younger generation particularly displayed one of the key qualities of the aspiring mind—a consuming passion for 'honor'" (*Aspiring Mind,* 87). In *Metamorphic Verse: The Elizabethan Minor Epic* (Princeton: Princeton University Press, 1981), Clark Hulse notes that Spenser had commented on this tendency earlier in his career. In commenting on Book III, Hulse says, "The upshot is that each martial encounter is erotic at base and each is of questionable worth. The result is not so much to test the moral status of desire—that is questioned quite enough already—but to call in question the psychological roots of heroic action and to break down any simple claim of the military hero to nobility" (265). Spenser may well have shared Arthur Kinney's insight into Sidney's *Defence:* "If we read the *Defence* closely, we find that it is a political document as well as a poetics; it is designed to enable the poet, to give him an unassailable position of power and authority. By teaching virtuous knowledge in the strongest and most permanent way, by encouraging readers to exercise virtue so as to know it—for that, Sidney says, is the true end of poetry—the poet become the moral leader, even the moral arbiter, of all men and women" ("Puritan Versus Royalists: Sir Philip Sidney's Rhetoric at the Court of Elizabeth I," in *Sir Philip Sidney's Achievements,* ed. M. J. B. Allen, et al. (New York: AMS Press, 1990, p.44). It was this role that Sidney abandoned in the hope of winning temporal glory.

20.   Margaret P. Hannay, *Philip's Phoenix: Mary Sidney, Countess of Pembroke* (New York: Oxford University Press, 1990), 63. Strangely enough, Hannay twice refers to the "Lay" as being inferior to *Astrophel* (67), thereby damaging her own argument: if we agree that the "Lay" is inferior, and if we think a woman would be capable only of inferior work, then Mary Sidney could certainly have written the poem. Surely Hannay could not have meant to prove Mary's authorship by pointing out the work's inferiority.

21.   Beth Wynne Fisken, "'To the Angell spirit . . .': Mary Sidney's Entry into the 'World of Words,'" in *The Renaissance Englishwoman in Print: Counterbalancing the Canon,*

ed. Anne M. Haselkorn and Betty S. Travitsky (Amherst: University of Massachusetts Press, 1990).

22.   In *The Psalms of Sir Philip Sidney and the Countess of Pembroke*, ed. J. C. A. Rathmell (New York: New York University Press, 1963), xxxv.

23.   In *The Complete Poetical Works of Spenser*, ed. R. E. Neil Dodge (Cambridge: Riverside Press, 1908).

24.   O'Connell, *"Astrophel,"* 32.

25.   There is, however, a reference to such a plant in the "Daphnaida":

> My little flocke, whom earst I lov'd so well,
> And wont to feede with finest grasse that grew,
> Feede ye hencefoorth on bitter *Astrophel*,
> And stinking Smallage, and unsaverie Rew . . .
>
> (344–447)

It is difficult to imagine Spenser using the phrase "bitter *Astrofell*" (even with this spelling) without being fully aware of what he was saying. The phrase is certainly appropriate as a description of the later poem.

26.   O'Connell comments that Clorinda's lament presents the Christian consolation and completes the elegy (*Astrophel* 32). I would argue that her lament uses Christian consolation, but that the elegy cannot be completed.

JEAN R. BRINK

Constructing the
View of the Present State of Ireland

THE *VIEW OF THE PRESENT State of Ireland,* because of its ad-
vocacy of the complete subjugation of the Irish by famine and military conquest, has long been a focal point for anti-colonial and
anti-English discourse. In this work attributed to Edmund Spenser, Irenius' proposals are to lead to a "vnion of manners and Con-
formitye of mindes to bringe them to be one people," but the goal
of achieving a nation of "one people," according to the author of
the *View,* depends upon a wholesale commitment of the resources
of the English crown to conquest and reformation.[1] Until· the
twentieth century the *View* was largely ignored by literary scholars
except for sporadic attempts to use it as a vehicle for attacking or
defending England's policies in Ireland. Irish school books, to be
sure, did not ignore the *View;* its highly quotable passages splen-
didly illustrated the brutality of the English and insured that Spenser was vilified as the archetypal English colonialist, a characterization of Spenser that has the merit, at least, of being simple. Perhaps,
because one of the basic tenets of New Criticism was that great
works of art must be apolitical, revisionist scholarship has become
obsessed in recent years with politics—its own politics and that of
the past. In consequence, it has become increasingly fashionable to
use the *View* to interpret Spenser's biography and to explicate *The
Faerie Queene.*[2]

203

Because of the lack of attention paid to textual scholarship, however, it is not generally recognized that we face significant challenges in constructing a context for this problematical text, a text first attributed to Spenser thirty-five years after his death and one for which there is no holograph manuscript. Recent literary theory has popularized the view that texts are unstable in meaning, that we inevitably reinterpret earlier texts and events according to our own needs. Nevertheless, general agreement that concepts such as "authoritative" and "standard" are constructed has not, in the case of Spenser's texts, resulted in widespread awareness of the need to reexamine primary sources and to critique the bibliographical principles employed in constructing "standard" editions. I hope to encourage this kind of critical approach to Spenser and his texts by interrogating assumptions about government censorship that have become entrenched in discussions of the *View,* showing that the text of the *View* is unfinished, and offering a critical survey of the evidence we have for attributing the *View* to Spenser. My purpose is to show that, until manuscript evidence is fully sifted, scholars should be very cautious about legitimizing aproaches to Spenser that interpret him or his work from the perspective of the highly unstable text we have of the *View.*

Was the *View* suppressed?

Recent studies of the *View* have been predicated upon the assumption that this dialogue circulated in manuscript because the English government prevented its publication. No documentary evidence, however, has been cited to demonstrate that either the Privy Council or the bishop of London suppressed it. Suppression of suspect works, the exercise of pre-publication censorship, would require a very efficient system of screening manuscripts.[3] From the surviving evidence, however, it appears that the English government, when it did attempt pre-publication censorship of contemporary works, was remarkably ineffectual. For example, even though the government, aided by the Company of Stationers, made a concerted effort to track down illegal presses and to prevent publication of the unlicensed Martin Marprelate tracts, these pamphlets circulated widely in print. The abundant evidence relating to the attempts to suppress "Martin" suggests that anyone determined to publicize his convictions, and willing to take the consequences, could get his views into print.[4]

Government censorship did occur, but surviving records suggest that when the government did object to a work and take action against the author and printer, reprisals took place after publication. Even then, efforts to prevent the circulation of seditious, libellous, or obscene books were usually ineffective. Copies have survived of the books ordered burned on June 1, 1599 by John Whitgift, archbishop of Canterbury, and Richard Bancroft, bishop of London (III.316).[5] Two well-documented instances of government censorship and retaliation, John Stubbs's *The Discoverie of a Gaping Gulf* (1579) and Sir John Hayward's *The First Part of the Life and Raigne of King Henrie the III* (1599), both occurred after the publication of these works. Stubbs's far from discreet tract was printed at a time when public sentiment opposed the queen's marriage to the duke of Alençon. Stubbs lost his right hand for writing what was described as a seditious and slanderous libel, but, somewhat ironically, was asked by Burghley in 1587 to write a polemical tract in defense of English justice.[6] Hayward's history did not cause immediate alarm.[7] He published it in January 1599 and dedicated it to Essex on the grounds that the earl would play an important role in deciding the succession. Although it was decided that Essex would go to Ireland by November 1598, English forces did not cross the Irish sea until April 1599. By March 1, 1599 John Chamberlain had written to Dudley Carleton: "Here hath ben much descanting about it, why such a storie shold come at this time, and many exceptions taken, especially to the epistle which was a short thinge in Latin dedicated to the erle of Essex."[8] On June 1, 1599 a number of books were burned by order of the archbishop of Canterbury and the bishop of London, but Hayward's history was not among them (III.677). Nevertheless, the printing of any English history was forbidden unless it was authorized by a member of the Privy Council (III.677). When Essex began to figure as a potential rebel, returning to England in defiance of the queen's orders on September 26, 1599, Hayward's history received new scrutiny. Events had made Hayward's history of the deposition of Richard II by Henry Bolingbroke appear to support the deposition of Elizabeth. Hayward himself was finally committed to the Tower in July 1600, more than a year and a half after his work was first printed. His imprisonment preceded the Essex rebellion by six months, but Hayward remained in the Tower until after James's accession.[9]

What evidence do we have that the *View* was suppressed? Even if we were to accept the notion of effective censorship, the suppression of the *View* is unsupported by documentary evidence in either the *Acts of the*

Privy Council or the state papers. In fact, the suppression of the *View* seems to be an invention of recent scholarship, which portrays the Elizabethan state as making extraordinary efforts to contain subversive texts. James Ware, who first attributed the authorship of the *View* to Spenser, does not mention any attempts to suppress its publication. Not one of the seventeenth- or eighteenth-century biographies of Spenser suggests that the *View* was suppressed by the government or even regarded as suspect. Later biographies are silent or tentative about the suppression of the *View.* Alexander Grosart, the nineteenth-century biographer responsible for early documentary work on Spenser's life, vigorously supported Spenser on the grounds that his defense of Lord Grey showed that Spenser was neither a "time-server," nor a "court-tool."[10] In 1928, Pauline Henley, though highly critical of Spenser's role in Ireland, tentatively suggested that official approval of the *View* may have inspired the government to recommend that Spenser be appointed sheriff of the County of Cork in 1598.[11] In 1949, Alexander Judson, author of the standard biography of Spenser, appearing as part of the *Spenser Variorum,* remarks that the *View* was entered in the Stationers' Register in 1598 pending further authority and very cautiously says, "but the authority seems not to have been obtained."[12] Grosart thus sees Spenser as the courageous and disinterested defender of Lord Grey; Henley thinks that the government may have rewarded him for writing his dialogue; and Judson begs the question.

Recent critical approaches to the *View* and its relationship to Spenser's biography are conveniently summarized by David B. Quinn in his article on the *View* in *The Spenser Encyclopedia* (1990). Quinn describes this work as Spenser's "considered opinions about the Ireland he knew so well after sixteen years of living (or exile) there" and concludes that the *View* "may be seen as Spenser's attempt to win the attention of English statesmen, perhaps even the Queen," and to advance himself, possibly even to secure a post in England.[13] Paradoxically, the other assumption repeated here and in recent studies of the *View* is that its publication was forbidden by the government.[14] Quinn, for example, states parenthetically that "the abortive attempt to have it published in 1598 was hopeless from the start as no English official would sanction it" (714).

The censorship argument is not new with Quinn. In fact, it is entrenched in recent Spenserian scholarship. In 1983 Jonathan Goldberg explained that the authorities suppressed the *View* because it "laid bare the premises upon which sovereign power operates," exposing the underlying savagery of reformation.[15] In 1986, Ciaran Brady stated that

"Spenser's work, on being submitted to the Master Stationer in 1598, was refused registration and blocked by the government" and concluded that "it was even then, as it has been since, a source of some embarrassment."[16] Also in 1986, David J. Baker assumed that Spenser wanted the *View* published and claimed that "Elizabeth's Council did not want the treatise published," but Baker concluded that the authorities must have misread the *View* because it is "royalist polemic."[17] In 1989, extending his earlier arguments, Brady maintained that the government had prohibited publication of the *View* because Spenser had rejected the efficacy of the common law as a means of reforming Ireland.[18]

Underpinning many of these arguments are two suppositions difficult to reconcile: Spenser wrote the *View* to promote his career, and the government intervened to prohibit its publication. If Spenser wrote the *View* to win the patronage of powerful people in the government, then we have to envision a singularly inept Spenser, if he failed so ignominiously that the government actually suppressed his work. Critical examination of the only documentary evidence upon which these suppositions are based makes the claim of censorship appear improbable.

The speculation that the *View* was suppressed by the government derives from an uncritical reading of a cautionary note in the Stationers' Register. The *View* was entered in the Stationers' Register on April 14, 1598 to Matthew Lownes under the hand of the Master Warden [Thomas] Man. The title given in the Stationers' Register is *A viewe of the present state of Ireland. Discoursed by waye of a Dialogue betwene EUDOXUS and IRENIUS,* and the entry carries the note "vppon Condicion that hee gett further aucthoritie before yt be prynted" (III.111). An entry in the Stationers' Register protected the rights of the publisher or bookseller, guaranteeing that another printer could not infringe on his copyright. In 1583, for example, it was determined that books entered in the Stationers' Register would have the same protection as books issued by her Majesty's privilege.[19] At least one of the wardens had to "allow" or approve a new book before the clerk made an entry in the Register. When Matthew Lownes entered the *View,* William Ponsonby was the recognized publisher of Spenser's works, and Ponsonby was on the verge of becoming a master warden. Thus, the cautionary note in the entry for the *View* could just as well signal a disagreement over publication rights as government censorship.

In fact, how frequent — or infrequent — an occurrence was it to have a conditional note recorded in an entry in the Stationers' Register? My rough survey of entries from January 1598 up to and including June

1598 indicates that over fifteen percent of all entries contain some kind of conditional note. A variety of possible reasons existed for mentioning the need for additional authorization or authority. As suggested above, protection of the rights of publishers was particularly important. On March 7, 1597 Thomas Millington entered a book called "JACK of Newbery," and the cautionary note reads, "so that he haue yt laufully Aucthorised" (III.81). This work was transferred to Humfrey Lownes on May 25, 1597, and the provision that it must be lawfully authorized was repeated (III.84). On the other hand, we might expect the authorities to ask questions concerning the licensing of libellous satires such as T. [John] Marston's *The Metamorphosis of PIGMALIONs Image, and Satyres* (III.116), a work that was later ordered burned in 1599, but Marston's work is entered without a provision.

If the entry concerning the *View* is compared with similar entries in April 1598, we have insufficient evidence to conclude that the government suppressed the publication of the *View*. On April 3, 1598 Thomas Bastard's *Seven bookes of Epigrammes,* a contribution to the epigram wars, is entered without comment (III.110). Sometimes, but not always, works that were entered before they had been translated required further authorization. That may have been the case with *the warres betwene the Turkes and the Christians from CHARLES the Vth untill the yeare of the lorde 1597,* a work entered to Robert Boulton on April 11, 1598 with the provision: "to be printed by him when he shall gett better aucthoritie" (III.110). An exceedingly cautious entry was later given to a translation of Herodotus from the French. On March 29, 1599 James Robertes entered his copy of a translation of *The preparatif treatis[e] to the Apologie for HERODOTUS.* The conditions are quite specific: "The Inglishe Wrytten Copye shalbe seene and laufully alowed / and Aucthorised to be putt in print before any Impression thereof be begunne / Otherwise this entrance to be voyd" (III.141).

On April 14, 1598, the very same day that the *View* was entered, Andrewe Harris entered his copy of *The second parte of HERO and LEANDER* by Henry Polone [Petowe] "vppon Condicon that hee gett further laufull aucthoritie for the publisheinge thereof. before yt be published" (III.111). The difficulty in this case was that Edward Blount had assigned his rights to *Hero and Leander* to Paule Lynlay on March 2, 1598 (III.105); Petowe's continuation of the story of Hero and Leander later appeared in print.

At the same time, the entry for *A viewe of the present state of Ireland. Discoursed by waye of a Dialogue betwene EUDOXUS and IRENIUS* more mildly stipulates that Matthew Lownes should obtain "further auc-thoritie." It is conceivable that the Privy Council suppressed the *View*, but the entry in the Stationers' Register, by itself, does not warrant that assumption. Spenser may have wished to stop the publication of an un-finished work, one that takes a highly critical view of English deputies in Ireland, but, again, there is no evidence that he made this effort, or that anyone made it on his behalf. We do know that Fulke Greville suc-cessfully intervened to prevent the publication of Sir Philip Sidney's *Ar-cadia* because this event can be documented.[20] In November 1586 Will-iam Ponsonby, who eventually printed the *Arcadia*, warned Greville that one of his competitors planned to print Sidney's work; Greville complained to Walsingham that the text of the Old Arcadia was inade-quate. The *Arcadia* did not appear in print until 1590 when a manuscript had been suitably edited based on Sidney's revisions.[21]

Before any conclusions can be drawn about government censorship, a cautionary note in the Stationers' Register has to be contextualized. Thomas Man, the Master Warden who approved the entry of the *View* to Matthew Lownes, was closely connected to the Lownes family. He was the father-in-law of Humphrey Lownes, the brother of Matthew Lownes.[22] To celebrate his marriage to Thomas Man's daughter, Hum-phrey hired the Stationers' hall for his wedding feast.[23] Thomas Man continued to promote Humphrey's career even after his daughter's death and his son-in-law's remarriage. At the same time, William Pon-sonby, who published all of Spenser's works printed during his lifetime, vigorously protected his own interests. We know that he managed to prevent a rival from printing the *Arcadia* in 1586. If William Ponsonby had entered the *View* in the Stationers' Register, the possibility that the cautionary note relates to government censorshop would be strength-ened, though not proved. As it is, the note tells us little. Matthew Lownes, aided by his kinsman Thomas Man, may have been attempting to encroach on the territory of William Ponsonby. Unless evidence other than the entry in the Stationers' Register is forthcoming, it is only prudent to assume that no official effort was made to suppress the *View*.

Is the *View* a finished work?

The existence of many extant manuscripts of the *View* also helped to energize the theory that its publication had been prevented, but, in fact, numerous tracts on Ireland survive in several copies, some of them still unprinted.[24] In many instances, textual scholarship might offer a reliable means of determining when the manuscripts of the *View* were copied, that is, before or after Ware's edition. Although interpretive commentary on Spenser is voluminous, much of it of high quality, textual scholarship is unreliable, particularly in the case of the *View*. If, for example, we examine the entirely straightforward question of which manuscript was submitted by Matthew Lownes for entry in the Stationers' Register, there are daunting inconsistencies in secondary scholarship. W. L. Renwick stated that Bodleian Library, MS Rawlinson B478 contained a note from Thomas Man, a Warden of the Stationers' Company, to the Secretary Mr. Collinges allowing Matthew Lownes to print the *View* when "he do bringe other authorytie."[25] Even though Renwick revised his commentary for the 1970 reprint of the *View*, he ignored Ray Heffner's argument that Bodleian, MS Gough Ireland 2, which contains an elaborate title page, was intended for publication.[26] Rudolf Gottfried says that Bodleian, MS Rawlinson B478 was intended for publication (507), but equivocates concerning Bodleian, MS Gough Ireland 2, remarking that it is important not only for its connection to a version in the Public Record Office, but also "because it seems to have been prepared for publication" (511, n.9). In his 1990 *Spenser Encyclopedia* article on the *View*, Quinn makes reference neither to Bodleian, MS Rawlinson B478, nor to Renwick's claim, but states that the Bodleian manuscript (MS Gough Ireland 2) was prepared for publication, probably by some of Spenser's friends (715). This kind of confusion can and should be avoided, but that will only be possible if far more attention is paid to Spenser's manuscripts. Renwick is correct in identifying Bodleian, MS Rawlinson B478 as the copy submitted for entry in the Stationers' Register; the note from Thomas Man appears on the last leaf of this quarto manuscript.

Both literary and historical interpretation depends upon accurate and thorough textual scholarship. No lengthy justification should be required to garner support for the position that every extant manuscript of a text, especially a text first printed after an author's death, should be examined, described, and collated with the standard edition. In his *Index of English Literary Manuscripts* (1980), Peter Beal identified four manuscripts of the *View* that were unknown to the editors of the *Spenser Variorum*, and a fifth has since been discovered by Dr. Christopher Ridgeway, Librarian, Castle Howard.[27] These manuscripts cannot be ignored. If additional manuscripts are discovered, they, too, must be described and collated with the standard edition. *The Spenser Encyclopedia* (1990) does not address the *View* in its article on critical bibliography; consequently, the only discussion of text available to scholars who wish to write interpretive commentary on the *View* is to be found in the textual apparatus of the *Spenser Variorum,* a work principally intended as a compilation of critical and historical commentary on Spenser. Rudolf Gottfried devotes only Part C of Appendix III to the text of the *View* (pages 506–24), while amassing interpretive commentary (pages 247–440).

We owe a debt of gratitude to both Renwick and Gottfried who worked on the text of the *View* prior to the existence of computers, when collation was a far more difficult task than it has since become. The problems we encounter in financing repeated trips to archives out of personal funds and of obtaining reliable microfilms were compounded for both of these editors. The best way to acknowledge the contributions of Renwick and Gottfried, however, is to examine the conclusions that they draw and confront their editorial procedures critically. The discussion of text in the *Spenser Variorum* was influenced by Francis Johnson's *Critical Bibliography of the Works of Edmund Spenser Printed Before 1700* (1933), a critical bibliography prepared before the work of R. B. McKerrow, W. W. Greg, and Fredson Bowers had been fully absorbed.[28] Johnson, for example, states that he has ignored manuscripts, even though he acknowledges that many manuscripts of the *View* were written prior to the printed edition (v–vi). There is as yet no critical bibliography of Spenser's manuscripts, and no article in *The Spenser Encyclopedia* addresses the bibliographical problems relating to the numerous manuscripts of the *View.*[29] Discussions of text in Renwick and the *Spenser Variorum* are arguably out-of-date, but they have never been corrected.

Let us now turn to the vexing question of what can generally be assumed about the suitability of the text of the *View* for the kind of close literary or historical analysis that it has begun to receive. Renwick, who was the first modern editor of the *View,* believed that the *View* was unfinished. He points out that "there are blank spaces in all texts, and plain errors of fact, that suggest that another revision was intended" (*Spenser Variorum,* 9:510). In terms of editorial practice, Gottfried seems to concur: he reproduces the blank spaces in Huntington Library, Ellesmere MS 1741 in the text of the *Spenser Variorum* (p. 113, 1942, f. 35V; P. 199, 4429, f. 80V; p. 230, 5291, f. 95R).

The methodology used to construct these modern editions also needs to be examined critically. Both Renwick and Gottfried selected a copy text with a known provenance and used other manuscripts to correct unclear readings (9:507). Omissions occurring in other manuscripts are for the most part silently ignored. These editorial practices are familiar because they are based on procedures developed to edit the printed texts of Shakespeare's plays. Procedures such as these, however, are unsuitable for handling a text existing in fifteen to twenty manuscript versions. No one would dream of ignoring an extant manuscript of *Hamlet,* if such a gem were known to have survived. And, if there were twenty manuscript versions of *Hamlet,* the editorial practice in Shakespearian textual studies would probably have been very different.[30] Manuscripts may differ radically from each other in ways that printed texts do not. Any single manuscript, for example, may preserve evidence of authorial revision and so be of unrivaled significance. In fact, the one manuscript that both Renwick and Gottfried identify as containing "fragments of an early, unrevised version of the dialogue" (*Spenser Variorum,* 9:509–510) was not collated against their copy texts, texts, making it impossible to check their conclusions without recourse to the original manuscript. This is understandable because when the standard editions of the *View* were constructed, the principal editorial objective was to produce the most complete text possible.

An important critical distinction needs to be made between a complete text and one that is finished. A text that has a beginning, middle, and end could loosely be considered complete, but it should not necessarily be treated as finished. Authors, as we are well aware, cut as well as add to their work. Any one of the abbreviated or condensed manuscripts of the *View* may preserve evidence of authorial revision, and so be more important than all of the others. The procedures used in constructing the standard editions of the *View* did not require the editors to confront these possibilities; in fact, their methodology probably prevented them from doing so.

We have several kinds of textual evidence that the *View* should not be treated as a finished text. First, we have the authoritative testimony of the modern editors who have worked most closely with the manuscripts. Renwick stated that another revision must have been intended in a passage that Gottfried took care to include in the *Spenser Variorum* (9:510). Second, we have clumsy examples of repetition (cf., 2611–2621 and 5028–5039), which would probably have been revised in a finished text. Third, we have the problem that editorial practices used to construct early twentieth-century standard editions were based on theories developed to produce conflated editions of printed works.

In spite of these significant textual problems, most interpretive commentary on the *View* has assumed that it was finished and that its finished

state is represented by these edited texts. Ciaran Brady, for example, offers the following argument concerning the text of the *View*:

> The *View* is a carefully researched, artfully constructed political
> treatise which went through several drafts before being pre-
> sented for publication: it should not, therefore, be compared
> with the casual fulminations of frustrated, scared or self-
> aggrandizing officials or planters which pepper the state corres-
> pondence of that period. . . . Significant comparisons, therefore,
> can only be made between the *View* and other items of its own
> kind, that it to say, formally constructed political tracts (23).

Brady assumes that differing manuscript versions of the *View* were
authorized by the author, that the text "went through several drafts,"
and that a finished text was then "presented for publication." But these
mistakes are understandable. The textual apparatus of the standard editions does not make the instability of this text clear, probably in large
part because the editors' primary aim was to furnish a complete text.

There is also external evidence that the *View* is unfinished: its tone,
when compared with that of the two authors whom Brady identifies as
appropriate for comparison, is undiplomatic. Comparing the *View* with
Richard Beacon's *Solon His Folie* (1594) and Sir William Herbert's *Croftus, Sive de Hibernia Liber* (c. 1588), Brady has argued that Spenser offers
a more desperate and brutal solution to the Irish question than either of
these contemporaries. In fact, comparison with the finished texts of
Beacon and Herbert calls attention to what is left out of the *View*. Presumably, if the author of the *View* actually wished to influence English
policy in Ireland, he would have included long diplomatic passages
praising the queen and might even have tempered his criticism of the
English colonial administration. If the finished texts of Beacon and
Herbert are those works most appropriate for comparison with the
View, then its author seems to have violated decorum by not specifically
exempting his sovereign from the harsh judgments meted out to her
servants: both Beacon and Herbert are critical of English policies in Ireland and advocate reforms, but their critical stances do not prevent
them from celebrating their queen.

Solon His Follie is a far more philosophical dialogue than the *View*:
Beacon has absorbed the lessons to be learned from careful reading of
classical history, and he has read and understood Machiavelli. Like the
author of the *View*, Beacon argues that force is necessary to reform a

commonwealth "gained by the sword and conquest" and "also corrupted in manners" (F1V), praises Lord Grey (F2V), and deplores the tyranny of the Old English or Anglo-Norman lords (K2V).[31] Beacon advises the queen to change certain policies; for example, he recommends disarming the Irish and not allowing them military training (N3V–N4R). Contrary to the Elizabethan policy in Munster of making hereditary grants to colonists, Beacon advises that lands be granted to colonists only during their lives because their offspring may intermarry or foster with the mere (or pure) Irish and become disaffected toward England (O3R). Nevertheless, Beacon frames his commentary with an "Epistle Dedicatorie" that unequivocally celebrates the queen, saying that if all "actes and monuments of former ages" . . . were "committed to oblivion, yet the recordes and monumentes of your Maiesties most happy governement, may sufficiently revive the same."

Even though later in his dialogue Beacon waxes eloquent on the abuses created by coyne and livery (F1V), his dedication tactfully praises Elizabeth for reforming the "detestable custome of Coiney and Livery, that fretter of the peoples lives and substaunce, that Nurse and teate which sometimes gave sucke and nutriment vnto all disobedience, rebellions, enormities, vices and iniquities of that Realme." Throughout his dedication Beacon is laudatory about the effectiveness of English policies and optimistic about their success, even though later he outlines reform of those policies. In 1594, the year that Hugh Maguire and Hugh Roe O'Donnell attacked Enniskillen, Beacon tells us that prior to Elizabeth's reign, life was "rude, cruell, and wilde" in Ireland, but now it is "for the most part . . . obedient, gentle, and civill." Praising Elizabeth and assuring her that she will find favor in God's sight for her "thorough reformation of this your Realme of Ireland," Beacon humbly excuses his presumption at giving the queen his advice, explaining that he has only done so, because he did not want to "suffer so honourable actions to bee buried in oblivion."

Sir William Herbert, the other author that Brady holds up as a comparison to the author of the *View,* like most of his English contemporaries in Ireland, wrote numerous letters and short tracts on Ireland preserved in the state papers. His Latin treatise *Croftus* remained in manuscript until it was printed by the Roxburghe Club in 1887. Herbert entitled his Latin treatise *Croftus* as a compliment to Sir James Croft, who had served as lord deputy in Ireland from 1551 to 1552. The treatise was written after Croft's death on September 4, 1590. Herbert had previously published a Latin treatise entitled *Sir William Herbert's confutation of Campion the Jesuit's Ten Reasons,* and his own death on March 4, 1593 may have prevented him from publishing *Croftus.*[32] Herbert begins his treatise with a lengthy philosophical preface that praises the acumen of Sir James Croft and explains that Herbert was moved to write this treatise because of his conversations with Croft.

Like Beacon and the author of the *View,* he is critical of the Old English, observing that colonies degenerate when the colonists adopt native customs. Herbert maintains that "there is no better way to remedy this evil than to do away with and destroy completely the habits and practices of the natives" (81). Like Beacon, however, Herbert extols the achievements of the "august hero, Henry VIII" and the "distinguished Elizabeth" (81). Applauding Elizabeth for passing legislation against Irish dress and rites, he blames the persistence of barbarous customs on those who have failed to enforce these laws (81). While Herbert does not explicitly criticize the queen's propensity to pardon rebels, as the author of the *View* does, he warns that sterner policies may be warranted if the Irish resist reformation. If persuasion and laws do not reform the Irish, Herbert predicts that some future king "of great prudence and power" will "disperse that entire race and will extirpate all the inhabitants there who have lapsed into the habits and customs of the Irish" (87).

Tactfully, he inserts an unqualified tribute to his monarch's administration of Ireland near the end of his treatise:

> Since our most illustrious and wise Elizabeth has vigorously and auspiciously and in a truly royal manner embarked on a system of administration for Ireland which is complete, carefully worked out and perfect in every detail, I pray from the bottom of my heart that this system which is designed for the everlasting happiness of that country may be blessed and made fast by the authority, council, power and care of so great a sovereign, so that this holy and heroic work for the happiness of Ireland, which is fit to be celebrated in all literatures and languages, may be blessed (117).

Thus, celebration of the monarch seems to have been conventional in political treatises advocating change or criticizing policy.

If the *View* were a text that its author regarded as ready for the press or for widespread manuscript circulation, we would expect to find the kind of tributes offered by Beacon and Herbert. Like these contemporaries, Edmund Spenser, although critical of foreign policy and court politics in the second part of *The Faerie Queene,* does not fail to celebrate the queen in a memorable dedication. Describing himself as Elizabeth's "most Humble servant," he assures her that he "doth in all humilitie dedicate, present, and consecreate these his labours to live with the eternitie of her fame." That the *View* departs from the politic conventions observed in the finished political treatises of Beacon and Herbert, and Spenser's own practice, supports Renwick's and Gottfried's editorial judgments that its text is unfinished.

That the manuscripts of the *View* lack both a dedication and a preface also suggests that it is an unfinished work. The manuscripts begin abruptly: Eudoxus comments to Irenius: "But if that Countrie of Irelande, whence youe latelye come be so goodlie and Commodious a soyle as yee reporte, I wonder that no course is taken for the turninge theareof to good vses, and reducinge that salvage nacion to better gouerment and Cyvilitye" (9:43). If the author of the *View* regarded his text as finished, we would expect him to have complied with convention and supplied a preface or a dedication. I am unaware of any sixteenth-century manuscript intended for presentation or any printed text that lacks both a dedication and a preface. If the *View* is finished and if Spenser wrote it, hoping to win patronage as well as influence policy, then it is puzzling in the extreme that only one extant manuscript has a dedication and, in that one instance, the dedication, addressed to King James, was written after Spenser's death.[33] Thus, that no contemporary dedication, or preface, for the *View* has ever been identified further substantiates Renwick's and Gottfried's conclusion that the *View* is an unfinished text, an unstable foundation upon which to construct interpretations of Spenser or his work.

DID SPENSER WRITE THE *View?*

Spenser may have written the *View,* and, if he did, we ought to be able to confirm his authorship by objective evidence. Unfortunately, the bibliographical evidence we have for attributing the *View* to Spenser is far less conclusive than we might wish, and too many questions about the publication facts have remained unasked. Thirty-four years after Spenser's death, James Ware, the first editor of the *View,* identified the author of *The Faerie Queene* as the author of this highly polemical and controversial text. Prior to 1633, there are certain instances in which we might expect to find references to Spenser's authorship, but do not.

Although Sir John Davies alludes to *The Faerie Queene* in his *Orchestra* (1596), Davies's *A Discovery of the True Causes Why Ireland Was Never Entirely Subdued* (1612) does not mention Spenser. Davies, like Spenser, spent almost two decades in Ireland, serving as solicitor and then attorney general. And, he had access to a manuscript copy of the *View* belonging to Sir Arthur Chichester, Lord Deputy of Ireland, whose name appears in the front of British Library, Add. MS 22022.[34]

The massive collection of state papers relating to Ireland attests to the fact that nearly every state servant at some point or another advised the government on the Irish question. Spenser, however, wrote no letters of advice that have survived. Geoffrey Fenton, Lodowick Bryskett, Barnabe Googe, Sir John Davies, Sir Philip Sidney, Sir John Harington, and Barnaby Barnes — all literary men — wrote letters or tracts on Ireland. Many of Spenser's letters written in the capacity of secretary to Lord Grey have survived, but we have no letters stating his personal views. Prior to 1633, nothing, other than Book 5 of *The Faerie Queene,* suggests that Spenser aspired to be regarded as an expert on the Irish question.

Even one contemporary reference to Spenser's authorship of the *View* prior to 1633 would make the issue of attribution less troublesome. If any manuscript, dating from before the Ware edition was printed, identified Spenser as the author by name or by "Ed Sp," an identification sometimes used on the title pages of printed works, Ware's attribution would be substantiated by an independent witness. However, there is no unambiguous confirmation of Ware's assertion. What manuscript evidence there is has to be examined critically because marginal notes in different handwriting may only indicate that those manuscripts were later attributed to Spenser. More than half of the manuscripts collated in the *Spenser Variorum* conclude merely with "finis" and a date; the rest of the manuscripts attribute the work to an unidentified E. S.[35]

Thus far, no systematic attempt has been made to date conclusively the manuscripts of the *View.* On the basis of physical evidence and provenance, I would date the two manuscripts used by Renwick and Gottfried as copy texts for their editions as deriving from the 1590s. It would be significant if either of these manuscripts unequivocally identified Edmund Spenser as the author of the *View,* but neither does. Renwick used the manuscript entered in the Stationers' Register by Matthew Lownes, Bodleian, MS Rawlinson B 478, as his copy text. The front matter indicates that this copy belonged to John Panton of Lincoln, perhaps as early as 1596, and afterwards to Richard Basnett. On extra leaves unrelated to the manuscript text and inserted at some later date than when the manuscript was copied, the following inscription appears: "A discourse touching the present State of Ireland wrytten Dialogue wise by Mr. Edmonde Spenser. A[nno] 1596." The title and text of the *View* are in secretary, and under the title the attribution to Ed: Spenser, gent. was later inserted in italic handwriting and black ink, both hand and ink differing from the hand and ink used to write the original title (f. 1R). This text of the *View* concludes in italic: "finis 1596 E. S.:" Thus, on the grounds of physical evidence, we cannot use this manuscript to confirm Spenser's authorship. Nor can we use the entry in the Stationers' Register, because it, like Rawlinson B 478, the manuscript from which it derives, does not specify the author of the *View*.[36]

Like Renwick, Gottfried selected as his copy text a manuscript with an identifiable provenance, Huntington Library, MS Ellesmere 7041, which once belonged to Sir Thomas Egerton, later Lord Ellesmere. This manuscript contains two watermarks: an urn of fruit and a dragon emerging from a fortress: the urn of fruit somewhat resembles a watermark in use in 1597, but, unless these watermarks can be traced to a specific paper manufacturer, dating by them is likely to remain inconclusive. Accompanying this manuscript are notes on the *View* written by Sir Thomas Egerton.[37] Egerton is most likely to have written these notes in 1599 when his son accompanied Essex to Ireland. Unfortunately, this manuscript, too, is attributed to an unidentified E. S. Gottfried speculates that Spenser himself might have presented this copy of the *View* to Egerton (9:606), but no supporting manuscript evidence can be found in the Ellesmere Collection. Among the Ellesmere manuscripts, there is no dedication that might have accompanied a copy of the *View*.[38]

The third important manuscript text, Cambridge, Gonville and Caius College, MS 188. 221, was used by Renwick to correct his copy text, Rawlinson B 478. Gottfried fully collated only three manuscripts: Ellesmere MS 7041, Rawlinson B 478, and Gonville and Caius College, MS 188. 221. No author is identified in the body of the text of Gonville and Caius, MS 188. 221. At the front of the manuscript, in a different handwriting than that used in the text, there is a note written in the left margin: "This book was written by Edward [crossed out] Edmund Spenser Clarke of the Counsell of the province of Mounster in Ireland in ano 1596." This note appears to be an attempt to confer authenticity on the manuscript by imitating seventeenth-century spelling and handwriting. A knowledgeable contemporary would have been unlikely to have identified Spenser as the Clerk of the Council of Munster because Lodowick Bryskett held the patent for that office until several years after Spenser's death. Grosart seems to have been the first of Spenser's biographers to mention that he may have served in this capacity, but this possibility was not widely discussed until the twentieth century.[39]

Any manuscript copied after the appearance of Ware's edition in 1633 is likely to attribute the *View* to Spenser, but problems of attribution are even more complicated than this possibility would suggest. Sixteenth-century manuscript notes on Ireland have been arbitrarily attributed to Spenser in hands dating from the late seventeenth, eighteenth, and even nineteenth centuries. The three manuscripts making up *A Brief Note,* for example, were first attributed to Spenser by Alexander Grosart in the late nineteenth century. Grosart attributed all three manuscripts to Spenser on the basis of the words "Edmund Spencer," appearing on the back of the third manuscript. It is unclear why he says that this note was written by Dudley Carleton because there is no way this conclusion could be reached by anyone examining the actual manuscript evidence. British Library, Harleian MS 3787, the manuscript that is supposed to confirm Spenser's authorship of *A Brief Note* — or at least of the third of the three documents — was written after Spenser's death, and the identification of Spenser as author appears to have been added after the manuscript itself was written.[40]

Two works were added to the Spenser canon, that is, editions of his complete works, for the first time in the late seventeenth century. The *View* and *Britains Ida* were first printed with Spenser's works in the 1679 folio. As we know from textual scholarship on Chaucer and Shakespeare, sorting out the canon of major writers most frequently requires the rejection of spurious attributions. *Britain's Ida* was included in editions of Spenser's works until 1923 when it was conclusively attributed to Phineas Fletcher.[41] It was not until the publication of the *Spenser Variorum* in 1949 that *Axiochus* was printed with Spenser's works. Rudolf Gottfried acknowledges that he has ascribed this work to Spenser because of its verbal resemblance to his poems and prose (9:495): thus, somewhat ironically, Spenser's supposed authorship of the *View* is used to confirm his authorship of *A Brief Note* and *Axiochus*.

Booksellers, and scholars as well, have an understandable propensity to identify E. S. as Edmund Spenser, W. S. as William Shakespeare, and I. D. as John Donne. So, it is important to point out that there was an E. S. who wrote tracts on Ireland who cannot have been Edmund Spenser. Huntington, MS Ellesmere 1746 is entitled "A Survey of the present estate of Ireland Anno 1615" (f. 8V) and is bound with a "Reporte of his Majesty's speech in Parliament XVIIJ day of november

1606." Ellesmere 1746 is bound in the same white calf as the Huntington copy of the *View* (Ellesmere 7041). This E. S. manuscript is dedicated to King James and covers many of the same topics as the *View*.
The author says that he is presenting to the king a "view in a confused
forme; the face of your kingdome of ireland which I took (as it were
running)" (f. 9R). The points covered in the manuscript are identified
in a marginal gloss and include such topics as "the effects of uniformity
in Religion" (f. 10R), "wherefore the naughty English kept Irish
tenants" (f. 11R), "the English & Irish must not plante together and
the reasons" (f. 12R), and "there can be no good plantation nor scarce
good subjects within 2 descents where the Irish are mixed" (f. 13R).

Our seventeenth-century E. S. is just as convinced as the E. S. who
wrote the *View* that the common law will not work in Ireland because
of jury fixing, and that the Old English (Anglo-Norman) nobility op-
press their tenants: "The Irish Lo: keepes his people ignorant of
religion, laws, and the English toung and strives as much as in them
lieth to keep the states of England and Ireland ignorant of them & their
lawles doings" (f. 14R). He describes at length the "miserable estate of
the tenante under the Earls" (f. 18R).

This E. S. also specifically describes Munster where Spenser's Kilcol-
man was located:

> All the plantations of Munster made uppon the Attainder of
> Desmond of forty lands ore Signories are nowe all consumed by
> the usurers or almost worne out by sutes of lawe; with which
> the Irishe have alwaies filled their handes (f. 11R). . . . For in
> suites of lawe against the English (whereof they are full) the
> whole countrey doth ioyne against the Englishman (f. 13V).

There is no solid evidence that our seventeenth-century E. S. wrote the
View. Likewise, "A Survey of the present estate of Ireland" is dated 1615
and so cannot have been written by Edmund Spenser. Nevertheless, the
similarities in topics and arguments between "A Survey" and the *View*
illustrate the problems with assuming that Edmund Spenser was the
only E. S. who ever wrote about Ireland.[42]

Unless further evidence is forthcoming, the credibiity of Ware's attribution of the *View* to Spenser hinges on our assuming that Ware
acted in good faith and that his connections in Ireland would have given
him personal knowledge that E. S. was Edmund Spenser and the author
of the *View*. Rudolf Gottfried attacked Ware's credibility as an editor by

listing instances in which Ware supposedly "doctored" Spenser's text (9:519–23). This is a serious charge, but it is not supported by the evidence cited. Gottfried, in effect, loaded the dice by collating Ware's text against his manuscript copy text Ellesmere 7041, rather than Bodleian, Gough Ireland 2 or PRO SP63/202 pt. 4/56, the two manuscripts that Gottfried himself says are closest to Ware (9:517–18).

Until the manuscript evidence is far more carefully sifted, the grounds for attributing the *View* to Spenser are highly circumstantial. In his 1633 edition Ware tells us that he printed the *View* from a manuscript in the library of James Ussher, bishop of Armagh.[43] Ussher (1581–1656) was seventeen when Spenser died and so could conceivably have known of him.[44] James Ussher's father, Arland, was a Dublin merchant who succeeded Spenser in the office of Register or Clerk in the Chancery of the Faculties in Dublin; the patent passed to Ussher on June 22, 1588. Bishop Ussher's mother was Margaret Stanyhurst, daughter of James Stanyhurst and sister of Richard Stanyhurst, contributor to Holinshed's *Chronicles* (1577). Richard Stanyhurst restructured and added to Edmund Campion's history of Ireland, a work that is first printed with the *View* in 1633.[45] James Ware (1594–1666), the first editor of the *View*, shared the antiquarian interests of Bishop Ussher, first publishing a history of archbishops (1626) and later of Irish and Anglo-Irish authors (1639). Ware includes Spenser in the latter work, but takes his biography of the poet almost verbatim from Camden. He does not repeat his statement in the 1633 edition of the *View* that the remainder of the *The Faerie Queene* was lost by a careless servant. It could be claimed that the antiquarian interests and accomplishments of either Bishop Ussher or James Ware would have given them the connections and resources to verify authorship. Nevertheless, if the manuscript copy text for Ware's printed edition can be identified and it can be proved that Ware did in fact radically tamper with the text of the *View*, then the reliability of his attribution to Spenser cannot be taken for granted.[46]

To introduce a particularly telling illustration of the numerous uncertainties attending to the attribution and publication of the *View*, let me summarize the later seventeenth-century history of Matthew Lownes's association with Spenser's texts. As discussed above, in 1598 the publisher Matthew Lownes attempted to obtain a license to print his copy of the *View;* his copy, Bodleian, MS Rawlinson B478 probably did not identify Spenser as its author. By the early seventeenth century, Matthew Lownes had obtained a license to print Spenser's works. Sometime before 1609, the enterprising Matthew Lownes turned up a manuscript of the

"Mutabilitie Cantos," which he added to the Spenser canon by printing them in the first folio edition of *The Faerie Queene*. Humphrey Lownes, who had married into the Man family, printed the 1609 folio for his brother Matthew. Since Matthew Lownes was the first publisher to print the "Mutabilitie Cantos" with *The Faerie Queene*, he clearly took an interest in the Spenser canon. Shortly after bringing out his folio edition of *The Faerie Queene* in 1609, Lownes decided to produce folio editions of Spenser's complete works. Between 1611 and 1617 Matthew Lownes oversaw the preparation of several folio editions; each of Spenser's works was printed separately, but then they were collected together under general title pages. Because of the manner in which these editions were assembled, it would have been very easy to add a new work. These editions too were printed by Humphrey Lownes. Although Ware attributed the *View* to Spenser in 1633, Lownes, who once had a manuscript of the *View* signed "E. S.," did not see fit to include the *View* in his seventeenth-century folio editions of Spenser's complete works.

Among possible explanations for Lownes's failure to include the *View* in his folio editions of Spenser's complete works are the following: (1) By 1611 Lownes had lost or disposed of his manuscript of the *View* and could not obtain another copy; (2) Lownes did not think that Spenser was the author of the *View*. To prove either of these hypotheses may be difficult because there may be insufficient evidence to warrant drawing definite conclusions, but Spenser's authorship of the *View* should not be taken for granted. From a purely bibliographical perspective, Lownes's exclusion of the *View* from his 1611, 1613, and 1617 folio editions of Spenser's complete works would seem to offset Ware's attribution of this work to him in 1633.

Tempting though it may be to scapegoat the author of *The Faerie Queene* for England's colonial policies, politics is not a post-Colonial invention. Did James Ware know that the *View* was written by Spenser or did he attribute the work of an unidentified E. S. to the distinguished author of *The Faerie Queene*? What motivated Ware to publish the *View* in 1633 shortly after Wentworth took office: eagerness to illustrate the success of James's policies "in these our halcyon days" (Dedication to Wentworth, 2R), antiquarian zeal to preserve records of Irish history (Ware's Preface to the *View*, 3V), interest in publishing a work written by a famous author (conjecture)? Is it possible that Ware's attribution of the *View* to Edmund Spenser was politically motivated?[47] Could Spenser's name have been appropriated to promote the political agenda of Anglo-Irish Protestants in the 1630s?

To summarize and draw conclusions from the above, the evidence for Spenser's authorship of the *View* has never been critically examined. Spenser may have written the *View,* but at this point the evidence for this attribution rests entirely on James Ware's edition in 1633. Since the manuscript copy text for Ware's printed edition has not yet been identified, his attribution is not confirmed by an independent witness. Further, even if we persist in assuming that Spenser wrote the *View,* it is still unclear which version has the most authority. Four new manuscripts identified in 1980 have neither been described nor collated against the standard edition. Far more attention should be paid to the evaluation of manuscript sources for this text, all of which need to be systematically dated.

There is no substantive evidence that the *View* is a finished work. On the basis of examining manuscripts consulted to prepare his edition, W. L. Renwick concluded that the *View* was unfinished. Rudolf Gottfried did not dispute this conclusion; instead he reprinted Renwick's comments in the *Spenser Variorum* (9:510). Numerous manuscripts leave gaps and blank pages, most notably after the devastating description of the scene in which Murrogh O'Brien's foster mother drinks her foster son's blood after his execution (9:112–13). Close examination of the text of the standard edition of the *Spenser Variorum* reveals instances of repetition uncharacteristic of a finished work (cf., 2611–21 and 5028–39). Comparison of the *View* with similar, more finished, political commentaries underscores its failure to offer a conventional praise of the reigning monarch. No dedication or preface for the *View,* written prior to Spenser's death in 1599, has ever been identified. Based on the cumulative weight of this evidence, we must conclude that the text of the *View* is unfinished and thus problematical, if not unsuitable, for close literary or historical analysis.

The conjectured suppression of the *View* by the Elizabethan government conveniently explains why the *View* was never published during Spenser's lifetime, but this suppression is a fiction for which there is no supporting documentary evidence. Censorship occurred after publication in cases that can be documented. Of course, Spenser, if he wrote the *View* (and if he was in England in 1598), may have intervened to prevent the publication of an unfinished text, but this, too, is pure speculation. Scholarship abhors a vacuum, but it is better to acknowledge and take into consideration uncertainty than to construct interpretations on foundations as weak as those in the House of Pride, which Spenser describes as having parts that "were ruinous and old, but painted cunningly" (I.IV.5).

Notes

I wish to acknowledge Northeast Missouri State University for inviting me to present a preliminary version of this paper on October 28, 1993, as an endowed lecture commemorating Barbara Early Vreeland.

1. *The Works of Edmund Spenser: A Variorum Edition,* edited by Edwin Greenlaw et al., 9 vols. and Index (Baltimore: The John Hopkins Press, 1949), 9:211. Rudolf Gottfried edited the prose volume containing *The View of the Present State of Ireland.* Unless otherwise noted, references to Spenser's text will be to this edition; page and line numbers will be cited parenthetically in the text.

2. For a cogent critique of such approaches, see Annabel Patterson, "The Egalitarian Giant: Representations of Justice in History/Literature," *The Journal of British Studies* 31 (1992): 97–132.

3. For an excellent analysis of the problem, see Richard Dutton, *Mastering the Revels: The Regulation and Censorship of English Renaissance Drama* (Iowa City: University of Iowa Press, 1991), 1–16, 74–96.

4. Leland Carlson, *Martin Marprelate, Gentleman* (San Marino: Henry E. Huntington Library, 1981), 75–91.

5. *A Transcript of the Registers of the Company of Stationers of London; 1554–1640,* ed. Edward Arber (1875; reprinted Gloucester, Massachusetts: Peter Smith, 1967), III:111. All further references will be to this edition and will be cited parenthetically in the text. Because of the confusion of two sets of pagination and numerous appendices, volume and page numbers will be cited exactly as they appear at the bottom of the page.

6. Burghley asked Stubbs to defend his *The Execution of Justice in England* in response to Cardinal Allen's *A True. . . . Defense of English Catholics that Suffer for Their Faith Both at Home and Abroad; against a False, Seditious and Slanderous Libel entitled, "The Execution of Justice in England."* For further information, see *John Stubbs's Gaping Gulf With Letters and Other Relevant Documents,* ed. Lloyd E. Berry, Folger Documents of Tudor and Stuart Civilization (Charlottesville: University Press of Virginia, 1968), xlii–xliii.

7. In his introduction to the Stationers' Register, Arber observes that cases such as these were "quite contrary to the general spirit and tenor of the Queen's government" (III.11). For an account of Hayward's problems, see Margaret Dowling, "Sir John Hayward's Troubles over his Life of Henry IV," *Library* 11 (1930): 212–24; S. L. Goldberg, "Sir John Hayward, 'Politic' Historian," *Review of English Studies* 6, n. s. (1955): 233–44.

8. *The Letters of John Chamberlain,* ed. Norman Egbert McClure, 2 vols. (Philadelphia: American Philosophical Society, 1939), 1:70.

9. The Privy Council prepared instructions for preachers regarding how they were to depict the Essex rebellion, and in these documents Hayward's history is described as "cunningly insinuating that the same abuses being now in this realm that were in the days of Richard II, the like course might be taken for redress." Great Britain, *Calendar of State Papers, Domestic,* 1598–1601, 449. See also 539–40. When possible, I have quoted the original state papers.

10. *The Complete Works in Verse and Prose of Edmund Spenser,* edited with a New Life, Based on Original Researches by Rev. Alexander B. Grosart, 10 vols. (London: Hazell, Watson, and Viney Ltd., 1882–84), 1:226–27.

11. Pauline Henley, *Spenser in Ireland* (Dublin and London: Cork University Press and Longmans Green, 1928), 154.

12. Alexander C. Judson, *The Life of Edmund Spenser* (Baltimore: The Johns Hopkins Press, 1945), 156.

13. *The Spenser Encyclopedia,* ed. A. C. Hamilton et al. (Toronto and Buffalo: University of Toronto Press, 1990), 713–15. A corollary view of Spenser as a "self-crowned laureate," who consciously fashioned his image as a poet, has also strongly influenced literary scholarship of the past decade. For especially influential studies, see Stephen Greenblatt, *Renaissance Self-Fashioning: From More to Shakespeare* (Chicago & London: University of Chicago Press, 1980) and Richard Helgerson, *Self-Crowned Laureates: Spenser, Jonson, Milton and the Literary System* (Berkeley: University of California Press, 1983).

14. W.L. Renwick seems to have been the first person to state that the *View* was suppressed; the only evidence that he cites is the entry in the Stationers' Register:

> It was a political document of practical and immediate intention, and as such it was recognized by the cautious Warden of the Stationers' Company who refused to take the responsibility of an unconditional entry in the Register, and by the authorities who apparently forbade its printing (*A View of the Present State of Ireland,* ed. W. L. Renwick [Oxford: Clarendon Press, 1970], 189–90.

This passage was reprinted in the commentary on the *View* in the *Spenser Variorum,* 9:501.

15. Jonathan Goldberg, in *James I and the Politics of Literature: Jonson, Shakespeare, Donne, and Their Contemporaries* (Baltimore, MD: The Johns Hopkins Press, 1983), 9.

16. Ciaran Brady, "Spenser's Irish Crisis: Humanism and Experience in the 1590s," *Past and Present* 111 (1986): 25.

17. 'Some Quirk, some Subtle Evasion': Legal Subversion in Spenser's *A View of the Present State of Ireland,*" *Spenser Studies* VI, ed. Patrick Cullen and Thomas P. Roche (New York: AMS Press, Inc., 1986): 147, 150.

18. Ciaran Brady, "The Road to the *View,*" in *Spenser and Ireland: An Interdisciplinary Perspective,* ed. Patricia Coughlin (Cork: Cork University Press, 1989), 25–45.

20. PRO, SPD 12/195/33 [Public Record Office, State Papers, Domestic].

21. Ronald Rebholz, *The Life of Fulke Greville, First Lord Brooke* (Oxford: Clarendon Press, 1971), 76–77.

22. *A Short-Title Catalogue of Books Printed in England, Scotland, and Ireland, 1475–1640,* compiled by A. W. Pollard & G. R. Redgrave, ed. Katharine F. Pantzer (London: The Bibliographical Society, 1991), 3: 109, 112. Hereafter cited as STC.

23. For a summary of Thomas Man's career, see Blagden, 78–91.

24. Two manuscripts of Patrick Finglas's "Breviate of the getting of Ireland and decay of the same" (MS 742) and "The breviat of the getting of Ireland and the keepinge of the same" (MS 786). Manuscript copies of Captain Thomas Lee's "A Brief Description of Ireland" are located at the Henry E. Huntington Library, MS Ellesmere 1731 and at Trinity College Dublin, MS 652; Lee's tract was not printed until the eighteenth century in *Desiderata curiosa,* ed. J. Lodge (Dublin, 1772), 1:81–150. Lee's numerous letters and commentaries on Ireland written between 1588 and 1599 are scattered throughout the state papers.

25.   Renwick cites this bibliographical note at the beginning of Edmund Spenser, *A View of the Present State of Ireland,* ed. W. L. Renwick (Oxford: Clarendon Press, 1970). The first edition of Renwick's text of the *View* was printed in 1934 under the title, *A View of the Present State of Ireland . . . from MS Rawlinson B. 487 in the Bodleian and MS 188.21 in Caius College, Cambridge* (London: Scholartis Press, 1934). Renwick, unfortunately, omitted textual notes from the 1970 reprint. Because Renwick's 1934 edition is not readily available to many scholars, I have cited his textual notes as excerpted in the *Spenser Variorum.*

26.   Ray Heffner, "Spenser's 'View': Some Observations," *Modern Language Quarterly* 3 (1942): 507–15.

27.   Peter Beal, *Index of English Literary Manuscripts* (London and New York: Bowker, 1980), 523–31. Dr. Christopher Ridgeway is preparing a new edition of the *View* that will take account of all extant manuscripts.

28.   Francis Johnson, *Critical Bibliography of the Works of Edmund Spenser Printed Before 1700* (1933; facsimile reprint, London: Dawsons of Pall Mall, 1966). The bibliographical description of Ware's edition of the *View,* for example, is flawed. He attributes the *View* to Spenser, but completely ignores two new poems introduced into the Spenser canon in this edition. I am indebted to David Lee Miller for calling my attention to this problem of provenance; Miller is preparing a critical study of these poems.

29.   Dr. Ridgeway and I are collaborating on a critical bibliography of Spenser's manuscripts. We would appreciate assistance in preparing this bibliography and especially welcome information regarding the possible existence of any Spenserian manuscripts not identified in Beal's *Index.* All contributions will be gratefully acknowledged and credited to those who make them.

30.   Ronald B. McKerrow, *Prolegomena for the Oxford Shakespeare: A Study in Editorial Method* (Oxford: Clarendon Press, 1939), 36.

31.   Richard Beacon, *Solon His Follie: A Political Discourse Touching the Reformation of Commonweals Conquered, Declined or Corrupted* (Oxford: Ioseph Barnes, 1594). Unless otherwise noted in the text, references are to the "Epistle Dedicatorie," which prefaces the printed text.

32.   Sir William Herbert, *Croftus sive de Hibernia Liber,* ed. Arthur Keaveney and John A. Madden, Irish Manuscripts Commission (Baldoyle: J & T Moreau, Colour Books of Baldoyle, 1992), xviii. All references will be to the English translation offered in this dual language edition.

33.   Dr. Ridgeway supplied this information to me. He is collating the Castle Howard manuscript in an article to appear in a forthcoming issue of *English Literary Manuscripts.*

34.   Barnabe Barnes, *A New Description of Ireland, Together with the Manners, Customs, and Dispositions of the People* (1610) also fails to mention Spenser's authorship of the *View.* In Chapter 1, he identifies Giraldus Cambrensis, Edmund Campion, and Richard Stanyhurst as "the only authors that have patched and pieced together the history of Ireland." Cited from *Elizabethan Ireland: A Selection of Writings by Elizabethan Writers on Ireland,* ed. James P. Meyers, Jr. (Hamden, Connecticut: Shoe String Press, 1983), 127.

35.   According to the collation in the *Spenser Variorum,* Spenser is identified as the author of the *View* at the beginning of C (Cambridge, Gonville and Caius, MS 188.221), R (Bodleian, MS Rawlinson B478), and H2 (British Library, Harleian MS 7388). The first two manuscripts are described and discussed below in the text. Brit-

ish Library, Harleian MS 7388 is a fair copy probably prepared for Sir Robert Harley after Ware's edition was published. This manuscript was bound with Harleian MS 1332, which includes a commission from Charles I dated 4 April 1642 appointing "Algernon Percy, Earl of Northumberland, Robert Devereux, Earl of Essex, Philip Herbert, Earl of Pembroke, . . . Sir Robert Harley, Knight of the Bath . . . John Pym, Henry Marten, and Oliver Cromwell" to be his "Commissioners and Counsell residing here in England . . . for the Government and Defense of Ireland."

36.   The 1598 entry in the Stationers' Register does not identify Spenser as the author. This is not especially significant, but it should be noted that the November 1594 entry for *Amoretti* and *Epithalamion* reads as follows: "William Ponsonby/ Entered for his Copie vnder th[e h]andes of the Wardens, A booke entituled *Amoretti and Epithalamion* written not longe since by Edmund Spenser" (Francis R. Johnson, *Critical Bibliography,* 29).

37.   I am indebted to Mary Robertson, Keeper of Manuscripts, Huntington Library, for confirming that these notes are in Egerton's hand and that they were probably written long before his death in 1617.

38.   I wish to thank the Henry E. Huntington Library for awarding me a fellowship during the summer of 1992; this grant enabled me to make a preliminary survey of Spenserian manuscripts and of Irish materials in the Ellesmere Collection. I also wish to thank the Huntington Library for permission to quote from manuscripts in that collection.

39.   Grosart, I:115; Judson, 112–14.

40.   In his article on *A Brief Note* in *The Spenser Encyclopedia,* 111–12, Ciaran Brady rejects Spenser's authorship of the first two manuscripts, but accepts him as the author of the third, largely on the basis of similarities in content between it and the *View.* I concur with Brady in rejecting Spenser's authorship of the first two manuscripts, but will argue that Spenser was not the author of any of these works in an article to appear in a festschrift for S. K. Heninger, Jr., edited by Peter Medine and Joseph A. Wittreich.

41.   Ethel Seaton, "Phineas Fletcher — A new MS," *Times Literary Supplement,* 22 March 1923, 199, and reply by F. S. Boas, 29 March 1923, 216.

42.   A tantalizing manuscript (PRO, SP63/203/119), dating from 1599, is presented as a dialogue between Spenser's two sons, Silvanus and Peregrine. Thomas Wilson is written at the bottom of the first page of the dedication, but is more likely to indicate someone who had possession of the manuscript than the author. The manuscript is formally dedicated to Essex. Bagwell attributed the manuscript to Spenser, but since it contains references to events occurring after 19 January 1599, when Spenser had already died, that attribution is impossible. The author of the dialogue was in the service of Sir Richard Bingham, whom he admires, and he describes outrages and causes of rebellion in King's county, South Leinster, Connaught, and Ulster. I have not transcribed this manuscript fully, but my preliminary examination does not suggest that the author was consciously imitating the *View.* It is more likely that the author selected the names of Spenser's sons for his interlocutors because of Spenser's recent death. Neither I nor the editor preparing the *Calendar* have found Spenser's name in this manuscript, but the reference to his sons merits further attention.

43.   James Ware, *The Historie of Ireland, Collected by Three Learned Authors, viz. Meredith Hanmer . . . Edmund Campion . . . Edmund Spenser* (Dublin: Societie of Stationers, 1633), Preface, 3V. References are to the edition located in the Henry E. Huntington Library.

44. John Aubrey, *Brief Lives,* ed. A. Clark, 2 vols. (Oxford: Clarendon Press, 1898), 2:232, 248.

45. For a biography and selections from Stanyhurst's works, see Colm Lennon, *Richard Stanihurst The Dubliner, 1547–1618* (Blackrock: Academic Press Limited, 1981), 24–40.

46. Gottfried argues that Bodleian MS Rawlinson B 479 belonged to Ware, but states that he made no use of it in preparing the 1633 printed edition, *Spenser Variorum,* 9:512. In the *Catalogi Librorum Manuscriptorum Angliae et Hiberniae* prepared by John Barnard in 1679 there is a reference to a manuscript of the *View* belonging to Peter de Neve dated 1584. Needless to say, if this manuscript has survived and can be identified or located, it would be of major importance.

47. For a discussion of the politics of why the *View* was printed in 1633, see Nicholas Canny, "Edmund Spenser and the Development of an Anglo-Irish Identity," *The Yearbook of English Studies,* ed. G. K. Hunter and C. J. Rawson, Modern Humanities Research Association, 13 (1983):17–19.

GLEANINGS

THE
DEFENCE OF

the Article:
Christ descended into Hell.

With Arguments obiected againſt
the truth of the ſame doctrine: of one
Alexander Humes.
All which reaſons are confuted, and the ſame doctrine
cleerely defended.

By *Adam Hyll,* D. of Diuinity.

Magna eſt veritas & praualet.

AT LONDON
Printed for *William Ponſonbie.* 1592.

By permission of the Houghton Library, Harvard University

230

ANNE LAKE PRESCOTT

Triumphing over Death and Sin

I N 1592, THREE YEARS before he published Spenser's *Amoretti,* William Ponsonby printed Adam Hill's *Defence of the Article: Christ descended into Hell,* a sermon preached on February 28, 1590. The title page does not show this descent but rather what it accomplished and what followed on Easter when, as Spenser's *Amoretti* 68 puts it, Christ made his "triumph over death and sin: / and having harrowd hell didst bring away / captivity thence captive us to win." On Ponsonby's title page Christ indeed triumphs, treading under heel the old serpent Sin and the skeleton Death.[1] In his hand he holds what looks to an English professor like a very large pen but is of course the palm of victory. Spenser did not need this picture to inspire the working of his sonnet, of course, but it might be of help when explaining to students the emblematic or iconic impulse accompanying so much Renaissance writing.

The text itself shows how much debate and even puzzlement lie behind Spenser's words. In a section insisting that while his soul was in Hell and his body in the grave Christ was nevertheless fully in both places (a point both relevant to issues such as the nature of Holy Communion and itself affected by arguments over the character of physical space), Hill explores some pertinent scriptural texts (sigs. D1-D1ᵛ). Concerning Psalm 68, for example, he

231

says that according to the learned Musculus — an authority unknown to me — "This God which was in Christ reconciling the world to himselfe in Christ, First descended into the lower parts of the earth, then he led captivity captive, and not only we are delivered from the captivity of Satan, sinne and damnation: but also Christ triumphing over them as tirants, hath ascended above all heavens to fulfill all things." Furthermore, just as by his death Christ "conflicted with his enemy on the crosse, so by his glorious descending into hell, resurrection and ascention he triumphed, as it is Ephes. 4. leaving his crosse lifted up as a monument of his victorye."

I reproduce the title page from the copy at the Houghton Library, Harvard University, bound in a collection of tracts that the catalogue card says once belonged to John Donne — another poet who wrote of victory over the "Mighty and dreadfull" death.

Barnard College

NOTES

1.   The image had been used already by the printer John Day for several books; see item 208 in Ronald B. McKerrow, *Printers & Publishers' Devices in England & Scotland 1485–1640.* (London, 1913).

Index

Contents of Previous Volumes

VOLUME X

DUE DATE

	201-6503	Printed in USA